Essays in Linguistic Ethnography

Full details of all our publications can be found on http://www.multilingual-matters.com, or by writing to Multilingual Matters, St Nicholas House, 31–34 High Street, Bristol, BS1 2AW, UK.

Essays in Linguistic Ethnography

Ethics, Aesthetics, Encounters

Adrian Blackledge and Angela Creese

MULTILINGUAL MATTERS
Bristol • Jackson

DOI https://doi.org/10.21832/BLACKL5594
Library of Congress Cataloging in Publication Data
A catalog record for this book is available from the Library of Congress.
Names: Blackledge, Adrian, author. | Creese, Angela, author.
Title: Essays in Linguistic Ethnography: Ethics, Aesthetics, Encounters/
   Adrian Blackledge and Angela Creese.
Description: Bristol; Jackson: Multilingual Matters, [2023] | Includes bibliographical
   references and index. | Summary: "This book argues for an approach to linguistic
   ethnography which departs from the perspective of the academic researcher, to
   amplify instead the voices of participants, researchers and collaborators. It reflects
   on ways of reporting research which add multiple perspectives and represent
   ambiguity more meaningfully than traditional academic prose"-- Provided by
   publisher. Identifiers: LCCN 2023010407 (print) | LCCN 2023010408 (ebook) |
   ISBN 9781788925594 (hardback) | ISBN 9781788925587 (paperback) |
   ISBN 9781788925600 (pdf) | ISBN 9781788925617 (epub)
Subjects: LCSH: Anthropological linguistics. | LCGFT: Essays.
Classification: LCC P35 .B553 2023 (print) | LCC P35 (ebook) | DDC 306.44--dc23/
   eng/20230501 LC record available at https://lccn.loc.gov/2023010407
LC ebook record available at https://lccn.loc.gov/2023010408

British Library Cataloguing in Publication Data
A catalogue entry for this book is available from the British Library.

ISBN-13: 978-1-78892-559-4 (hbk)
ISBN-13: 978-1-78892-558-7 (pbk)

Multilingual Matters
UK: St Nicholas House, 31-34 High Street, Bristol, BS1 2AW, UK.
USA: Ingram, Jackson, TN, USA.

Website: www.multilingual-matters.com
Twitter: Multi_Ling_Mat
Facebook: https://www.facebook.com/multilingualmatters
Blog: www.channelviewpublications.wordpress.com

Copyright © 2023 Adrian Blackledge and Angela Creese.

All rights reserved. No part of this work may be reproduced in any form or by any means without permission in writing from the publisher.

The policy of Multilingual Matters/Channel View Publications is to use papers that are natural, renewable and recyclable products, made from wood grown in sustainable forests. In the manufacturing process of our books, and to further support our policy, preference is given to printers that have FSC and PEFC Chain of Custody certification. The FSC and/or PEFC logos will appear on those books where full certification has been granted to the printer concerned.

Typeset in Sabon and Frutiger by R. J. Footring Ltd, Derby, UK

Contents

Acknowledgements	vi

Part 1. Encounters in Linguistic Ethnography

Essay 1. Linguistic Ethnography	3
Essay 2. Developing an Ethical-Aesthetic Perspective in Linguistic Ethnography	17

Part 2. Enacting Linguistic Ethnography

Essay 3. Polyphony	33
Essay 4. Poetry	59
Essay 5. Ethnographic Drama	74
Essay 6. Performance	90
Essay 7. Politics	107

Part 3. Relations in Linguistic Ethnography

Essay 8. Relational Ethics	127
Essay 9. Responsibility and Trust	144
Essay 10. Strangeness and Proximity	160
Essay 11. Difference	174
Essay 12. Movement and Affect	192
References	210
Index	217

Acknowledgements

This work was supported by the Arts and Humanities Research Council (April 2014 – March 2018) as a 'Translating Cultures' Large Grant: *Translation and Translanguaging. Investigating Linguistic and Cultural Transformations in Superdiverse Wards in Four UK Cities* (AH/L007096/1), Principal Investigator, Angela Creese. With Mike Baynham, Adrian Blackledge, Jessica Bradley, John Callaghan, Lisa Goodson, Ian Grosvenor, Amal Hallak, Jolana Hanusova, Rachel Hu, Daria Jankowicz-Pytel, Li Wei, Agnieszka Lyons, Bharat Malkani, Sarah Martin, Emilee Moore De Luca, Jenny Phillimore, Mike Robinson, Frances Rock, James Simpson, Caroline Tagg, Jaspreet Kaur Takhi, Janice Thompson, Kiran Trehan, Piotr Wegorowski and Zhu Hua. Further information about the research project is available at https://tlang.org.uk.

Part 1
Encounters in Linguistic Ethnography

Essay 1. Linguistic Ethnography

> And so we are all bystanders now: we know that something
> needs to be done, but also know that we have done less than
> needs be, and not necessarily what needed doing most.
> (Bauman, 2007: 130)

In linguistic ethnography we document and analyse the communicative practice of human encounters, in all their ambivalence and multiplicity. Ambiguity is at the heart of interaction. The interpretation of meaning is alert to individual difference and disposition. Social togetherness is not so much a meeting of minds, as a sea of abundant possibilities and responsibilities. Analysis of human relations therefore must account for multiplicity and ambivalence. In encounters between people we see both the potential and the limits of solidarity. The essays in this collection bring to bear thought and practice developed in the arts and in philosophy. At the same time as analysing the ways in which semiotic signs create and convey meaning, we explore new directions which add depth to understandings of the complexity of people's lives.

The depiction of ambivalence in human encounters requires a form of representation which enables a range of ethical and moral perspectives to be made evident. We need modes of representation which do justice to the multiplicity of outlooks and standpoints we document in linguistic ethnographic research. In this book we describe ways of reporting research which incorporate multiple perspectives. This journey has taken us away from the singular perspective of the academic researcher, to amplify instead the voices of research participants, researchers, collaborators and bystanders. We have set ourselves the challenge of writing polyphonically, so that we account for the complexity of individual voices, while incorporating the social and historical contexts which inform them. This has meant paying explicit attention to the intersection of the social and the individual. In these essays we propose that a polyphonic approach to ethnographic writing represents the experiential, aesthetic, emotional, moral and ethical values people bring to encounters with others.

A polyphonic approach to ethnographic writing does not conceive of ethics or morality as systematic or codifiable. It rejects practices of moral policing. In adopting this approach we view human diversity as anything but uniform. A comprehensive or unitary account of other people's values is inconsistent with the aims of linguistic ethnography, which sets out to portray the intricacy of individual lives. Ethnography approaches social life as fluid, heterogeneous and under-patterned. It accepts fragmentation, contingency, indeterminacy and ambivalence. Morality in practice is not universal but, rather, personal and social. Individual subjectivity is formed through the *inter*subjectivity of social encounters, where values and beliefs are played out. In linguistic ethnography we unpick trails of indexical signs, so that it becomes possible to see how 'truth' is fashioned.

Is there anything further to say about meaning in linguistic ethnography, beyond identification of indexicality? Are there other ways to approach the analysis of signification, in which meaning is not underpinned by social positions? While the analysis of indexical signs produces powerful accounts of social reproduction and sedimentation, are there other features of encounters which escape indexical analysis? The arts have a long history of engagement with ethical ambiguity, providing accounts of lives unknown, and revealing difficult moral decisions. However, linguistic ethnography has tended to be less ambitious in this respect. In this book we seek to open up ethnography to the unknown. We will explore writing styles which disrupt the orderly logic of the ethnographic account, in favour of forms which allow those we encounter in research to 'imagine possibilities, weigh alternatives, shift mindsets, and act without knowing what lies in the future' (Ochs & Capps, 2001: 6). In our effort to make sense of the actual and possible lives we observe, we work towards incomplete and unresolved ethnographies, exploring different genres, including ethnographic poetry, ethnographic drama and narrative, 'to air, probe, and otherwise attempt to reconstruct and make sense of … life experiences' (Ochs & Capps, 2001: 7). Our intention in the essays in this book is to illustrate how different genres can open up linguistic ethnography, and in so doing engage with unfixed and unfinished aspects of experience. We will consider genres which maintain close allegiance to the lived experiences of real people, while presenting stories through artistic and narrative media. To do so, we will refer to four recent publications, each of which takes a form different from conventional linguistic ethnographic accounts. These are:

- Adrian Blackledge and Angela Creese (2019) *Voices of a City Market: An Ethnography*. Multilingual Matters.
- Adrian Blackledge and Angela Creese (2021) *Interpretations – An Ethnographic Drama*. Multilingual Matters.
- Adrian Blackledge and Angela Creese (2021) *Volleyball – An Ethnographic Drama*. Multilingual Matters
- Adrian Blackledge and Angela Creese (2022) *Ode to the City – An Ethnographic Drama*. Multilingual Matters.

It is not necessary to have read these four books in order to understand the essays which follow. We provide extended examples from each text. In each of the four books we have departed radically from traditional ethnographic writing practice. While careful sociolinguistic analysis took place before the books were even imagined, ethnographic material is represented very differently there. Data are transformed, as field notes become poems, and audio-recordings become play scripts. The four books are examples of a trajectory of change from evidence-based academic writing to experience-based engagement. The essays collected here describe this process of change. Each of the four books is an outcome of research conducted as part of a large linguistic ethnographic research project in a particular location in Birmingham, UK. The full title of the research project is *Translation and Translanguaging. Investigating Linguistic and Cultural Transformations in Superdiverse Wards in Four UK Cities* (www.tlang.org.uk). We will refer to the project as 'TLANG'. *Voices of a City Market* is a curation of observations made in Birmingham's Bull Ring market. *Interpretations* is a play based on advice and advocacy meetings recorded in a Chinese community centre. The context for the *Volleyball* play is observation of a men's volleyball team, which trains and plays together in a city sports hall. *Ode to the City* dramatically represents staff working in Birmingham's city centre library during a period of austerity and financial cuts.

Alongside the essays in Part 2, which refer directly to the four books, is a further set of essays in Part 3, which expands on methodology in research teams. These essays address relationships in ethnographic teams, and relationships between researchers and research participants, as values, beliefs and ideologies are contested and navigated. Differences between team members become an important contributing factor in ethnographic research. We will consider the productive and potentially detrimental possibilities afforded by difference and diversity in research teams. In these essays we analyse primary data in the form of researchers' field notes and vignettes. We discuss how researchers' reflections conceive of responsibility for difference. We approach these narratives through the prism of relational ethics. We examine ways in which researchers encounter difference. To do this we move beyond understandings of 'othering' as a socially harmful and discriminatory process of social categorisation, to reconfigure otherness as a potentially unifying and communal experience. Focusing on the relationship between the researcher and the researched, we explore field notes and research vignettes to understand how researchers build relationships which cannot be fully explained through social categorisation. In these methodological essays we show how researchers draw upon, resist, negotiate and transcend social categories. We listen to the voices of researchers who participated in the linguistic ethnographic research project. We are particularly grateful to the eight researchers who gave permission for their vignettes to be included in discussion of these issues. The researchers are:

- Amal Hallak
- Rachel Hu
- Agnieszka Lyons
- Bharat Malkani
- Daria Jankowicz-Pytel
- Janice Thompson
- Kiran Trehan
- Zhu Hua

These researchers' field notes and vignettes appear in essays in Part 3 of the book. Each of the researchers had the opportunity to comment on, and contribute to, the discussion of their narratives. In some instances we have included their comments, in order to illustrate the polyphonic, dialogic nature of team ethnography, where knowledge is disputed, cumulative and collegial. Each researcher gave permission for their work, and their comments, to be reproduced here.

TLANG

Throughout the book we will make reference to the TLANG research project. TLANG was funded by the UK Arts and Humanities Arts Council, from 2014 to 2018. The project studied encounters between people in contexts of social and linguistic diversity. The research project was a multi-site linguistic ethnography, which set out to examine how people communicate in contexts where they do not necessarily share similar historical, biographical, economic, legal, national or linguistic backgrounds. Over the four years of the project the research team conducted detailed ethnographic research in 16 research sites, four in each of four cities in the UK. The research sought to make explicit what is often taken for granted, and to make accessible new ways of understanding. The project developed a linguistic ethnography approach which relied on learning from research participants, with whom the researchers were closely involved. The research team set out not to inform but, rather, to forge a 'partnership of equals' (Blommaert, 2010: 5), earned through researchers' investment and involvement in the research site. Hymes (1980: 105) proposes that ethnographic research is:

> the most open, the most compatible with a democratic way of life, the least likely to produce a world in which experts control knowledge at the expense of those who are studied.

Blommaert (2010: 5) argues that ethnographers attempt to counter and transform existing social orders through flattening the relationship between researcher and researched. He suggests that there is reward to be gained from being 'an agent of improvement, not of continued or exacerbated oppression and exclusion' (Blommaert, 2010: 5). This was the approach pursued in the TLANG research project. A team of researchers in each of Birmingham, Cardiff, Leeds and London identified research sites for linguistic ethnographic study. The researchers were interested in locating places where communicative practice was observable. The research sites were situated in superdiverse wards, or neighbourhoods, and were selected as public points where people with different histories, biographies and languages came into contact with each other. Across the four cities, research sites were united thematically. That is, in order to maintain coherence in the overall design of the research, and also to ensure a diverse spread of ethnographic research locations, the research teams worked simultaneously across sites which were thematically related. In the first four-month phase of ethnographic investigation, we observed small business settings; in the second phase, cultural heritage sites; in the third, community sport settings; and in the final period of four months, we conducted ethnographic research in welfare advice and legal advocacy sites. The 16 research settings included market stalls and corner shops, libraries and community centres, capoeira, karate and football clubs, and welfare benefits advice centres. The research team was interested in all forms of communication in these sites. However, linguistic ethnography in superdiverse settings is dependent on the research team having at its disposal the linguistic resources to interpret and translate the communicative repertoires of participants in the research. This required us to determine the linguistic make-up of the neighbourhoods in which we would work, and to ensure that our team was equipped with appropriate linguistic resources to conduct the research.

The 2011 Census asked UK residents to name their most commonly spoken language other than English (Office for National Statistics, 2011). The results of the Census thus revealed the languages reportedly spoken most widely in city neighbourhood wards. While the Census question was a blunt and imprecise instrument, it nevertheless provided starting-points for the research teams. Analysis of the Census led to decisions about the selection of research sites, and of key research participants. In London, speakers of varieties of Polish were invited to participate in each phase of the research; in Cardiff, speakers of varieties of Arabic; in Leeds, speakers of varieties of Czech, Slovak, Romani and Portuguese; and in Birmingham, speakers of varieties of Chinese languages, including Mandarin, Cantonese, Fujianese, Hokkien and Hakka. In each city, researchers whose linguistic resources enabled them to participate, interpret and translate in these linguistic settings were recruited as field workers and analysts. In each of the 16 research sites teams of researchers conducted close and repeated observations of communicative practices over a period of four months. In each case, at least two researchers were involved. The researchers wrote field notes of their observations, audio-recorded and video-recorded participants' spoken interactions, collected social media and other online and digital communication, interviewed stakeholders, took photographs, gathered relevant documentary material and asked research participants to audio-record themselves in domestic and/or leisure settings.

Eighteen key participants took part in the 16 ethnographic case studies across the four cities. Of the 18 key participants, all but one was born outside the UK: two in China, two in Hong Kong, three in Iraq, one in Malaysia, one in Mozambique, one in the Netherlands, five in Poland, two in Slovakia and one in Sudan. The multilingual nature of the study meant that in addition to English, we worked in Arabic, Cantonese, Mandarin, Polish, Portuguese, Romani and Slovak, as well as in many different varieties of these languages. This was made possible by the multilingual backgrounds of the research team members, eight of whom were themselves born outside the UK: three in China, one in Syria, one in Slovakia and three in Poland. Other members of the research team were born in the UK but spoke between them a number of different languages. Multilingualism and migration histories were therefore prominent features of personal biographies and current practices, for both research participants and researchers. Interactions in research sites often took place in English. However, this was by no means always the case. For example, Chinese butchers in the Birmingham market regularly served customers in a range of Chinese languages. The translator in Leeds operated, for the most part, in Slovak, as she responded to the needs of her clients. The karate coach in London spoke mainly in Polish to his class of young students. The advice and advocacy worker in a Chinese community centre in Birmingham largely worked in Mandarin and sometimes in Cantonese and other varieties of Chinese. And the football coach from Sudan regularly spoke in varieties of Arabic as he coached a group of boys attending a madrassa in Cardiff. While English was the language we most commonly heard throughout our observations in the TLANG project, translanguaging was a normative means of communication, as people drew on extensive semiotic repertoires.

Our primary research question in the TLANG research project asked how people communicate in contexts of social and linguistic diversity. This brought us to the study of encounters between people from different linguistic and social backgrounds. Because research participants were welfare rights advisors, artists, butchers, customer assistants, librarians, shopkeepers, sports coaches, interpreters and translators, their work was normally public facing, and therefore demanded interaction with strangers. We saw that visible and linguistic difference sometimes attracted commentary, and that social, cultural and linguistic backgrounds often led to convivial conversation. The highly repetitive speech acts of greeting, buying and selling, and giving advice, created environments conducive to both commercial enterprise and public service. Indeed, we observed that reference to linguistic and social differences was often at the centre of interactions between strangers.

The people we observed typically saw social, cultural and linguistic difference not as a problem, but as a resource for getting on with others during their work and leisure routines. Perceived difference was an opportunity for curiosity, surprise and engagement. This is not to suggest that all the encounters we observed were characterised by a generous response to difference. In the four-year ethnographic project we came across instances of racism, misogyny, insensitivity, ignorance and distrust. There were examples of discriminatory othering across all city contexts. We have documented these in case study reports, which are available on the TLANG project website (www.tlang.org.uk). However, for the most part we witnessed little in the way of serious division and discord in the research sites we investigated.

The TLANG research team consisted of academic researchers from a range of disciplines. Members of the wider project team also included a number of partners from organisations beyond the academy. In all we were a team of 33 researchers and partners. We are particularly grateful to the following organisations for their formal partnership with the TLANG research project. Many others generously participated through involvement in data collection and community engagement, but are too numerous to list.

- Birmingham Museums Trust
- Business in the Community
- The Law Centres Network
- The Library of Birmingham
- Migrants' Rights Network
- Sporting Equals
- Women & Theatre

Artistic Representation in Linguistic Ethnography

In the course of the TLANG research project we worked with artists to explore ways to enhance and amplify representation and analysis of ethnographic material. We wanted to consider what might be gained through an approach to representation and interpretation of linguistic ethnographic data when it was facilitated by creative practice. We commissioned a theatre company to devise, produce and perform a theatre piece which responded to the outcomes of the research. We ran workshops in collaboration with museum curators and directors of art collections. We also invited award-winning artists and creatives to collaborate with members of the academic research team in a series of 'Creative Arts Labs'. The artists and creatives included a dancer/choreographer, an artist who works in large-scale participatory practice, a museum curator, a visual artist, a theatre maker, a socially engaged artist and a composer of opera and song. Academic researchers working with arts-based practice beyond the TLANG project team were also invited to participate. The programme was facilitated by an independent artistic director. The Creative Arts Labs took place towards the end of the four-year funded period of the TLANG project. The aim was for academic researchers to collaborate with artists, to collectively think about the potential of arts-based practice to augment linguistic ethnography, and to consider the potential of linguistic ethnography to enrich arts-based practice.

At the beginning of the first day of the Creative Arts Lab, researchers from the TLANG team made presentations of data they had collected during fieldwork. The artists also introduced the group to their creative practice. As part of the process of becoming familiar with the research material, the academics and creative artists visited the local research sites where observational research had been conducted during the project, including Birmingham Bull Ring market and the Library of Birmingham. The following day the artists ran practical sessions which responded to the linguistic ethnographic research. The choreographer/dancer led participants as they danced their response to a transcript of a Chinese butcher's interactions with his customers, which we had audio-recorded in the meat and fish market. The composer directed a group of researchers and creative artists to produce a short operatic piece based on SMS messages collected during the project. Participants performed their new creative pieces for the larger group. After a period of reflection and further planning, there was a second instalment of the Creative Arts Lab, involving the same artists, but with an expanded cohort of interested academic researchers. Throughout the Creative Arts Lab sessions, provocations and discussions were recorded and transcribed.

Researchers and artists alike saw creative possibilities for collaboration and for mutual learning. For the academic researchers, working with the arts offered a means of public engagement, an opportunity for wider dissemination of research outcomes, and a way to push at the limits of interpretation. Researchers also identified clear potential for the development of a creative approach to research methods through the arts. Choreographing sporting action as dance and singing everyday voices of the market were proposed as innovate research practice. A creative approach provided the prospect of seeing research findings anew, from a different perspective, with fresh eyes. Both researchers and artists recognised the potential of creative approaches to research and of research-based approaches to creative practice. One of the artists, who usually worked on large-scale outdoor arts installations, said:

> It makes me think about the experience of communication – from language, and languages, to listening, gesture, body, gaze…. Makes me think about the potential for a dual-purpose research/art, art/research project that works for both academic and arts disciplines – and is the richer for it. It makes me reappraise public spaces like the butcher and the

corner shop as social spaces for more than economic exchange. It makes me think about social media – multiple identities, how we communicate by text or online. It makes me think about how we use body, voice and rhythm in communication, and how we could interpret or explore that creatively. I was struck by how much shared language there was: conviviality, repertoire, etc.

The common ground shared by linguistic ethnographic researchers and creative artists was pointed out by several of the Creative Arts Lab participants. The opera composer elaborated on this, saying that the initiative had reawakened his interest in finding the operatic in the everyday:

There is much in common between the processes of academics and of artists. There is a location or context in which research is to be done, or a piece to be made; exploration and inquiry is going on; a 'eureka' lightbulb moment, the impulse to make a particular piece or follow a particular line of inquiry; data gathered from the outside world or from the imagination, or both; a narrative created or imposed on the material as the work is composed/written; in performing arts there is rehearsal, which involves further analysis and perhaps a metanarrative; dissemination through performance, lecture, conference, publication.

Another artist similarly saw the potential of artistic representation and interpretation of ethnographic material:

I was struck by some of the similarity in areas of interest – diverse voices, participation, narrative, storytelling, listening, audio, public space, bringing together people who otherwise might not come into contact. I'm very interested in the development of an arts/research project that is engaging both artistically and academically.

An academic researcher who had not previously given serious consideration to the artistic representation and interpretation of social practice said the workshops had opened his eyes:

Creative engagement with research ideas can make thoughts and stories more tangible, more audible. Creative engagement with research ideas as a focus of joint knowledge construction can be transformational.

Another academic researcher who had viewed collaboration in the arts mainly as an opportunity to disseminate research to a wider audience now saw that it could also be an important part of the interpretation process, helping researchers to understand and conceptualise data. The museum curator agreed, saying 'artists can play a key role in exploring an idea or concept in new ways, to discover new meaning'. The aim of the Creative Arts Lab was to invite a collision of practice, an exchange of ideas and experience between researchers and artists, to understand how each other think, how each other work, to gain an insight into each other's ways of working. If specific collaborations did not immediately emerge, there was a definite sense of learning. Artists saw the dramatic, musical and visual potential of practice observed over time. Academics recognised the potential of the arts to enhance the curation, representation, interpretation and dissemination of research outcomes. Angela Creese saw possibilities in ethnographic drama:

> I would be interested in co-writing a play script based on some of our data, and seeing it produced. Some themes which I think have theatrical potential are: the carnivalesque in community sport; the absurd in mediating the social/welfare system; the comedy, pathos and ritual of highly repetitive service encounters in public institutions; the banter of the multilingual marketplace.

Here was perhaps the first inkling of what was to emerge. Five years later, we have published three play scripts based on research conducted in the Birmingham segment of the TLANG project. In addition, we published *Voices of a City Market: An Ethnography*, a polyphonic representation of the sound, sights, smells, tastes and textures of Birmingham Bull Ring market. The energy, insight and imagination of the artists and academic researchers who attended the Creative Arts Lab gave us the confidence to explore artistic means to enact and show outcomes of the TLANG research project. The essays in this collection offer accounts of the development of the four books that are artistic outcomes of the Birmingham research. In the final four essays in the collection, we give space to the voices of researchers in the TLANG project who were based in Cardiff, Leeds and London, as well as Birmingham. In doing so, we make visible the research process. We do not attempt to tidy away the messiness and unpredictability of linguistic ethnographic research. Rather, we make available the researchers' accounts of research practice from their own point of view. The choreographer/dancer who participated in the Creative Arts Lab said:

> I am interested in how connected the researchers become with the participants they work with. I am very interested to hear how they manage their emotions and their feelings, through discussions, debriefing sessions, writing field notes and talking to each other as a team. I think there is something very interesting about how research affects you emotionally. I would be interested to know if the researchers had profound or even crisis moments. What did they feel, what happened, how did it affect them and how did they deal with it? Did anything make them really angry? Did they ever get upset in front of the participants?

Relationships within research teams, and relationships with research participants, were the focus of field notes and vignettes written by the researchers. In the essays in Part 3 we make these accounts visible.

Structure of the Book

In this book we discuss aspects of the TLANG research project in 12 essays, organised in three sections. **Part 1, Encounters in Linguistic Ethnography**, sets out the orientation of the book.

Essay 1, 'Linguistic Ethnography', has outlined the rationale, organisation and orientation of the book. We have provided an overview of the essays in the collection, which offer a theoretical and practical account of linguistic ethnography. In this introductory essay we have summarised the aims and structure of the TLANG research project, and indicated the main outcomes of the research. In the essay we refer to the four books which are creative outcomes of the TLANG project and which are the subject of several of the essays. We list organisations which participated throughout the project and we name eight researchers whose reflexive methodological accounts open up the research process in the final four essays of the collection.

Essay 2, 'Developing an Ethical-Aesthetic Perspective in Linguistic Ethnography', introduces the theoretical orientation of the essays in Part 2 and Part 3. Here we describe an approach to linguistic ethnography which seeks to flatten traditional hierarchies in the research process, making visible and audible the voices of researchers and researched. We develop a perspective on ethnographic research which does not seek to explain or endow with meaning the culture of the other; a perspective which does not claim to know the other, but which retains ambiguity and complexity. We propose that researchers and research participants can bring an affective sensibility to field and team relations, through narrative reflections in research vignettes, producing accounts of subjectivity constituted both in and beyond indexical discourse. We argue for creative practice as a means of representing the unfinishedness of observed social action. In particular, we suggest that poetry and theatre offer fertile means by which social and linguistic experience may be represented in all its complexity. We engage with responsibility, temporality and spatiality in considering an ethical-aesthetic approach to linguistic ethnography.

Part 2, Enacting Linguistic Ethnography, describes ways of writing and performing linguistic ethnographic research which represent social practice through creative means. In five essays we describe how outcomes of research may be recontextualised and recreated for new audiences through theatre, poetry and creative curation.

Essay 3, 'Polyphony', refers to *Voices of a City Market: An Ethnography*, a book-length artistic outcome of the TLANG project which represents the everyday practice of Birmingham Bull Ring market. This essay describes an approach to ethnographic writing which relinquishes the omniscient perspective of the academic researcher, in favour of polyphonic representation of the myriad voices of the market. We propose a way of writing ethnographically that is akin to curation, placing alongside each other the voices of market traders and their customers, without authorial comment or explanation. By these means we seek to mitigate the structures of power that often privilege academic voice above the voices of research participants. This essay suggests that voices collected and curated ethnographically may stand for themselves, call attention to the quotidian and represent the heteroglossia of everyday life.

Essay 4, 'Poetry', explores the potential of poetry in ethnographic writing. We submit that poetry has the capacity to incorporate the rhythm and rhyme of everyday life in ethnographic accounts. In *Voices of a City Market: An Ethnography* poems are part of the fabric with which to represent the sounds, smells, tastes, textures and visual experience of the city centre market. The shout-outs of butchers as they advertise their wares, the signage on a hardware stall, observations made in a nail parlour, description of the severed head of a goat, all become the stuff of poetry. The music of the city centre market is evoked through the music of the poem. Citing poet John Burnside, we argue that poems provide a means by which the noise of time can be re-experienced as the music of what happens. In ethnography, the poem has potential to offer new ways of seeing and new ways of saying.

In Essay 5, 'Ethnographic Drama', we explore the potential for dramatic approaches to linguistic ethnography to expand knowledge, to heighten the representation of social life and to bring research to new audiences. We consider the potential of ethnographic drama as a powerful medium through which to present research outcomes to a public audience. In the context of *Interpretations – An Ethnographic Drama* we suggest that the performance of research outcomes has the ability to move audiences to reflective, critical action. In this essay we propose that enacting observed practice involves a combination of curation and creation. Ethnographic drama can create a validity, authenticity and integrity which go beyond the scope of the conventional academic report. In this essay we propose that the representation of social practice on stage lends it an exponential quality, opening out the interpretive potential of research.

Essay 6, 'Performance', takes up the possibilities offered by ethnographic drama. Located in the context of observation of a volleyball team over four months as it practised, competed and socialised, this essay explores the potential of ethnographic drama to push its audience to reflect critically on everyday practice. With reference to *Volleyball – An Ethnographic Drama*, we examine theatre techniques devised to create distance between the audience and the dramatic performance. Such techniques include the constant presence of researchers on stage, their role to show to the audience outcomes of research, while at the same time participating in the world of volleyball. Shadowing, choreographed dance, stylised movement and simultaneous speech, all have the effect of denying to the audience that they are looking on the real world, insisting that they interrogate everyday life with a critical eye.

Essay 7, 'Politics', accounts for the representation of observations conducted in a major city centre library at a moment of political tension. *Ode to the City – An Ethnographic Drama* is set in a new, state-of-the-art library, when government austerity measures mean that staffing of the library is to be radically cut and opening hours reduced. In the play, four characters show the social world to the audience through discourse. It is a world subject to the contingencies of global economics, institutional power and local and national politics. It is a world constrained by big social structures, yet open to the possibility of transformation. In this essay we discuss the making of ethnographic drama from research. We suggest that ethnographic drama is neither a verbatim account of research data nor fiction. It is a creative curation of field notes, transcripts, audio-recordings, video-recordings, conversations and observations. It is creative non-fiction.

In **Part 3, Relations in Linguistic Ethnography**, we move from researched to researchers. In five essays we engage with researchers' accounts of relations in research teams and of relationships with research participants.

In Essay 8, 'Relational Ethics', we consider encounters in research through the lens of the philosophical works of Emmanuel Levinas. Here we look beyond familiar social categories to understand how compassion, humanity, empathy and understanding are common features of human encounters. In our ethnographic observations we constantly noticed that people sought contact and involvement with one another. Relational ethics provides a point of entry which allows us to understand people's willingness to go beyond the transactional and instrumental in everyday exchanges. This willingness, even desire, for human contact was occasioned not so much by preconceived identities as by the possibilities afforded by relating to others. For Levinas, people become individuals, and become ethical, through their relations with others. In this essay we develop a theoretical framework which guides our analysis in the remaining essays, as we engage with relations and relationships in research.

In Essay 9, 'Responsibility and Trust', we introduce the concept of 'moral spacing' as a dimension of linguistic ethnography. Relationships between researchers and research participants are replete with moral possibilities, which require an openness to one another's perspectives. In this essay responsibility is explored from the perspective of relational ethics, with the suggestion that responsibility has little to do with either duty or accountability, but is more concerned with an orientation towards other people. The essay explores two researchers' dispositions towards encountering difference. Focusing on trust and mistrust in field relations, we show how researchers investigating business and cultural heritage sites were able to transcend social categories, and transform relationships in the field. We describe how the researchers frequently faced moments of decision-making which required ethical and moral judgements.

In Essay 10, 'Strangeness and Proximity', we critically revisit the notion of 'making the strange familiar' in linguistic ethnography. We argue that strangeness is not something to be overcome, and made familiar, but, rather, is an essential quality of human togetherness. The essay documents a specific case study in the TLANG research project, in which political categories proved to be harmful in developing field relations, closing down ways of knowing rather than opening them up. In this essay, relations between researcher and researched are explored through the metaphor of proximity. We demonstrate that proximity does not erase strangeness, but maintains plurality and difference.

Essay 11, 'Difference', addresses interdisciplinarity and ethics. Developing an anti-subjectivist perspective to the generation of knowledge in research, this essay looks at meaning construction as a communal and critical process in a team of inquirers. An ethical perspective is required to reflect on the possible outcomes of research and the human consequences of those outcomes. As researchers, we encounter others whose perspectives differ from our own. In such encounters, difference between researchers and participants is conceived as a fundamental alterity, a vulnerability common to all. This essay draws on vignettes from three researchers in the TLANG project whose areas of expertise were not in linguistic ethnography, but who contributed their specialist knowledge in the fields of law, business and entrepreneurship, and sport, exercise and public health. In this essay we also explore concepts of responsibility, vulnerability and susceptibility in fieldwork relations in a quasi-legal setting, as a researcher engaged with stories of trauma.

Essay 12, 'Movement and Affect', explores ambiguity and uncertainty in written accounts of emotions, feelings, ideas, values, thoughts and beliefs in linguistic ethnography. Drawing on field notes and vignettes from participant observation in sports settings in the TLANG research project, the essay explores the relevance of 'irrelevancies'. An interest in the mundane, undramatic and apparently ordinary nature of everyday practice opens up space to contemplate fleeting moments in ethnographic research. In some cases, researchers participated in this phase of the research by learning to play the sports they were investigating. Their written accounts articulate their perception of their own and others' bodies under pressure as they attempted to learn new skills.

The essays in the book are complementary and incremental. A guiding principle of the book is polyphony, as we do what we can to let voices stand for themselves, without bowing to the insistent hand of the authors. Voices of butchers, welfare advisors, capoeira coaches, shopkeepers, librarians, artists, academic researchers and more are curated, sometimes created, and wherever possible given space to speak. Their voices vividly articulate the process of making linguistic ethnography.

Essay 2. Developing an Ethical-Aesthetic Perspective in Linguistic Ethnography

Introduction

The essays which make up Parts 2 and 3 of this book can each be read as free-standing and independent. The essay differs from the more typical academic 'chapter' in that it is an interpretive genre which deals with its subject from a personal perspective. The essay provides a literary convention more suitable to our purpose than other genres. Although the essays in this book are theoretically and methodologically linked, we do not attempt to impose on them an overall coherence. While we hope there is lucidity in the collection as a whole, each essay makes its own set of arguments. Acknowledging the researcher's inability to do justice to ethnographic observation in academic accounts, Ruth Behar (1996: 20) offers the essay as a promising mode of representation. She proposes that the essay is:

> an amorphous, open-ended, even rebellious genre that desegregates the boundaries between self and other.... Through the essay anthropologists can come closest to fulfilling those illicit desires of longing to write poetry, fiction, drama, memoir, anything but ethnography.

The essays in this book not only come close to fulfilling such desires, but they offer detailed reflections on the practice of writing poetry, drama and research vignettes to represent observed social life.

In terms of authorship, the essays are jointly curated. We bring a history of more than 20 years working together, over multiple linguistic ethnographic projects, invariably publishing co-authored accounts of our research. However, our early trajectories mark different routes into linguistic ethnography. We both studied the arts as undergraduate students. Adrian took a BA in English Literature. He won the national Eric Gregory Award for poetry. Adrian has continued to write and publish poetry outside his academic professional life. He served as Birmingham Poet Laureate from 2014 to 2016. More recently, he has extended his writing of poetry in the representation of ethnographic research. Adrian has also taken the lead in the development of ethnographic drama. Angela took a BA in Drama, and after graduating set up a theatre-in-education company, performing in primary and secondary schools in Cornwall, UK. During the early days of her career, she designed and taught language classes which drew heavily on drama techniques, took part in theatre performances and participated in improvisation classes. However, the last 20 years had seen a hiatus in her drama and theatre activities, until she led a small project to develop multilingual drama with international students. Angela and Adrian collaborated with doctoral researchers and a theatre practitioner to run drama and translation workshops with international students to devise and rehearse scenes from *Interpretations – An Ethnographic Drama*, which is an outcome of the TLANG research project. A short film of the multilingual workshop is available at https://youtu.be/tqey4qnUndA. We bring different skill sets to creative practice in linguistic ethnography, but our close collaboration means that we both take ownership of artistic and academic research outcomes.

An Ethical-Aesthetic Approach

The ethical-aesthetic approach we propose offers a means to represent multiple voices without an insistence on the imposition of meaning or explanation. Our aim is to step back from the authoritative, authorial voice of the academic researcher, allowing space for the inclusion of the voices of others. Once we accept that the perspective of the ethnographic researcher is not the only perspective, we are confronted with questions of how to go about including other voices, finding ways to articulate the complexity of experience. Ana Deumert (2022: 9) challenges us as researchers to broaden our understanding of what it means to collect data, and what counts as data, and asks, 'If empiricism is about sense experience, then how can we capture the complexity of what we sense?' Deumert urges us to capture the 'manyness' (2022: 9) of worlds of sense. In these essays we respond to this challenge, proposing that an ethical-aesthetic approach is equipped to articulate the complexity of what we sense in linguistic ethnography. In responding to the challenge to include many voices and perspectives in the representation of social life, we have turned to creative practice in the arts.

Representation of the polyphony of the communicative practices we encounter and observe in linguistic ethnographic research requires an openness to a range of artistic forms. Accounts of the complexity of what we sense in empiricism require creativity as well as accuracy, imagination as well as precision, the figurative as well as the literal. In order to move beyond the referential we must continue to develop an expanded ethnographic repertoire. This repertoire potentially includes ethnographic drama, the visual arts, dance, song and musical composition. Adopting modalities other than academic writing allows us to formulate a sociolinguistics that attends to the world as multi-sensuous and multi-sensed (Deumert, 2022). This is perhaps where the greatest potential lies in the development of the arts in ethnography. It opens up our thinking, so that we are able to go beyond 'the naïve empiricism that has shaped sociolinguistic work over the decades' (Deumert, 2022: 1). It pushes us to be self-conscious about what we are saying, whom we are including or omitting from the picture, and how we describe or explain what is going on. These are ethical as well as aesthetic issues. Deumert proposes a sociolinguistics of the spectre, suggesting that cultural presences in research might best be represented by those with a poetic sensibility and a hermeneutic orientation to meaning.

Many artists work to destabilise, disrupt and confound commonly accepted meanings. In the essays that follow we refer to the literary and artistic contribution of documentary novelist Svetlana Alexievich, dramatists Samuel Beckett and Bertolt Brecht, photographer Dorothea Lange, and poets Don Paterson and John Burnside, among others whose creative output has shaped our thinking. Their curation, writing, production and performance have inspired us to approach the relationship between semiotic subject and object more openly, focusing on affect and on the poetic function of language. This direction produces its own set of ethical issues, as we consider our own subjectivity in relation to those to whom we listen and those with whom we work. We also reflect on how we may represent the voices and social practices of those we encounter in the research process.

An Ethical-Aesthetic Perspective on Not Knowing

For the linguistic ethnographer it is a challenge 'not to know' when working with language. As discourse analysts we are used to tracing language through interactions to wider ideologies. In language we categorise, label, position, judge, name and know. We reflect social order, but also shape social order. As Jaworski and Coupland (1999: 3) put it, 'discourse is an inescapably important concept for understanding society and human responses to it, as well as for understanding language itself'. The analysis of discourse is central to sociolinguistics. It offers a window into understanding of human subjectivity and into processes of objectification. Indeed, linguistic ethnography approaches the human subject as initiated in, and individuated through, discourse.

One of the most familiar approaches to discourse analysis in linguistic ethnography, as in sociolinguistics, is through the study of indexical signs. A recent and powerful example can be found in the seminal scholarship of raciolinguistics, which describes racial and linguistic category-making. For example, Jonathan Rosa (2019) shows how historical and institutional discourses shape colonial constructions of reality in relation to US-based persons of Latin American descent. Rosa describes the assemblage of categories, racial and linguistic, which produce a 'colonial logic' (2019: 3) in the creation of Latinx as a particular 'recognisable coordinate'. Drawing on Inoue's (2003) concept of the listening subject, Rosa shows how signs are rearticulated in order to create and maintain a historical, political, economic and semiotic vantage point, which privileges all that is 'more or less normatively European' (Rosa, 2019: 5), across institutional and interactional scales. The privileged listening subject is already formed in discourse through the normative social categories and linguistic varieties of racial capitalism and liberal democracy. We visit this work in more detail in Essay 8.

Linguistic ethnography is indebted to the scholarship on indexicality of the philosopher and linguist Charles Sanders Peirce (1839–1914). Peirce characterised icons, indexes and symbols as matching relations of similarity and contiguity between sign and object. Although these sign–object relationships become 'intertwined in countless, indeterminate ways' (Rosa, 2019: 212), an indexical analysis involves tracing the relationship between linguistic signs and social phenomena. Michael Silverstein's (1992) work on indexicality established how the interactional moment is linked with larger ideological discourses across spatial and temporal scales. Rosa provides a helpful definition of the indexical sign, drawing on Silverstein's scholarship on metapragmatics:

> [A] sign – any utterance or object that people find culturally meaningful – has meaning only with respect to a 'metapragmatic' or 'metacultural' model of it. Such models make available the types of people that can be enacted in a given social context. Without them, we could not identify who people are or what they are signaling about themselves and others. (Rosa, 2019: 113)

In our research we have worked with a similar understanding of indexicality, pointing to the ideological underpinnings of sign–signifier relations in a variety of social settings. Indexical analysis approaches identity, agency and subjectivity as shaped through structures and categories which are produced linguistically. This approach has served us well to date.

Now, however, we find ourselves moving away from a position in which we claim to be able to explain the lives of those who are the subject of our research. Ethnography typically seeks to make transparent the experience of the migrant, the market trader, the low-paid worker, the small-business owner, the community activist, the butcher, the baker and the candlestick maker. An ethnographic perspective aims to understand the experience of the 'other' through their eyes. Linguistic ethnography aims to make audible the voices of those who participate in research. However, we increasingly retreat from the imperative to explain the life or meaning of the 'other'. A creative approach to ethnography allows us to stand with those whose voices we represent, to stand beside them but not above them, resisting the urge to say 'I know'. In adopting ethnographic poetry and ethnographic drama to represent the voices of participants in research, we have found the means to produce those voices as vital, vibrant and visible. As we will see in Essay 5, Édouard Glissant precisely argues for *not knowing*, for accepting things as they are, without explanation, leaving some things opaque. Opacities, wrote Glissant, can coexist and converge, weaving fabrics. Then 'every Other is a citizen, and no longer a barbarian' (Glissant, 1997: 190). Opacity drives every community and has the potential to bring people together. If Glissant's optimism might be read as utopian, so be it. Glissant's assertion that it is not necessary to grasp the other, to know the other or to become the other resonates with our practice in linguistic ethnographic research. Ethical-aesthetic research resists preconceived transparency, instead retaining the complexity of human interaction. It is an approach to research in which social phenomena are not reduced, but are expanded upon and elaborated.

Glissant (1997) reminds us that it is impossible to reduce anyone to a truth they would not have generated on their own. This is an ethical stance in research. We resist the ethnographic urge to explain the other, to make claims of familiarisation, to reproduce the other by naming them. In an ethical-aesthetic approach to research we confront our own actions as listening subjects, mindful that the last thing we want is to reproduce the iniquities of history. In confronting our actions we view subjectivity as not only indexically formed in discourse, but also as ethically shaped through temporal and signification orders. As white Europeans we acknowledge our ethical responsibility for injustices in which we have historically and institutionally been implicated. We continue to draw on indexical discourse analysis to understand how these injustices are structured in discourse, and how they are reproduced through language. In doing so we rethink the responsibilities of the social and linguistic researcher.

While Silverstein's (1992) conceptualisation of indexicality shows how micro-instantiations of language-in-use are ideologically linked to larger discourses, he paid less attention to the relational and ethical agency people bring to human encounters. Deumert (2018: 10) suggests that we should listen to the way people

> produce ways of speaking and writing that are ... skilfully crafted, directed towards an audience, and aimed at producing a felt and sensual experience in both speaker/writer and listener/reader.

This does not mean advocating for agency outside structures of power, but it does imply a reimagining of existing relations in the moment. As Deumert puts it,

> Creativity, our ability to bring a sense of newness into the world, enables us to overcome not only the fatigue of language, but also – and this is important in, especially, decolonial–postcolonial contexts – its violence: how can we speak ourselves to others through the language of the (former) colonizer? (Deumert, 2018: 10)

The indexical sign continues to be central to the analysis of discourse in linguistic ethnography. But we turn to creative practice in the arts to represent the contingency and complexity of ethical relations.

We find Peirce's thinking on indexicality to be more open to agency than that of Silverstein:

> Anything which focuses the attention is an index. Anything which startles us is an index. Indexical signs direct the attention to their objects by blind compulsion. (Peirce, 1931: vol. 5, 2.285)

Peirce emphasises surprise, attention and focus in his definition of the indexical sign. His definition explicitly refers to the senses. Peirce is concerned with perception and with reaction to the sign. While the indexical sign is powerful in compelling the agent's attention, it is the noticing of the object which is called into being by human agency. Peirce points to the dynamic force in any moment of saying. The indexical sign, as defined by Peirce, is therefore an opening for (re)interpretation. The 'interpretant' is a core element of Peirce's conception of the sign. The interpretant is the aspect of the sign which disrupts sign–object relations. Peirce saw that the reaction to any sign is itself a sign and comes with a readiness to create new meaning (Peirce, 1958). In other words, each moment of saying scrutinises the moment of the said. Through the concept of the interpretant Peirce established the interplay between the conventional and the creative, as he sought to account for the emergence of meaning in socially situated contexts. Peirce's observation, putting the interpretant at the centre, is important because it captures the possibility of indeterminacy in discourse and therefore of human agency.

Peirce (1935) names three sign types: the iconic, the indexical and the symbolic. We propose to add to this list the ethical sign. An ethical sign disrupts the culturally meaningful interpretations of sign–object relationships in order to engage with difference as a feature of human relations. The ethical sign shifts attention away from ego towards alterity, making demands of the listener to respond in ways which avoid categorising, knowing and essentialising. The ethical sign questions the certitude of the indexical, iconic and symbolic sign. While Peirce does not include the ethical sign in his lists of sign types, he does pay attention to both ethical and aesthetic features of signification. As we explain in Essay 11, when Peirce speaks of the aesthetic he is not concerned with beauty, taste or appreciation but, rather, with values, ideals and beliefs. This comes close to what we mean by an ethical-aesthetic perspective. The aesthetic is concerned with the manner and disposition of performance and representation, where listening to the other involves disruption, and possibly discomfort. The ethical sign thrives on exigency. It brings to signification an understanding that the Other comes before self. We will discuss the distinction between the 'other' and the 'Other' in Essay 8.

To shift away from the ethnographic urge to explain the life and culture of the other is to accept that the meanings of other lives may remain opaque to the researcher. A positive stance towards opacity has required a reorientation in our approach to research. It has meant rethinking our relationship to discourse; it has meant a shift away from an emphasis in discourse analysis on category-making. If we cannot know, or are not prepared to claim to know, or to name and to speak for another, what forms of discourse are available to us to represent the social world and to examine our own responsibility towards it? We have had to catch up with our own thinking in this journey, our understanding becoming clearer only after we started writing ethnographic research outcomes in different modes and genres. Before we write plays and poems as outcomes of linguistic ethnographic research we engage in several stages of analysis. We continue to write up our work in academic articles, analysing indexical discourse in ways familiar to sociolinguists. Careful listening to the polyphonic voices of large research teams has been part of our long-term commitment to reflexive research practice. However, as we come to reflect more on the aesthetic direction our work is taking, and as we discover the ethical implications of this pathway, our thinking about representation and responsibility has begun to change. We find inspiration in Kazuo Ishiguro's (2017: 35) thoughtful contemplation on literature:

> It's hard to put the whole world to rights, but let us at least think about how we can prepare our own small corner of it, this corner of 'literature' [social science], where we read, write, publish, recommend, and denounce.

Encounters in Research

Ethnographic research involves interactions between research participants and researchers, and between researchers within teams. The way the researcher constructs 'field' relations is a deeply value-laden process. The ethnographer faces questions of responsibility towards others involved in the research. To speak of responsibility is to consider one's subjectivity in relation to another's, and to acknowledge the ethical stance this entails. Ontologically, the ethnographer views each and every individual as irreducible in their distinctiveness and complexity. The individual remains a curiosity to the ethnographer, and the differences that make up unique lives can never be fully accounted for. Notwithstanding ethnographic reflexivity or empathy, the individual research participant or co-researcher remains unfathomable in their essence. The ethnographer upholds difference, resisting the urge to make the strange familiar, while simultaneously acknowledging that 'the aesthetic appreciation of everyday life requires defamiliarisation, making strange, or casting an aura' (Saito, 2015, in Deumert, 2018: 12). The ontology of the human subject is at the heart of this discussion, an ontology which maintains the singularity of the individual, while emphasising the complex interconnectedness of human relations in socially and historically formed regimes (Butler, 2005). We pay attention to the listening subject's orientation to difference, arguing that 'difference from' and 'in difference' are two distinct but overlapping dimensions of what it means to build ethical kinship in research practice. The perspective of 'difference from' considers the ways in which a unique subject articulates difference from an other (Biesta, 2016). Biesta describes 'difference from' as an instrumental difference, which involves the naming of identities. Here, difference is an effect of discourse in which people become categorised, and knowable to themselves and others. This conceptualisation is familiar to us as sociolinguists. The second theorisation refers to 'in difference' (Williams, 2021), in which difference is a feature of being human and demands an ethical response to the Other's vulnerability. To be in a state of 'in difference' is to respond to the ethical demand to trust the stranger, with all of the attendant hopes and disappointments such a position brings (Løgstrup, 1956/1997).

Our orientation to the individual in research demands that we consider our own responsibilities. Representation of ethnographic material through artistic practice brings new responsibilities for the researcher. Linguistic ethnography defines itself through detailed, repeated observation of social and linguistic practice. It is characterised by rigour, attention and care in the recording of voice, action and context. The linguistic ethnographer goes to great lengths to build trust and confidence with their subject, spending time with them, getting to know them. They do anything they can to level unequal relations of power, to be an attentive listener, to be present without being intrusive. They collect material by a number of means: writing field notes of their observations, audio-recording their subjects' interactions, taking photographs of the immediate environment, drawing sketches and diagrams, making video-recordings to capture embodied communication, conducting informal interviews and conversations, gathering documents and artifacts. As they collect their evidence they begin the long and laborious process of transcription, translation (where appropriate) and analysis. They annotate field notes and transcripts, write summaries and vignettes, look across data sets, share thoughts with team members and colleagues, make notes, annotate their annotations, summarise their summaries, and start to build arguments from what they have noticed. When that is done they typically begin to write their ethnographic account, ensuring that it is securely situated in the evidence as it was collected and analysed. By these means we might say that the linguistic ethnography can claim to take responsibility for the representation of a version of 'truth'.

What need, then, does the linguistic ethnographer have of artistic forms which claim their own truth, but are equally at home in the realm of the imagination? What does creativity offer to the science of linguistic ethnography? In proposing a sociolinguistics of the spectre, rooted in radical empiricism, Deumert (2022: 1) argues for research which acknowledges 'the sensuous and affective nature of social life', which refuses to work with the boundaries, binaries and demarcations that are located within the linearity of modernity. If our empirical studies are to incorporate responses to the social world which are beyond familiar limits and margins, we need means of articulating these responses. Melisa Cahnmann (2003) reports her experience of writing ethnographic poetry while doing observational work in a school in North Philadelphia. Her identity as both poet and researcher gave her licence to adjust what was 'true' in the detail and accuracy of her observations, and to also capture the 'Truth', or depth of feeling and music in the original situation. Cahnmann found that ethnographic poetry had the potential to make her thinking clearer, fresher and more accessible, and to render the richness and complexity of the observed world. She concluded that the literary and visual arts 'offer ways to stretch our capacities for creativity and knowing' (2003: 34).

Aesthetic merit and ethnographic validity can be difficult to attain simultaneously. For ethnographic validity, 'data' must be grounded in empirically 'true' experiences in a way that may conflict directly with the notion that it is better to be true to aesthetic judgement than to fact. A poet may not be loyal to historical locations, direct quotation or chronology, yet write a poem that is highly achieved technically, and which is true to experience or observable phenomena (Maynard & Cahnmann-Taylor, 2010). Poetry develops its own form of rigour, different from that of science, but no less demanding (Maréchal & Linstead, 2010). We expand discussion of ethnographic poetry in Essay 4. Correspondingly, the ethnographic playwright operates in a space which insists on both fidelity to observed social practice and on the creative imagination to entertain an audience.

The responsibilities of the linguistic ethnographer have less to do with duty, benevolence or altruism, and more to do with the subjectivity they bring to careful looking and listening. We take this up in more detail in Part 3. Acts of charity or mercy have no place in ethnography, but 'events of subjectivity' do (Biesta, 2016: 22). Biesta approaches the encounter relationally, in that being in the presence of another singularises the listening subject, and makes them responsible. Biesta describes this as 'subjectivity-as-responsibility' (2016: 21), in which it matters less what the person is and matters more what the person does in relation to the other. As we will outline in Part 3, we are working with a concept of subjectivity which is defined not in terms of sovereignty but, rather, relationally, in terms of non-sovereignty (Kelz, 2016; Butler, 2005). Following Levinas (1996), we argue that liberalism is unable to transcend the logic of utility, barter and exchange. Levinas argued that liberalism fails to account for generosity, trust, love and being-for-the-other. According to Tahmasebi-Birgani (2014: 97), he saw that 'an unhindered movement of sovereign ego, in its autonomy and its absolute freedom, is tyranny'. Levinas presents an alternative, in which ego is in the service of alterity. Relations are therefore asymmetrical, rather than symmetrical. In a revision of the normal order of hierarchies in liberalism, ego is commanded by the Other. The sufferings of the Other become my responsibility, not because I am remiss or guilty of inaction, not because I am under a sense of duty, or because I am feeling benevolent or charitable, but because the sufferings of the Other are mine too. I sense the other in me, recognising the vulnerability that resonates across humanity. Tahmasebi-Birgani (2014: 107) summarises Levinas's ethical project as a treatise against the effort of the ego 'in existing, sustaining, and projecting itself into the world, erasing the face of the Other'.

In an inversion of liberal politics, Levinas resists the self-referential prioritisation of ego. Liberalism presents a mode of agency founded in conceptions of autonomy and self-fulfilment. While we recognise the individual as singular, we do not conceive of them as autonomous. Rather, we approach the individual as relationally connected through ethical responsibility. The researcher has a responsibility to others in fieldwork relations, including in relations with colleagues. As the researcher listens, they create an ethical space. Theirs is an embodied space, in which they are open to the address of the proximal Other. We came to this ethical dimension of linguistic ethnography through close examination of the relationships people form with one another in quotidian interactions in research practice. Perhaps Levinas's most important contribution is to situate the ethical not as a relationship between human and God but, rather, in the concrete encounters which make up human relationships. That is, the ethical comes into being in the presence of others (Biesta, 2016). Levinas (1996) conceives of the human agent in terms of social change, and argues that relations are not formed in discourse, but in listening to and seeing the humanism of the Other. Levinas emphasises the face in his account of signification. The expression and proximity of the face is an invitation and an opening to social change. This orientation to research asks that we consider subjectivity beyond indexical discourse, and that we engage with both real and imagined temporal and spatial frames.

Temporality and Spatiality in an Ethical-Aesthetic Orientation

Bringing different understandings of temporality and spatiality to the fore contributes to an ethical and aesthetic account of human connectedness. In both Part 2 and Part 3 we explore temporality which does not follow the linear progression of past, present and future. While temporalities that link past, present and future are crucial for indexical analysis, we explore other time/space arrangements, which bring an aesthetic and ethical sensibility to relationships. In the forthcoming essays in this book we rethink dominant temporal narratives in linguistic ethnography, considering our role in cultivating 'an attitude of care towards the unknowable, but [nevertheless] formable future' (Kelz *et al.*, 2022: 6). In Part 2 we show how ethnographic drama and ethnographic poetry approach the plural temporalities and counter-histories (Kelz *et al.*, 2022) of the past. We argue that forms of representation such as the poem, the play script and the narrative vignette bring diverse values, voices and viewpoints, to reveal how past injustices are felt in the present. Kelz *et al.* argue for more nuanced engagement with theories of time and temporality, seeking to show how the future becomes a politicised space:

> It is necessary to consider the past not just as preceding the present, but as an integral part of any present and future politics. Past catastrophes and injustices continue to be felt in the present, and must play a more important role in the consideration of sustainability measures and efforts for more participative politics. (2022: 3)

In the essays in Part 2 we explore the possibilities of creativity in reordering events and scenes that do not follow the usual demands of chronology or linear plot. Here we learn from playwrights, poets, photographers and novelists, engaging with their ability to move in freer ways to represent different worlds. For example, novelist Kazuo Ishiguro (2017) describes how through his reading of Marcel Proust he learned to move between episodes diachronically, bringing together associations and memories across time and space. He describes the process as aligned to painting, in that,

> I could compose in something like the way an abstract painter might choose to place shapes and colours around a canvas. I could place a scene from two days ago right beside one from twenty years earlier, and ask the reader to ponder the relationship between the two. (2017: 17)

Moreover, Ishiguro observes that unconvincing characters in novels and films fail because the characters do not connect with other characters in an 'interesting human relationship' (2017: 27). He learns that paying attention to relationships in his novels, rather than to characters, produces better literature. He notes,

> Stories can entertain, sometimes teach or argue a point. But for me the essential thing is that they communicate feelings. That they appeal to what we share as human beings across our borders and divides … in the end, stories are about one person saying to another: This is the way it feels to me. Can you understand what I'm saying? Does it also feel this way to you?

Ishiguro's focus on relationships brings us to time/space configurations. Learning from philosophical critiques of synchronic time we conceive of relationships as points of ethical contact which re-describe history in non-linear terms, and understand the future as a realm of the unexpected and new. The subject is formed not solely in discourse but through human contact and relational ethics outside and beyond any specific linear time/space setting:

> The 'I' receives or welcomes the other at the same time as it is addressed by the other – it comes into existence (and remains as 'coming into existence') as an 'I' through this very act of invitation. Address, response, and constitution of the subject cannot be thought of as temporally distinct, separate phases. (Kelz, 2016: 102)

The listening subject is bound to the Other ethically in ways which are outside synchronic temporality. The subject and the Other are interrelated and interwoven in their constitutions of one another's being.

Jean-Luc Nancy (2007: 5), a philosopher of music, defines listening as an 'intensification and a concern, a curiosity or an anxiety', in which the self enters an attentive state. In this perceptible realm, listening becomes a sensibility towards sound. Don Paterson similarly notes that poems are 'semically overwired' (Paterson, 2018: 228), so that any detail in a poem is already overconnoting, and charged with an extra, motivated valency: it is already seeking out a thematic domain to which it wants to connect and from which it can draw power. The poem, says Paterson, has two authors hell-bent on expressing themselves – the poet and the reader; between them, poems are double-charged. In poetry, as in music, the past is not finished, fixed or final, but open to oncoming time. Seamus Heaney (2003) speaks of the energies beating in and between words that the poet brings into half-deliberate play. Heaney is concerned with the relationship between the word as articulate noise and the word as etymological occurrence, as symptom of human history, memory and attachment. John Burnside (2019) argues that music is what matters most in a poem, yet it is too often curtailed by mere denotation. The poet reinterprets the noise of time and makes of it a kind of music. As music-making is a way of making sense of noise, of giving noise order, so poetry is a way of ordering experience, of giving a meaningful order to lived time. Burnside (2019: 2) points out that temporality has been fundamental to humanity for many centuries:

> The first human communities calculated time by looking at the sun and the moon, and by observing changes in the natural world as they happened. Later, time was measured by man-made devices: the flow of water, the movement of shadows, the trickling of sand. Later still, clocks, watches, digital measures of time appeared. We came to inhabit a world of infinite temporal subdivisions.

In Essay 4 we will see that the poem can reveal what is happening, offer a context to events, and propose a means by which quotidian life can be reimagined in rhythm and rhyme.

Levinas is similarly concerned with time; not with the negation of synchronic time, but with its diversion and interruption (Tahmasebi-Birgani 2014: 103), so that it might be open to justice for those whose pasts have not been heard. Levinas's project is an ethical one, seeking ways to push back against liberal and neoliberal conceptualisations of the individual. Tahmasebi-Birgani (2014: 108) describes Levinas's work as a treatise against violence which 'unmask[s] the violence at the heart of ego's effort in existing, sustaining, and projecting itself into the world', a violence which ultimately has as its intention effacing the other's face. Throughout the essays in this book we consider the ethnographer's ethical and aesthetic responsibilities in representing others, while asking questions about researchers' responsibilities to themselves and others in human relations.

Part 2
Enacting Linguistic Ethnography

Essay 3. Polyphony

Introduction

Voices of a City Market: An Ethnography is a polyphonic text which is an outcome of linguistic ethnographic research conducted in Birmingham Bull Ring market as part of the TLANG project. The text is in three parts. Part 1 and Part 3 are dramatic dialogues between a group of characters – two butchers, a researcher, a dramaturg, a photographer, an entrepreneur, a poet and a documentary novelist. They discuss social research and debate the artistic representation of social life. Part 2 of *Voices of a City Market* represents the voice and action, the sound and smell, the taste and touch of Birmingham Bull Ring market. Taking as its starting-point a butcher's stall run by husband-and-wife migrants from China and Malaysia, the text includes shout-outs of butchers selling their wares, haggling of customers seeking discounted prices, sharp-edged banter between stall-holders, conversation at the family dinner table, stories of becoming and belonging, signage on posters and notices around the market hall, and much more. There are pigs' hearts, chickens' feet, goats' heads and exotic fish. There are children's shoes and Wellington boots, music tee-shirts and balaclavas, nail bars and tattoo parlours, greasy spoon cafés and noodle shops. This part of the book is constructed from a total of more than 100,000 words of observational field notes, 35 hours of audio-recordings and video-recordings in the market hall, 30 hours of audio-recordings in the butchers' home, more than 200 photographs, 150 online, digital and social media screen shots, and transcripts of 18 interviews with market stall holders.

What is it we are trying to represent in Part 2 of *Voices of a City Market*? Included in the usual aims of a linguistic ethnographic monograph is an intention to explain the motivations and meanings of the voices and actions of the social actors represented in the research. Often, explanation is corroborated with reference to research of a similar kind which has gone before, to situate the study in the context of existing theory and method. In the conventional format, analytical commentary on select examples of 'data' illustrates theoretical points. In this way arguments are built and theory invoked. Meanings of aspects of social life emerge and are tentatively asserted. We stand by, and are committed to, the rigorous process of knowledge generation from observations of social life through careful analysis. An open-access Working Paper reports the research we conducted in Birmingham Bull Ring market (Blackledge *et al.*, 2015). Eleven articles in peer-reviewed journals and edited book collections also take a familiar approach, each article reporting academic outcomes of the research.

Having engaged in the process of writing ethnography conventionally, we wanted to do more. We also wanted to do less. We wanted to do more to allow the voices and actions of the market to stand for themselves. And we wanted to do less to explain the meaning of those voices and actions. Literary scholar Mikhail Bakhtin (1963/1984) points out, with reference to Dostoevsky's novels, that the human being cannot finally be explained, that there are things only characters themselves can reveal. Bakhtin celebrates Dostoevsky for affirming the moral and existential irreducibility of the other, allowing characters to stand for themselves, without explanation. This ethical imperative is central to Bakhtin's account of Dostoevsky's polyphonic aesthetic. It is also the ethical imperative that drives the form and structure of Part 2 of *Voices of a City Market*.

Polyphonic Writing

When documentary novelist Svetlana Alexievich received the Nobel Prize in Literature in 2015, the Nobel Committee's citation commended 'her polyphonic writings, a monument to suffering and courage in our time' (Svenska Akadamien, 2015). The Nobel Committee's use of the term 'polyphonic' is close to Alexievich's own description (2015) of her writing as a 'novel of voices' (*roman golosov*) or 'super-literature' (*sverkhliteratura*), while Russian-language publishers typically categorise it as 'documentary prose' (*dokumental'naia proza*). Polyphony refers to the multifractal coherence that is achieved through the representation of multiple voices and worldviews within a single text (Bartlett, 2012: 14). Alexievich's (2005, 2016) journalistic method is to collect witness evidence in the form of extended narrative interviews about people's experiences of Soviet and post-Soviet times. Her series of five books, 'Voices from Utopia', is a pioneering blend of documentary material and literary art, a genre, she says, where human voices speak for themselves, where she intentionally blurs and even disregards the line dividing 'fact' and 'fiction' (Myers, 2017). Alexievich hears and sees the world as a chorus of individual voices and a collage of everyday details. Her literary method, she says, allows the closest possible approximation to real life.

The narrations presented in 'Voices from Utopia' do not straightforwardly correspond with the voices of the biographical persons interviewed by Alexievich. They are the voices of her interviewees, but ordered and arranged by her. They are at once her curation and her creation. Although Alexievich writes according to the same principles as a novelist, she does not write fiction. In Alexievich's texts there need be no clear threshold, no contradiction, between fact and fiction. The question is not whether the voices represented by Alexievich are 'true' but, rather, whether the implied author makes the implied readers believe in these voices as bearers of truth (Lindbladh, 2017). The historical value of 'Voices from Utopia' is inseparable from its artistic value. Regardless of the fact that the voices she represents are the creation of a supposed author, they are testifying to events that are real, in the real world. The polyphonic composition of 'Voices from Utopia' emphasises the ambivalence experienced by witnesses in relation to the act of representation. The implied author provides a representation of their experience while avoiding an external perspective, thus preserving the testimonies as unfinalised.

Bakhtin (1986) says he hears voices in everything, and dialogic relations among them. Polyphony does not merely refer to the coexistence of different voices. It also refers to engagement with the voice of the other and to engagement with difference. Bakhtin (1963/1984: 6) describes Dostoevsky's novels as polyphonic because they represent 'a plurality of independent and unmerged voices and consciousnesses, a genuine polyphony of fully valid voices'. For Bakhtin, Dostoevsky's polyphonic novel is a fundamentally new novelistic genre. Here, a character's word is just as fully weighted as the author's word. It is not merely one of their characteristics, nor does it serve as a mouthpiece for the author's voice. It is independent, speaking alongside the author's voice, combining with it and with the voices of other characters. It is not only unfinalised but also unfinalisable. In order to ensure the polyphony of independent ideological voices, an author avoids interposing the authoritative voice, and world view, between character and reader. The essence of polyphony lies precisely in the fact that voices remain independent. Characters in a polyphonic novel are no longer objects manipulated by the author, but subjects coexisting with the author and contending for the reader's attention (Krasnov, 1980).

Bakhtin (1963/1984) argued that Dostoevsky's novels are organised in a profoundly different way from those that precede them. The narrator renounces the right to the last word, and grants full and equal authority to the voices of the characters. The notion of polyphony addresses the question of narrative authority and discursive hierarchy – the view that novels are made up of a hierarchy of voices, with the author/narrator speaking the language of omniscient truth. The polyphonic novel undoes that hierarchy. It does not strive for authorial explanation or resolution. It opens on to the future rather than seeking to explain the past (Dentith, 1995). Bakhtin offers an aesthetic that is attractive in its anti-authoritarianism and its pluralism, seeing the novel as a form which counters the author's claim to speak with authority, to explain and to have the final word. In addition to the authorial voice, the world of the polyphonic text is populated with the stratified speech of its characters. The speech of characters points to positions in the social hierarchy. The language used by each character possesses its own belief system. A character's speech may refract the belief system of the author. At the same time, a single utterance, of author, narrator or character, may point to competing perspectives, beliefs and ideologies. That is, an utterance may simultaneously point in different directions. Discourse which represents the engagement of different wills, worldviews and intentions has come to be termed 'heteroglossia'. It is a key dimension of the polyphonic novel.

Heteroglossia in the novel serves two or more speakers at the same time, and expresses simultaneously two or more different intentions: the direct intention of the character(s) speaking and the refracted intention of the author. In such discourse there are multiple voices, multiple meanings and multiple expressions. Bakhtin (1981) argued that language in use and in action represents specific points of view on the world, each characterised by its own objects, meanings and values. That is, the speech of a character or narrator indexes a certain point of view, ideology, social class, profession or other social position. What is distinctive about heteroglossia is its focus on social tensions in language (Bailey, 2012). The use of certain words in a certain way indexes a social position (or some positions) because these words are characteristically used by members of a certain group. In this way, speakers inevitably position themselves with respect to others, making associations and evaluations. Bakhtin saw that what we talk about most are the words of others. Our speech is overflowing with other people's words. We weigh, evaluate, refute, repudiate, celebrate, affirm and so on not only the words of others but also the political/ideological position represented by those words. Any utterance, in addition to its own themes, always responds in one form or another to others' utterances that precede it, and speech inevitably becomes the arena where viewpoints, world views, trends and theories encounter each other.

A keystone of Russian literature, Aleksandr Solzhenitsyn, understood the polyphonic novel as a novel without a main hero, in which the author feels responsible for multiple characters but does not accord preferential treatment to any single voice. The author, he said, must understand every character and motivate his or her actions. Solzhenitsyn described his three major novels, *The First Circle*, *Cancer Ward* and *August 1914*, as polyphonic. These novels, together with *One Day in the Life of Ivan Denisovich*, were chiefly responsible for the award of the Nobel Prize in Literature to Solzhenitsyn in 1970. In *The First Circle*, for example, Solzhenitsyn demonstrates his ability to hear, comprehend and imitate not only different ideological voices but different languages as well. In *Cancer Ward* Solzhenitsyn allows the reader to see the world from the perspectives of patients and doctors, former labour camp prisoners, and those who send them to the camps. He allows the reader to see the world through the eyes of Communists, Christians and atheists. In *August 1914* Solzhenitsyn constructs a polyphony of ideological voices, diverse, articulate and virtually independent of the author (Krasnov, 1980). What unfolds in the novels of Alexievich, Dostoevsky and Solzhenitsyn, then, is a plurality of consciousnesses which combine but are not merged in the unity of the event. The polyphonic novel can be defined as a diversity of social speech types and a diversity of individual voices, artistically organised. This diversity of voices includes what Bakhtin (1963/1984) called social dialects, characteristic group behaviour, family jargons, professional jargons, generic languages, languages of generations and age groups, languages of the authorities, languages of passing fashions and languages that serve the specific sociopolitical purposes of the day. The polyphonic novel orchestrates this heteroglossic diversity of voices through authorial speech, the speech of narrators and the speech of characters. These languages struggle and evolve in an environment of social heteroglossia.

The originality of Dostoevsky's polyphonic novel lies not in its content but in its form. In a polyphonic novel the central idea is expressed through the work's structure (Krasnov, 1980). The dispersion of voices into 'the rivulets and droplets of social heteroglossia' (Bakhtin, 1981: 263) is a distinguishing feature of the polyphonic novel. Polyphony avoids the representation of finalised dialogue and narration. That is, the polyphonic text is not finished; it is not a coherent unity, with a beginning, a middle and an end. In Alexievich's work, life is not represented according to a finished narrative. It is continuous, ongoing life, which from the perspective of the subject is never finalised but always in the process of becoming. Through selection, juxtaposition and commentary, Alexievich presents in literary form the evidence she has gathered from her extended interviews (Brintlinger, 2017). The author's curation of the narrative transforms history into a story, blending facts with literary form. This stylistic liminality between oral history and literature creates a dramatic effect that sets Alexievich's narratives apart from contemporary literary and historical works (Karpusheva, 2017). She is not concerned so much with the facts of a case as with its universal qualities, and for this reason her intention is to capture and represent the history of the experience. She emphasises the places where stories trail off, indicating in parenthetical asides when her interviewees weep, or laugh, or stop to smoke, or bemoan their inability to express their feelings, or refuse to try. The appearance of these 'stage directions' in the text is a constant reminder that the stories narrated to Alexievich coincide only imperfectly with the words that have been reproduced.

The unfinalised nature of Alexievich's documentary novels is further evident in the fact that she has always continued to rewrite. Variations between editions of the works that make up 'Voices from Utopia' exist, from the level of words and phrases to that of entire monologues and essays. These changes to the text involve additions and deletions, as well as rewording and rephrasing. Another common change involves moving a word or phrase from one place to another or, less commonly, moving a monologue from one essay to another (Myers, 2017). Alexievich's literary technique is not just a matter of 'truthful' depiction but of restoring experience to those who have been deprived of the opportunity to tell about it. In Alexievich's work, as in Dostoevsky's, the ordinary pragmatics of the plot play a secondary role. The structural elements of the text are devoted less to the unity of the narrative than to the task of constructing a polyphonic world. The consciousness of the author, binding together plot, style, tone and narrative, is no longer at the forefront. New principles appear for an artistic combination of elements and for the construction of the whole. A belief that there must be more than one way of understanding the world is essential to a polyphonic conception of art, and it is this belief that governs the structure of the polyphonic novel.

Polyphony in Ethnography

Alexievich's polyphonic documentary novels lay the groundwork for an understanding of the human world, and the human condition, that attempts to give precedence to the once marginal and peripheral. Her work asserts that matters of representation are also matters of justice (Bush, 2017). In ethnography, likewise, independent voices create their social world but also point beyond that world, to structural forces. Reading ethnography connects individuals whose completely different points of view may be at odds, and even clash, in real life. Although the voices heard in ethnography stem from the implied author, they are not fictional. They are voices which are unfinalised, and which testify to everyday human life. The ethical imperative of polyphony, which insists on the engagement of self and other, and displays the human condition through representation without explanation, has enormous potential for ethnography. It is 40 years since James Clifford (1986) wrote of the challenge of representing the communication practices, and intercultural influence, with which people interpret themselves and others in a multivocal, heteroglossic world. In this condition, said Clifford, it is increasingly hard for anthropologists and ethnographers to conceive of human diversity as inscribed in bounded, independent cultures. Not only this, it was clear that styles of cultural depiction were, historically, limited. Ethnographic writing was undergoing something of a crisis. How could the complexity of everyday experience be transformed into an authoritative written account? How could the encounter shot through with power relations be represented as characteristic of some other world? How could the full range of multi-semiotic, multimodal practice be represented in the written word?

Ethnographers were seeking new ways to adequately represent the lives of their informants, but finding few models to help them. The central, dominant voice was still that of the ethnographic writer aspiring to a Flaubertian omniscience. Clifford saw that the textual embodiment of authority was a recurrent problem in ethnography. He was drawn to what he saw as the useful – if 'extreme' – standpoint provided by Bakhtin's analysis of the polyphonic novel. It was in the polyphonic novel that speaking subjects could be represented in a field of multiple discourses. It was the polyphonic novel that grappled with, and enacted, heteroglossia. Polyvocality in ethnography had been restrained and orchestrated, by giving to one voice a pervasive authorial function, and to others the role of sources, informants to be quoted or paraphrased. Perhaps the extensive use of quotations from informants could be a strategy to break up the monophonic authority of the ethnography. If dialogism and polyphony were recognised as modes of textual production, monophonic authority may be questioned, and revealed to be characteristic of a science that had too easily claimed to represent cultures. Clifford proposed reading ethnography against the grain of the dominant voice, seeking out other, half-hidden authorities, reinterpreting the descriptions, texts and quotations gathered together by the writer. However, he was perhaps not ready to relinquish the control traditionally exercised by the academic researcher over the representation of the voices of participants in research. He worried that ethnography had been 'invaded' by heteroglossia. Polyphonic works, he counselled, were open to unintended interpretations.

The crisis in ethnographic writing (Geertz, 1973) was unresolved. The problem was to write ethnography in such a way as to bring interpretations of some society, culture or way of life into an intelligible relationship with its members, carriers or representatives. The crisis was one in which ethnographic authors had become nervous about claiming to be able to explain the lives of others on the grounds that they had spent time observing them in their 'native habitat'. In an age of decolonisation, Geertz recognised that the moral and epistemological foundations of ethnography were sinking into quicksand. Ethnography relies on its capacity to persuade readers that what they are reading is an authentic account by someone personally acquainted with how life proceeds in some place, at some time, among some group. Whatever else ethnography may be, said Geertz (1988: 143), 'it is above all a rendering of the actual, a vitality phrased'. At the same time, he acknowledged that writing ethnography was a creative process, a work of the imagination, involving telling stories, making pictures, concocting symbols and deploying tropes.

Acceptance of creativity in ethnography was resisted because the imagined was confused with the imaginary, the fictional with the false. Whether ethnographers have recovered from the moral and epistemological crises of the 1980s is a moot point. Fred Erickson (2018) asserts that ethnographic research reports are often partial renderings done from the standpoint of the life experience of the researcher, and suggests that their validity may be compared to that of novels and poetry – pointing toward 'truths' that are not literal. Part 2 of *Voices of a City Market* reaches for the condition of the polyphonic. The content is a curation of disparate materials: service interactions between butcher and customer as they barter over the price of chickens' feet and pigs' trotters, WeChat orders for pork and beef from a local restaurant, complaints about the city council's decision to move the bus stops further away from the market hall, narratives about the tough early days of setting up a business. These are the independent voices and consciousnesses of the marketplace. They are voices that stand for themselves, without authorial explanation.

We have seen that in a polyphonic novel the central idea is expressed not so much through one character or another, as through the work's structure and form. We can say the same about polyphonic linguistic ethnography. Part 2 of *Voices of a City Market: An Ethnography* is constituted as 304 separate sections, in six groups, representing the voices, actions, sounds, interactions, opinions, memories, digital communications and linguistic landscape of Birmingham Bull Ring market. Of these sections, 150 are excerpts from field notes. Of the 150 field note excerpts, 116 include dialogue, while the other 34 do not. Ninety of the 304 sections are extracted from interviews with market stall holders, including the Chinese and Malaysian butchers who were key participants in the research. Seventeen sections rely entirely on transcripts from audio-recordings, without field notes, and one section relies on the transcript of a video-recording. Seventeen sections represent examples of signage from the semiotic landscape of the market. Fifteen poems are based on aspects of the social life of the market. Twelve photographs taken in the market are included. In addition, at the heart of the book, a set of 51 rhyming haiku offer a creative version of the voice of the market's Hygiene Operative, uniquely placed as he constantly circulated the market hall. The 304 sections of Part 2 are ordered and arranged neither randomly nor according to a prescribed system. There is perhaps a rhythm to the arrangement of dialogues, narratives, descriptions, transcripts, lists, advertising signs and WeChat messages. If such a rhythm is discernible, it is the rhythm of the market.

In 1965 Dorothea Lange, the pioneering photographer of migrants in dust-bowl America, curated an exhibition of her photographs at the Museum of Modern Art, New York. As she prepared the exhibition, she looked through her photographs, which she said were about nothing very much, but which described human life. She selected some, rejected others, as she did so talking through the process of ordering and arrangement. How do you tell others about what you think is worth telling, she asks. How do you tell others what you have discovered, or uncovered, or learned, or been endowed with in one way or another? Not that one, she says, examining and evaluating her work. Yes, that one; put that with the other one, yes. She holds a negative up to her eyes. You try, she says. You find your way. And no one can assure you when you've been successful and when you haven't. You never really know that. But that's what the job is. She was not enthusiastic about the process of putting together the exhibition. But she realised its importance. Get that exhibition together, she said. Put it on the wall for other people to look at, to spell out what I would like to speak about in photography.

As she worked, Lange said she would like to produce an exhibition so that people's minds might be stirred by the immense variety and richness of human life. She said what will stir people's minds is not merely the content of the work, but its form. This group of pictures, she said, is just like all my groups of pictures, they just suggest the possibilities of the medium. It's all I hope ever to do, with this show or anything, not to achieve it, but to suggest it, for someone else to carry it on. She expressed her ambition as a feeling. I feel it in terms of possibility, provocation, the potential of this medium. We're just on the threshold of it, and I'd like to give it a push, a slight push. What was needed, according to Lange, was a new repository of cultural history which focused on the development of cities. Such a repository would enable people to see what was really there, what it looked like, and in so doing reveal the underpinning human condition.

Lange hoped that the viewer of the new photography would say, oh yes, I know what she means, though I never thought of it, I never paid attention to it. Calling attention to the mundane, the everyday, the familiar, would enable people to see as if for the first time something they had passed by a thousand times. Lange's vision was for a new photography of the metropolis (or, as she put it, the 'megalopolis'), a new form, one that resisted explanation but represented the world as she saw it. Like Svetlana Alexievich, Dorothea Lange made representations of people in their ordinary, extraordinary lives. She set them alongside each other, not systematically, but also not randomly. Alexievich's arrangement of narratives and witness memories, which she called a chorus of individual voices, a collage of everyday details, had much in common with Lange's curation of the everyday. Asking no explanation, the photographs and the witness narratives stand for themselves. And of course they do more than call attention to the mundane. Unfinalised, and unfinalisable, they represent the human condition.

Form

In the process of analysing the material collected in our observations of the market, we did everything we could to combine data types and sources. An interaction at the butcher's stall would be audio-recorded at the same time as two or three sets of observational field notes about the same event were written by researchers. The process of analysing these encounters between people does not regard the different data sets (field notes, audio-recordings etc.) as separate. Rather, they are integral to each other. In the remainder of this essay, a small number of complete sections from the book are presented as examples of material (entirely or partly) collected using familiar technologies – biro and notebook, camera, digital voice-recorder, video-camera, smart phone. These typical examples enable us to argue that the structure and form of Part 2 of *Voices of a City*

Market: An Ethnography is polyphonic, and represents the heteroglossia of the social and commercial life of the market.

Field notes that include dialogue

A fundamental means for the ethnographer to begin to construct and record the voices and actions of people in the social world is by writing field notes. Ethnographic field notes describe social action, and create voices of characters through direct and indirect reported speech and by paraphrasing (Emerson *et al.*, 2011). An important aspect of the process of representation is the selection of excerpts from the corpus of field notes. Given that we wrote more than 100,000 words of field notes in the market, how did we select some for inclusion in Part 2 of *Voices of a City Market* and choose to omit others? A perceptive author, say Emerson *et al.* (2011: 207), looks for excerpts – especially those rich in talk and action – that reveal people's different views and concerns, as well as consequential moments in interactions. That is, the perceptive author looks for excerpts which, taken together, provide a polyphony of voices. This is a matter of form as well as content. Artistic form, argues Bakhtin (1963/1984: 43), does not shape already prepared and found content, 'but rather permits content to be found and seen for the first time'.

Not everything in the orbit of the researcher can be recorded. Speakers under observation may be at a distance from the linguistic ethnographer, or speech may be quiet, or otherwise indistinct. However, when the research participant is wired with an audio-recording device, gaps in field notes can be filled in from transcripts of audio-recordings. Observation, of course, continues uninterrupted when audibility is limited, and the researcher continues to write field notes. Conversely, at other times the research participant and her interlocutors may be consistently audible, but may temporarily disappear from view – into a store room, outside for a smoke, to chat with a friend or neighbour. Again, the audio-recording becomes crucial. Although we may miss some relevant observable action, much can be recovered from audio transcripts. The following is one of the 304 sections of Part 2 of *Voices of a City Market: An Ethnography*. It is a typical example based on both an audio-recording transcript and two sets of field notes written during observation of the butcher's stall:

> Two women in headscarves, long skirts, cardigans and striped socks stop at the stall. One is older than the other. The pragmatic butcher, the genial butcher and the loyal assistant butcher are on the stall. The women buy a large bag of chicken wings. They also want to buy a hen, but are unimpressed with the price. The loyal assistant butcher holds up a hen in two hands, stretching it from end to end.
> Look at the size of that! he says.
> The women buy the hen.

Now a young man appears and joins the women. He starts by asking the pragmatic butcher how to say good morning in Chinese. How do I greet good morning?
The pragmatic butcher says good morning.
The young man says, no, in your language.
Now the pragmatic butcher understands what is being asked of him. Zaoshang hao, he says.
Zaoshang hao, says the young man.
Zaoshang hao, says the pragmatic butcher again.
Zaoshang hao, says the young man again.
Ah, says the pragmatic butcher, confirming that the greeting has been learned, and that the impromptu lesson is at an end.
Zaoshang hao, says the young man one more time.
The young man now bends forward with the upper half of his body, sticks out his bottom, and extends his left arm and the forefinger of his left hand out behind him. Everyone laughs. The loyal assistant butcher understands that the elaborate mime represents the young man's request for pig tail. Oh, the tail? he says.
However, the pig tails have not yet been delivered. They will arrive later in the morning.
The loyal assistant butcher says, I gotta wait for delivery.
The pragmatic butcher mimes with his hands driving a car, and says, car coming later.
The genial butcher says, delivery coming later.
The pragmatic butcher adds, driver.
The loyal assistant butcher says, eleven, eleven o'clock, picking up a small mantelpiece-style clock from its usual position next to the till and pointing to it.
The customers echo him, eleven, eleven.
The loyal assistant butcher laughs, and says, yeah, walk around, come back.

The young man wants to know whether it is all right for him to leave his purchases at the stall and return later to pick them up. He says, I leave it here everything?
His wife adds her voice, saying, I buy, leave here.
Before he leaves the scene, the young man asks how much his purchase of meat has cost so far. Twenty-six so far, the loyal assistant butcher replies.
The older female customer says, that's too much. However, she does not pursue the point.

The pragmatic butcher turns to the genial butcher and nods towards the women. This must be her mum, he says in Mandarin, this must be her mum, she's a spitting image of her. He turns back to the customers, and addresses the man, your wife's mum? No, her sister? His joke is a compliment to the older woman.
The young man says, not sister.
The loyal assistant butcher picks up the pragmatic butcher's cue, pointing

to the pragmatic butcher and saying loudly, my brother, this one my brother, he's my brother, yeah, hahaha!!
Everyone laughs again.

The above section of the book was constructed from the two sets of field notes and the audio-recording transcript, all of them synchronous. The relevant field notes are reproduced here, together with the transcript of the audio-recording.

Adrian's field notes

In Adrian's field notes 'Mr C' is the butcher; 'B' refers to the assistant butcher.

Two women in headscarves, long skirts, cardigans and striped socks stop at the stall. They are perhaps Romanian (although I am guessing). They buy a large bag of chicken wings. They also buy a hen, and are unimpressed with the price. B holds the hen up in two hands, stretching it from end to end. 'Look at the size of that', he says. The women buy the hen. 'Anything else?', asks B. The two women discuss between them. They buy a tray of pork belly. 'Ten pounds', says B. The older of the two women wanders over to All Seasons. Now a young man appears and joins the women. He starts by (I think) asking Mr C how to say 'good morning' in Chinese. Mr C tells him and the man mimics him two or three times. The customers want to leave their purchase behind the stall to collect later. There are gestures here I don't quite understand. Mr C mimes driving a car, and asks 'car?' The young man at this point bends forward with the upper half of his body, sticks out his bottom and extends his left arm and the forefinger of his left hand out behind him. They all laugh. I'm sure the mime means something, but at the same time it might be untranslatable. B picks up the tiny mantelpiece-style clock from its usual position next to the till and points to it, saying 'eleven o'clock'. This seems to be the time arranged for the collection of the meat. There is much besides in this translation zone. I can't identify the language of the group, and would be guessing at their nationality/ethnicity. But I hope that if we have recorded this interaction we will be able to translate their talk. Mr C points to the two women and says 'same', then 'sisters?'. B points to himself and Mr C and says 'my brother'. The group all laugh together. The ability to joke and laugh in a context in which there is such a differential range of proficiencies in the main language in use is remarkable.

Rachel's field notes

In Rachel's field notes 'KC' is the butcher; 'BJ' refers to the assistant butcher.

Two south European women stopped by the counter. They looked like mother and daughter age wise and were both wrapped up in baggy sweaters and long skirts draped down above their ankles. They also both wore a sparkled, sequined head scarf, finished with gaudy coloured stripy socks tucked in slippers. They were checking the meat in lazy steps before telling BJ what they wanted. They kept chatting between themselves in their own language, which I didn't even know what language it was.

When the women were just about to finish their shopping a lean, tall young guy walked to the counter and said 'Nihao' to KC in high spirit. He had dark hair and dark beard, looked Asian to me at first so I didn't realise that he's actually the husband of the younger one of the two women there. He asked KC how to say Good Morning in Chinese. 'Zao Shang hao!' KC told him and he mimicked the pronunciation, sounded not bad actually. 'How much?' He pointed to the purchase his wife just took off BJ's hand which gave me the idea that they were together. '26' BJ answered, waiting for payment. The man took out a wallet from his jacket and paid for the meat.

KC was watching them at the side and said to the man 'Same, same', pointing at the two women. KC must have felt both women were dressed up in the same way, trying to tell the man that these women looked quite similar to each other. KC asked the man 'Your wife?' The man nodded his head 'Yes, man!' The mother was a bit unhappy so she spoke up for her daughter as well, pointing at the other woman with one finger, said to KC 'My daughter!' KC continued and asked the man: 'No sister?! Are you sure they are not sisters?!' and they all laughed loudly. BJ tipped his thumb at KC and said to the man: 'This is my brother!' louder laughter exploded from them. While the 'live show' was on the young woman drifted to the other side of the counter, starting to check other stuff. She bought a huge bag of chicken wings and paid herself this time with a 20 pound note. The man said something to KC and BJ, waved his arms and moved his legs at the same time, as if putting on a pantomime show. Finally KC and BJ understood the man was trying to tell them he wanted to leave his shopping bags at the counter and would come back later around 11am as they were going shopping somewhere else first. Three of them left empty handed. Adrian and I were quite amused by their jokes and we were pleased that we recorded these interesting bits. 'It's like a translation zone' Adrian later on commented excitedly. I really hope the recordings could come in handy when we come to the data analysis.

Transcript of the audio-recording

The following transcript is of the audio-recording of the same event as that described in the field notes. The transcript begins as the 'tall young guy' arrives.

[Female customer (FC); male customer (MC); Bradley (BJ); Kang Chen (KC). (xxxx) refers to unintelligible speech.]

1 MC good morning
2 KC good morning
3 MC how do I greet good morning?
4 KC eh?

5	MC	good morning
6	KC	good morning
7	MC	no, in your language
8	KC	早上好
		<zaoshang hao>
9	MC	zaoshang hao
10	KC	早上好
		<zaoshang hao>
11	MC	zaoshang hao
12	KC	ah
13	MC	zaoshang hao
14	FC	(xxxx)
15	BJ	the tail? Are we waiting for delivery?
16	FC	yea (xxxx)
17	BJ	I gotta wait for delivery
18	KC:	car coming later
19	MC	pork
20	BJ	yea
21	MC	delivery coming later
22	KC	driver
23	BJ	eleven, eleven o'clock
24	MC	eleven
25	FC	eleven
26	MC	(xxxx)
27	BJ	yeah, walk around, come back, hahahaha
28	MC	I leave it here everything
29	FC	I buy, leave here (xxxx)
30	BJ	okay, yep
31	MC	how much?
32	BJ	twenty six so far
33	FC	that's too, that's too much
34	KC	这个是她妈, 这个肯定是她妈, 跟她一样一样的!
		<this must be her mum, this must be her mum, a spitting image of her>
		your wife's mum? (xxxx) yea, no sister?
35	MC	not sister
36	BJ	my brother, this one my brother, he's my brother, yea, hahaha, four pounds, thank you

Both sets of field notes and the audio-recording are essential to the representation of the encounter. The field notes written by researcher Rachel Hu, a Mandarin speaker, were complemented with those written by Adrian Blackledge. The scene as presented in *Voices of a City Market* was thereby reconstructed from the field notes in conjunction with the audio file and its transcript.

The field notes describe what was in many ways a typical and everyday interaction between the butcher, Kang Chen, his wife, Meiyen Chew, his assistant, Bradley, and three customers looking to buy chicken wings, a hen and pigs' tail. The customers complain about the price of the hen, and the butcher's assistant responds with good humour, but refuses to drop the price. The researchers, stationed relatively unobtrusively four or five yards from the action, with their notebooks, are not able to hear everything that is going on. Moreover, if they were able to hear everything, they still might struggle to interpret the fine grain of rapid-fire interaction in the marketplace. This was the kind of interaction observed repeatedly during our four months of observations of the butcher's stall. However, two aspects of the interaction mark it as less than typical. First, one of the customers asks Kang Chen to teach him how to say 'good morning' 'in your language'. This was not a unique instance of this kind of request, but nor was it typical. In turn 1 of the transcript the customer initiates contact with the butcher as he approaches the stall, saying 'good morning'. Kang Chen responds in kind, also saying 'good morning'. As soon as Kang Chen understands what it is the customer is requesting, he is more than willing to engage in the linguistic game of teaching the customer how to say 'zaoshang hao'.

More unusual than this was the customer's subsequent mime. We had become used to customers pointing to the cut of meat they wished to purchase. We had also noticed customers using other physical gestures to order their meat – a man touched his own tongue when he wanted ox tongue; a man pointed to his own head when he wanted to buy pigs' head. Another man widened and narrowed his arms repeatedly, as if pulling a piece of elastic, as he asked for pigs' intestine. The mime described in the field note here, however, goes beyond these examples, in that it was of the order of performance rather than merely communication. As the field note describes, the man 'bends forward with the upper half of his body, sticks out his bottom and extends his left arm and the forefinger of his left hand out behind him'. Neither of the researchers observing the performance and writing field notes understood the meaning (if any) of the mime. As the field note reports, although it was assumed that the physical performance probably meant something, it 'might be untranslatable'. Only later, when the audio-recording of the same incident was listened to repeatedly and transcribed, did it become clear that the young man's wife (or mother-in-law – it was not clear which) had asked the butcher's assistant for 'tail'. Then it was clear that the man was making a physical representation of a pig in order to support his wife's request. The mime was probably unnecessary, as the butcher's assistant, Bradley, understands the woman's question immediately (turn 15). The mime is convivial, and part of the entertainment for an audience comprising the market traders and the man's wife and her mother, two researchers and any passers-by. During our four months in the indoor meat and fish market we frequently heard and saw traders shouting their wares and putting on larger-than-life performances to attract customers to their stall. As such, performance and conviviality were part of the everyday fabric of the market. It was certainly less usual for customers to put on a performance for traders than vice versa, but the performative aspect of this customer's repertoire was permitted, and was deployed, because in the market hall clowning around is commonplace and acceptable. Also, the particular type of performance presented on this occasion was not inappropriate because embodied communication was a common feature of the discourse of the market hall.

The corporeal dimension of the interactants' repertoires is further evidenced when Adrian's field note comments 'Mr C mimes driving a car, and asks "car?"' The audio-recording transcript shows that while acting out this mime Kang Chen said 'car coming later' (turn 18) and 'driver' (22). In the field note we find evidence of more visual cues, this time for a more explicit communicative purpose, as Bradley 'picks up the tiny mantelpiece-style clock from its usual position next to the till and points to it'. At the same time Bradley says 'eleven, eleven o'clock', indicating with both words, the clock as supporting prop, and his pointing gesture that the delivery of pigs' tail will not arrive before eleven and that they should return at that time. The male customer says something which we were not able to hear in the audio-recording clearly enough for transcription, and Bradley says 'yeah, walk around, come back, hahahaha' (turn 27). At this point the male customer says 'I leave it here everything', asking whether it is all right for him to leave his purchases at the stall and return later to pick them up. His wife adds her voice, saying 'I buy, leave here'. Before he leaves the scene the male customer asks how much his purchase of meat has cost so far, and when Bradley replies 'twenty-six so far', the female customer says 'that's too much'. She appears to want to argue about the price, and perhaps to negotiate down the cost of the meat. We saw many customers attempt to do this during our time in the market. We spoke to market traders who were happy enough to engage in this kind of haggling, and were prepared to do a favour for some of their customers. Others were less enthusiastic about the practice. On this occasion, however, the female customer did not push the point.

It was not uncommon for the couple, Kang Chen and Meiyen Chew, to comment to each other on their customers, creating a private moment in the parochial space of the market. Kang Chen looks at the two women customers and says to his wife, in Mandarin, 'This must be her mum, this must be her mum, a spitting image of her'. The comment on the appearance of the older woman, good-natured and good-humoured, creates a point of communicative overlap between the protagonists in the interaction. Bradley joins in with Kang Chen's joke, picking up his cue and contributing his own version, pointing to Kang Chen and telling the customers: 'my brother, this one my brother, he's my brother, yea, hahaha'. Everyone present laughs at the joke. When Bradley says (three times) that Kang Chen is his brother it is funny because it is a comment on visible difference – Kang Chen is ethnically Chinese, while Bradley is not, so the idea that they are brothers is humorous. The comment on difference has the potential to limit difference, as Bradley validates and rewards Kang Chen's joke by repeating his own version of the same.

The polyphonic ethnography orchestrates a heteroglossic diversity of voices through the discourse of field notes and the recorded speech of characters in the market. These languages live a real life in an environment of social heteroglossia. They are, at minimum, the language of convivial commerce ('Look at the size of that!'), the language of unfolding access to interaction ('How do I greet good morning?'), the language of accommodation ('Zaoshang hao, says the pragmatic butcher again'), the language of embodied action ('The young man now bends forward with the upper half of his body'), the language of repetition as consent ('The customers echo him, eleven, eleven'), the language of request ('I leave it here everything?'), the language of negotiation ('The female customer says, that's too much'), the language of compliment ('her sister?') and the language of humour ('he's my brother, yea, hahaha!!'). Diverse languages coexist, jostle together, organised into a structured artistic system. Alongside the languages of characters in the market is the voice (we might say the voices) of the field notes, which acts as the voice(s) of the narrator. Description of action ('The pragmatic butcher mimes with his hands driving a car') and visual detail ('headscarves, long skirts, cardigans and striped socks') brings the scene vividly to life. In addition to the descriptive voice, and the narrative voice of the field notes, the scene is ordered and arranged so that it is acted out as a drama. The authors, backgrounded but not erased, leave their mark, arranging the elements of the scene in such a way that the drama plays out with dynamism and humour. In this section of Part 2 of *Voices of a City Market* the diversity of speech types, the coexistence of unmerged voices and the relatively backgrounded author and narrator are characteristic features of the polyphonic text.

Field notes that do not include dialogue

Whereas some sections of the book are principally based on dialogue, others are excerpts from observational field notes which do not include dialogue. In these instances the focus of the researchers was on what they could see, smell, taste and touch, rather than mainly on the detail of what they could hear. The following section of *Voices of a City Market* reproduces notes written on the first day of fieldwork, as Adrian Blackledge sat in the market café waiting for the stalls to open:

> A large mug of strong tea. Salt and pepper pots, a plastic ketchup bottle in the shape of a tomato, chipped blue Formica. Signs on the wall – STEAKS BURGERS COOKED DINNER BEEF POTATO'S GRAVY TAKE-AWAY FISH & CHIPS. A young woman places a bacon sandwich on the table in front of me. The bread is thick and white. The young woman's left arm wears tattoos from shoulder to wrist. The inside of her right arm is

inscribed with Chinese characters. Her dyed black hair has been shaved at the back and sides. Outside the window, but inside the market hall, a poster: POULES PLUVERA C'EST DELICIEUX. Hundreds of brightly coloured tins, packets and bottles line the high shelves of REMMISON LTD AFRICAN FOODS. The tattooed woman conducts a loud conversation about her social life with a man in the kitchen. He is frying bacon and wears a heavily stained blue-striped apron. They both have broad local accents. Union Jack bunting hangs from the ceiling in constant celebration. Paint peels from the walls like dead skin.

Again, form is as important as content. There are characters here, but they are broadly drawn: a tattooed woman, a man in the kitchen. The narrator takes up a position in the first person ('on the table in front of me'). But this is not the perspective of the all-seeing, all-knowing author. It is an external perspective. We know nothing of the internal worlds of the protagonists in the market café. The external landscape of the market hall is in evidence in signage, both within and without the café. The register of signs inside the café may index levels of literacy associated with a certain position in the social or educational hierarchy: 'POTATO'S'.

Adrian included with the field notes a photograph, taken on his iPhone, of a sign at the rear of a frozen-meat stall near the café. The sign advertises a product with the brand name 'PLUVERA'. The sign also has a line drawing of a cooked chicken. The main slogan on the sign reads 'POULES PLUVERA C'EST DELICIEUX', with 'PLUVERA' inscribed in blue and the other words in red. A symbol that resembles an Arabic character appears after the word 'DELICIEUX'. A little detective work reveals that 'pluvera' is a neologism, an invented word recontextualised from a Dutch phrase 'PLUimVEe-RAvels', meaning 'poultry from Ravels'. Ravels is a town in the Belgian province of Antwerp. 'Pluvera' is a trademark of N.V. Klaasen & Co., a poultry slaughterhouse in Ravels. Close by the sign in the market is a stall called 'Remmison African Foods'. 'Poules Pluvera' are imported to the UK by traders with a focus on the African and African Caribbean market, especially the Congolese diaspora. The sign is apparently 'in French'. However, the brand name is also 'in Dutch'. At the same time we might say that it is partly 'in Arabic'. If the sign can be said to be 'in French', it is French with an African accent, as those in the know are privy to the fact that this is a product intended for the Francophone African diaspora market. The sign reinscribes a history of mobility, taking in, at the very least, Kinshasha, Antwerp and Birmingham. It is a record of mobility and experience, responsive to time and (dis)location. It is a text with a narrative, or at least it is a text that prompts and suggests a narrative. It is constituted in histories of colonialism and post-colonialism, and in histories of migration and post-migration. These histories are known to some, partially known to others, unknown, perhaps, to more. They are not explained in *Voices of a City Market: An Ethnography*. The sign is itself, part of the polyphony and heteroglossia of the market hall. The text stands alongside other texts in this brief section – including 'COOKED DINNER', the name of the African foods store, the tattoos on the young woman's left arm and the Chinese characters inscribed on the inside of her right arm. In these cases, too, the texts stand for themselves, without academic explanation. Texts rub up against each other, bearing the traces of ideologies, histories and world views. They are nothing if not the marks of social heteroglossia.

Interviews

Ninety of the 304 sections of Part 2 of *Voices of a City Market* are constructed from transcripts of interviews with market stall holders. Interviews were transcribed without addition or substitution. Transcripts of interviews were rearranged to the extent that they were edited into sections and distributed throughout the book. Again, the ordering of sections of interviews may have a discernible rhythm, but no attempt was made to introduce a repeatable system. Two sections of Part 2 are third-person narratives created from first-person interviews with Kang Chen and Meiyen Chew, the key participant butchers.

Interviews were conducted by Rachel Hu and Adrian Blackledge, usually together. Stall holders willingly answered questions about their history in the market, changes to customer demographics, management of the market environment, ongoing commercial challenges and relationships with customers. Some traders ventured beyond answers to specific questions, setting their own agenda. In the interview transcripts the voices of the stall holders speak for themselves. Their arrangement is different from Alexievich's arrangement of interview transcripts, in that Alexievich typically represents (edited versions of) entire interviews. We cut the transcripts into sections, so that the form of the text corresponds to the often fragmentary discourses of the market hall. Here we take a brief look at just one of the 90 sections based on interviews. It is from an interview with a trader who sells flowers outside the main entrance to the market hall. In this section of the interview he is discussing migration:

> THE FLOWER SELLER. I'm not saying it was a good thing to open the floodgates, I'm not saying that at all, but now that we have we might as well make the most of it, rather than trying to fight it, we might as well just embrace it. I don't know if that's an English sort of thing to say. You're not going to win any wars in this country. They're still going to come. You're better off embracing it. You have to believe it. There needs to be more support for the markets because it's a meeting place for people in the city.

In his analysis of the polyphonic novel, Bakhtin suggests that a single utterance, in the voice of a single speaker, may point to competing perspectives, beliefs and ideologies. This notion of dialogism envisions voice as collectively produced through the play of different and competing voices within an utterance. The flower seller's discourse is permeated with opposing discourses about migration. He says he is 'not saying' that historical government policy to allow immigration to the UK ('open the floodgates') 'was a good thing'. His discourse is so constructed that his argument is shaped and penetrated by someone else's argument, the argument he is *not* making. The way his speech is organised is determined by awareness of, and reaction to, the speech of the other. Dialogical relationships can penetrate an utterance, or even an individual word, when two voices collide within it. Here the voice of the illiberal other, which stands *against* immigration, clashes with the voice of the liberal self, which stands *for* immigration. The flower seller emphasises the tension between the two arguments ('I'm not saying that at all'). In Bakhtin's terms his speech answers and reacts to the invisible interlocutor. It points outside itself, beyond its own borders, to the other person's unspoken word. The opposing discourses seem to clash with each other, each taking a turn to put its case: 'but now that we have we might as well make the most of it, rather than trying to fight it, we might as well just embrace it'.

One voice expresses limited enthusiasm for immigration ('now that we have'). The other takes a different stance, urging, 'make the most of it'. But even this relatively positive statement acknowledges the opposite discourse ('we might as well'). Within the single utterance the collision of ideological world views persists – the construction of 'rather than trying to fight it' and 'we might as well just embrace it' again determined by awareness of the speech of the invisible, inaudible other. The flower seller's discourse is polyphonic, articulating more than one point of view. The flower seller even now appears to distance himself from his own subjective view, suggesting that his discourse may be a generalised, national, or nationalist, perspective ('I don't know if that's an English sort of thing to say').

The to and fro of dialogue continues: 'You're not going to win any wars in this country', the flower seller says, apparently taking on the discourse of the illiberal other, but without hostility. Immigrants will still come, he says, and 'You're better off embracing it'. Still seeming to speak back to the voice of the invisible other, he says, 'You have to believe it'. In the discourse of the flower seller, different voices confront each other, and competing perspectives engage in dialogue. Here, two (or more) belief systems intersect and rub up against each other in a single utterance. The speech of the flower seller represents the speech of another in another's language, clashing with it and contesting it, while at the same time acknowledging it. No authorial voice explicitly frames the speech of the flower seller. The utterance stands beyond the authority of the author. Disagreements and oppositions within a single utterance are what Bakhtin saw as the untamed elements in social heteroglossia, manifestations of oppositions which are contradictory and saturated with a fundamental speech diversity. Unfinished, and unfinalised, the dialogic speech of the flower seller bears the marks of conflict and contest in discourse which is constructed as internally clashing. That is, it is the *form* of discourse that bears the marks of social heteroglossia.

The 90 sections from interviews in Part 2 of *Voices of a City Market: An Ethnography* stand without authorial commentary, evaluation or intervention. As we have seen, they are at times the site of dialogism, as opposing discourses and speech types come into contact and are contested. Their separate, unmerged consciousnesses constitute the polyphony of the market hall.

Audio-recording

Three members of the team working on the butcher's stall wore audio-recording devices while being observed. In all, 35 hours of workplace interactions were audio-recorded. On two occasions video-recording of the butcher's stall was done by a filmmaker, in conjunction with field notes and audio-recording. As we have seen, transcripts of audio-recordings were integrated with field notes and became a fundamental resource in the construction of 116 sections of Part 2 of the book. We asked the proprietors of the butcher's business, who lived together as a couple, to audio-record themselves at home. In all, they audio-recorded 47 hours of family and domestic interactions. These audio-recordings are the basis of 17 sections of Part 2 of the book. They are not integrated with field notes, because researchers did not visit the family home, and so did not write field notes related to these interactions. The following example of one such section is typical of the representation of domestic life in *Voices of a City Market: An Ethnography*. In the book the male and female butchers are respectively referred to as 'the pragmatic butcher' and 'the genial butcher'. In this section the pragmatic butcher's father-in-law is with the pragmatic butcher and the genial butcher. The exchange is translated into English from Cantonese and is framed with authorial reporting verbs to indicate who is speaking.

> How is your new assistant working out? asks the pragmatic butcher's father-in-law.
> I fired him this afternoon, says the pragmatic butcher. He was no use. It was really busy on Saturday, there were so many customers, at first he was all right if I kept an eye on him, but when I wasn't standing over him he did virtually nothing.
> All day, says the genial butcher, he was asking how much is this, how much is that. You don't have time.
> I thought I'd give him one more day, says the pragmatic butcher, but really he's not good enough. This morning I bought a sausage-and-bacon

sandwich for him, he just ate the two pieces of bread and threw away the rest. Not so much as a thank you.
Maybe he can't eat pork, says the genial butcher.
No, he can, it's not that. He can eat it, I asked him. Also sometimes I don't understand what he's saying. It's better to have someone who has done the job before.
Or at least knows the prices, she says.
I sometimes think, says the pragmatic butcher, even someone with thirty-five years' experience isn't going to be good enough. Are you able to work tomorrow? he asks her.
It's not that I can't do it, but I would prefer if you can get someone else to help out, she says.
It would be better if we didn't do so many deliveries, says the pragmatic butcher.
I could switch to part-time, maybe, only work on busy days, she says.

In response to a question from the pragmatic butcher's father-in-law, the genial butcher and the pragmatic butcher narrate a brief story about a temporary member of the team working on the butcher's stall. Again, the *form* of the scene contributes to the polyphonic nature of the text. Voloshinov (1973) points out that reported speech may be represented in such a way that it merges with the representing speech, or so that it stands outside the reporting, or representing speech. Fairclough (1995: 58) introduces the term 'boundary maintenance' to refer to the extent to which the voices of reporting and reported speech are kept apart or merged. Merging of reporting and reported discourse can mean that both voices are speaking at once, travelling in the same direction. The reported discourse may overwhelm the reporting discourse, so that the reporting and reported voices come to closely resemble each other. Alternatively, the boundary between the speech doing the reporting and the speech being reported may be firmly in place, as is often the case when the reported speech is represented as a direct quotation in speech marks. In the example here, the boundary between reporting and reported speech is securely maintained. No speech marks are deployed, but it is clear where the speech of each of the butchers and the father-in-law begins and ends. The author makes no evaluation of the speech of the characters. The maintenance of the boundary between reporting and reported speech assures the independence of voices in the polyphonic text.

However, in the discourse of the two butchers resides another reported voice. The new assistant is the subject of the brief narrative of the pragmatic butcher and the genial butcher, and they represent his voice in several different ways. After the pragmatic butcher tells his father-in-law that the new assistant was fired because 'He was no use', and 'he did virtually nothing', the genial butcher joins in: 'All day, says the genial butcher, he was asking how much is this, how much is that. You don't have time'. Enclosed in the direct reported speech of the genial butcher is the direct reported speech of the new assistant, 'how much is this, how much is that'. Unlike the neutral authorial framing of the reported speech of the butchers, the reported speech of the new assistant is negatively evaluated by the genial butcher as narrator, in the constructions 'All day', and 'You don't have time'. Now the pragmatic butcher adds an anecdote about a sausage and bacon sandwich. His narrative is critical of the behaviour of the new assistant, and also negatively evaluates his speech in two ways: first for its absence ('Not so much as a thank you'), and second for its unintelligibility ('sometimes I don't understand what he's saying'). These representations of silence and incoherence in reported speech function to further damn the dismissed assistant. The genial butcher offers a possible defence ('Maybe he can't eat pork'), but the pragmatic butcher summarises the speech of the assistant in indirect discourse ('He can eat it, I asked him').

In this section of Part 2 of *Voices of a City Market* there are two aspects of reported speech. Authorial framing of the speech of the pragmatic butcher and the genial butcher is more or less neutral, and without evaluation. But the speech, and lack of speech, of the new assistant, reported in the narrative of the pragmatic butcher, is subject to negative evaluation by the butchers. Within the reporting voice of the butchers as narrators are direct discourse, indirect discourse, and silence and incoherence. Voloshinov argues that representing reported speech is not located in the individual but in society (1973: 117). Between the reported speech and the reporting context, dynamic relations of high complexity and tension are in force. A failure to take these into account makes it impossible to understand any form of reported speech (Voloshinov, 1973: 119). For Voloshinov, the true object of inquiry is the dynamic interrelationship between the speech being reported and the speech doing the reporting. Looking closely at this section offers insight into the overall construction of Part 2 of *Voices of a City Market*. The perspective of the authors is backgrounded, limited to simple reporting verbs, offering very little in the way of evaluation or commentary. The perspective of the characters in the text – the pragmatic butcher and the genial butcher – is distinctly evaluative. The authors renounce the right to the last word, and grant full and equal authority to the discourse of the characters. The creative vision of the text does not finally permit explanation of the characters. They speak for themselves.

Semiotic landscape

Seventeen sections of Part 2 of *Voices of a City Market* are devoted to representation of the semiotic landscape of the market hall. An aspect of the heteroglossia of the market, recorded in photographs, field notes and video-recordings, was a diversity of types of signage. We have seen description of signs inside and beyond the market café. Other signs included prices and descriptions of goods for sale, price lists, menus, hand-written job vacancies, names of businesses and so on. A number of signs were written in Chinese characters. The following section of *Voices of a City Market* is a textual representation of a sign advertising international phone charges:

Afghanistan	1p landline	9p mobile
Kenya	1p landline	5p mobile
Mauritius	4p landline	6p mobile
Pakistan	4p landline	4p mobile
Portugal	1p landline	3p mobile
Sri Lanka	3p landline	3p mobile
Turkey	1p landline	5p mobile
Vietnam	3p landline	3p mobile

Out of this world bundles

1000 free minutes   unlimited UK texts

The advertising sign, placed outside a mobile phone shop, like other examples from the semiotic landscape of the market hall, is represented without explanation or commentary. Something might be inferred about globalisation, migration and mobility. However, the role of the sign in Part 2 of *Voices of a City Market* is not to be subject to explanation. It is not our intention to explain the sign. It stands for itself, alongside the sign advertising the price of having button holes sewn by hand, the sign promoting Curry Beef Fried Rice for £6 and many others. It is part of the heteroglossic life of the market.

Online and digital communication

Seven sections of Part 2 of *Voices of a City Market* represent WeChat messages. Kang Chen and Meiyen Chew were asked to copy and share with the research team a selection of their social media and other online communication during the period of fieldwork. The major digital platform for their online activity was WeChat. Here we reproduce one of those sections, an exchange of digital messages between Kang Chen and his brother:

The pragmatic butcher contacts his brother in China by WeChat.

do you know the treatment for appendicitis?

let me search for it
who is it for?

                                    the Brit working on my stall
                                    the Western doctor here won't
                                             remove it for him

in China it's called lanwei yan
if it is serious the Chinese way
is to remove it with a surgical operation
is it acute or chronic?
there is keyhole surgery

The brief WeChat interaction is introduced in the authorial voice. This provides context. The remainder of the section represents four transcribed WeChat messages. No further explanation is given. The exchange refers to other sections of Part 2 of the book, in which the genial butcher in particular had expressed concerns about the health of the 'loyal assistant butcher'. In the discourse of the pragmatic butcher and his brother there appears to be a common view of a tension between 'Western' and 'Chinese' approaches to medicine. This ideological view stands alongside other discourses, unfinalised and unexplained.

Most of the online and digital messages represented in Part 2 of *Voices of a City Market: An Ethnography* are oriented to commerce, as the pragmatic butcher takes orders from local restaurants (e.g. 'Tomorrow 70 kg pork belly'). There is also an extended sequence of messages in which the pragmatic butcher inquires about the health of the Chinese student butcher, who is in hospital following an accident at work. WeChat messages are not immediately evident in the heteroglossic life of the market. However, they constitute a significant means of communication for the butchers.

Summary

In Part 2 of *Voices of a City Market: An Ethnography*, field notes, audio-recordings, interviews, online and digital exchanges, and market signage are curated and arranged as a collage of everyday details, a chorus of disparate voices. Offering no explanation, the sections of text stand for themselves. They call attention to the mundane and they represent the heteroglossic life of the market.

The intention is not to explain characters in socio-historical terms. Nor is the purpose to represent the internal life of the characters of the market, but to represent the external world of their everyday practice. Here we see and hear a plurality of voices, which combine but are not merged in the unity of the event. The text allows the closest possible approximation to real life. It is polyphonic, a diversity of social speech types, a diversity of individual voices. At once a curation and a creation, the text orchestrates the heteroglossic diversity of voices through authorial framing, the speech of narrators and the speech of characters. These are voices which are not closed or resolved; they are neither finalised nor finalisable. They are about nothing very much, but they describe human life.

Essay 4. Poetry

Introduction

One of the ways in which ethnographers have responded to the supposed crisis of representation in ethnography is by adding the poem to their repertoire. The poem offers a language that researchers can access when other modes of representation are not fit for purpose, enabling them to paint social realities in ways that may prove difficult through ethnographic prose. Ethnographic poetry has the potential to embody the rhythms, time and space of observed practice. In this essay we consider the poem in ethnography.

The Poem in Ethnography

Why do we propose that poetry has a place in ethnography? It is – even now, with a resurgence of interest in spoken-word poetry in the UK, at least – a minority interest. Why take the trouble to represent ethnographic material in a form that is often dauntingly succinct, robust and difficult? Why learn techniques that call on us to deploy rhythm, metre, rhyme and figurative forms, and risk alienating our audience? The answer is that when we do it well, the pay-offs are considerable.

Ethnographic researchers have long used poetry as a medium for expressing their sense of connection to their field and their subjects (Phipps & Saunders, 2009). The poet and social scientist share commonalities in approach: both ground their work in meticulous observation of the empirical world and are often reflexive about their experience. But the poem reaches for something more. It is in the enhancement of, and elaboration upon, social research outcomes that the ethnographic poem has rich potential. The poem in ethnography can be a creative response to questions of representation (Prendergast, 2009). It has potential to offer analytical and reflexive approaches, as well as a representational form. It is a means of inquiry which challenges notions of authenticity, acknowledges complexity and contests the single, unimpeachable account of events (Butler-Kisber & Stewart, 2009). Ethnographic poems rely on a belief in the ability of poetry to speak to something universal, or to clarify some part of the human condition. They come into their own as a means to enrich ethnography when researchers want to explore knowledge claims, write with greater engagement and connection, mediate understandings, and reach diverse audiences (Faulkner, 2009).

The poem can incorporate the rhythm and rhyme of everyday life in ethnographic accounts. Ethnographic poems are able to provide insight by resonating with the voices of research participants and representing difference without resorting to easy, determinate answers. In order to be useful for research, however, the ethnographic poem must first be a poem (Maréchal & Linstead, 2010). The best examples of ethnographic poems are good poems in and of themselves (Prendergast *et al.*, 2009). They should not be judged by more forgiving criteria than poetry at large. The purposes of ethnography are not well served by writing inferior verse. Poetry operates within its own established conventions, the same as other forms of ethnographic writing. We do not escape that by assuming that we do not need to be trained as poets on the grounds that we are really ethnographers (Maynard & Cahnmann-Taylor, 2010).

Technical and formal excellence are the first ambition, and the first requirement, of the poem. Sandra Faulkner (2009: 74) complains of being 'tired of reading and listening to lousy poetry that masquerades as research, and vice versa'. The ethnographic poem is doubly challenged: to be technically and formally sound, and to maintain validity as an outcome of research. A poem may articulate what is not yet known; an ethnography orients more to a report of what has already been learned. The ethnographic poem must do both. That is, like historical fiction, the ethnographic poem must be faithful to experience, while reaching beyond or through it to a sense of aesthetics that enhances everyday voices and practices rather than diminishing them. Poets have much to teach ethnographers about how metaphor, metonym, rhythm and rhyme can illuminate and enhance understandings of social life. However, that is not to say that ethnographic poetry is necessarily more insightful, or more privileged, than prose (Maynard & Cahnmann-Taylor, 2010).

What Is an Ethnographic Poem?

Ethnographic poetry has the same responsibility to technical features as does any other poem. It is not sufficient to chop up transcribed speech, or field notes, into shorter lines, in the hope that this makes it into a poem. We need to be familiar with the technicalities of form, what it is that makes a poem a poem, and what it is about a poem that affords artistic representation of experience. Whatever else may be claimed for the poem is best achieved through attention to formal and technical means. Does this mean that reading and writing poems is therefore the preserve of specialists? Does it mean that the ethnographic researcher with little or no experience of poetry is excluded from writing ethnographic poetry? By no means. We are committed to the democracy of the poem. Everyone can write poems and everyone can read poems. But the poem is a technical art form, and there are things we need to know, things we need to learn, in order to write poems which enhance ethnographic research.

In the polyphonic text *Voices of a City Market: An Ethnography*, we include poems as part of the music with which to represent the sounds, smells, tastes, textures and visual experience of the city centre market. At the heart of the book is a poem in 51 sections. The poem represents a panoptic view of everyday life in the market. Here we reproduce a selection of 10 of the 51 sections, with brief commentary. The poem is based on field notes written by Adrian Blackledge and Rachel Hu, interviews, photographs, audio-recordings and video-recordings made in the market. It is written in the voice of one of the characters in the market, the Hygiene Operative, as he makes his rounds of the market hall:

> I
> I start work at six
> when souls of pigs and pixies
> are up to their tricks.
>
> X
> She was here last week
> from the university
> noting how we speak.
>
> XIV
> The pungent perfume
> of pig offal calls to mind
> one Leopold Bloom.
>
> XX
> Doherty's fish stall
> claim to have landed the year's
> biggest conger eel.
>
> XXIV
> It's a canny squid
> peddles residual ink
> for three or four quid.
>
> XXXIX
> I take out my book
> to record an incident
> with a butcher's hook.
>
> XXXVIII
> The couple who run
> the Polish deli turn out
> to hail from Bodrum.

XL
Not a methane leak
but a box of durian.
Closed for a whole week.

XLII
Something to be seen:
sardines in their very own
Busby Berkeley scene.

XLIV
It didn't take long
for that Leviathan eel
to be dubbed King Kong.

Each section of the poem is a rhyming haiku (a poem of three lines of, respectively, five, seven and five syllables). The haiku is not habitually a musical form. Originating in Japan, haiku depend on syllable count rather than metre, and they do not normally rhyme. The emphasis is instead on a meditative image, which quietly (and not rhythmically) implies more than it says. However, the poet Paul Muldoon has taken the traditional Japanese form and, we might say, set it to music. That is, he introduces both rhythm and rhyme to the haiku. Muldoon's book *Horse Latitudes* (2006) includes a set of 90 rhyming haiku. Each short poem, or section, rhymes the first and third line. End-stops, caesurae and line breaks create rhythm. Unavoidably, and anyway not to be avoided, haiku in English find their rhythm and metre. The set of 51 rhyming haiku in *Voices of a City Market: An Ethnography* become the means with which to give voice to the city market's Hygiene Operative, and to represent a polyphonic account of the market hall.

Perhaps uniquely in the market, the Hygiene Operative constantly moves around the market hall, mopping floors, cleaning toilets, clearing spillages and checking that the environment is safe. As such, he comes into contact with almost everyone who works there. The haiku represent the protagonist in direct, straightforward terms, with reference to his role essentially as a health and safety officer. The first and third line are generally three-stressed (have three discernible 'beats'), the middle line generally four-stressed. The poem articulates the sensuality of the market hall – the smells, sounds, tastes, textures and sights of the busy commercial environment. Taken together, the 51 haiku make audible the music in the diverse spaces of the market. Perhaps the most defining characteristic of the poem is its strong rhyme across each of the haiku. This is most vividly achieved when the poem is read aloud, or when the sound of the poem is imagined (in what is sometimes called 'the auditory ear') by the silent reader. This effect is at least partly to do with rhyme. When we speak of rhyme we often refer to the repetition of the same or similar sounds at the ends of lines in the poem, as in the set of haiku. However, rhyme also includes the repetition of the same or similar sounds *within* lines in the poem. That is, we are interested in the repetition of sounds at the ends of lines, repetition within individual lines, and repetitions of sounds between lines which are not at the ends of lines. We are interested in repetition of vowel sounds, consonant sounds and combinations of these. Furthermore, we are interested in the repetition of sounds within words. Nor is rhyme merely a matter of surface finish or verbal ingenuity. As well as adding aesthetic quality, it has a structural function, binding together the poem and intensifying logical (or even illogical) connections.

Rhyme is important because sound and sense are aspects of the same thing. The sound of a word or phrase is fundamental to how we understand the poem (Paterson, 2018). Rhyme in the poem offers technical challenges to the writer, holding things up and slowing things down. Rhyme becomes resistance in the writing process, limiting the words available to those which chime with words elsewhere in the poem. Paradoxically, however, at the same time as this apparent limitation, options proliferate. In the need for end-rhyme, in particular, words suggest themselves which would otherwise have remained out of sight and out of mind. End-rhyme is one of the defining characteristics of what are known as verse forms, or poetic forms. That is, long-established frameworks are available to act as structures to support the poem. This at the very least means the writer does not have to reinvent the wheel (although it is quite acceptable to do so, and this can be a creative process). The great advantage of making use of traditional or more recently developed frameworks for the poem is that the given structure offers both resistance and catalysis in the making of the poem. The chosen form requires adherence to both metrical and rhyming patterns. The sonnet, for example, rhymes, in prescribed ways, each of 14 lines, usually of five stresses, and the final six lines often comment or expand on the first eight. The ballad stanza is of four lines, in which the first and third lines are usually of four stresses, while the second and fourth lines are three-stressed. And so on, through verse forms that include the villanelle, terza rima, rondeau, rondelet, pantoum, sestina, ode, cinqain, limerick, tanka and others which have fallen into disuse. Verse forms offer resistance because they guide the poem to be concise, economical and rigorous. They offer catalysis because the prescribed rhythm and rhyme offer to the poem words which would otherwise have remained beyond its scope.

Poems need originality if they are to breathe. Yet originality is hard to come by. Everything we want to say has been said before, and probably in the way we want to say it. So we need whatever assistance we can find to pull originality from its hiding place (Paterson, 2018). The surprising rhyme, the word we would never have found in our imagination without the requirement for rhyme, brings originality out into the open.

A second series of poems in *Voices of a City Market: An Ethnography* responds to the striking visual world of the market hall. This series of six poems is based on close observation of the market traders' stalls. Although the poems are dispersed throughout the volume, they are linked in terms of their form. They are of eight lines, each one taking as its starting point a description of produce for sale on the butchers' counters in the market. We reproduce here four of the six:

> Cows' feet line glass countertops.
> Each hoof, or toe, or toenail, or is it
> fingernail, is painted vibrant pink
> not carefully, but roughly, clumsily
>
> as if the very last thing to be done
> before the sacrifice
> was the application
> of a small touch of glamour.

—

> Every Monday morning this man nods
> to a plastic ice-cream tub
> and holds up gnarled fingers and thumbs:
> ten pig hearts for five pounds.
>
> When the butcher weighs each heart in his hand
> and turns it to the light
> it shimmers like a creature washed up
> still wet from the sea.

—

> These tongues will not speak, not now, not ever.
> How big they are lying side by side
> like new-born babies;
> you can almost hear them breathe.
>
> Stippled and coarse as red sandstone
> heavy as stone too. Somewhere oxen
> heave slowly forward,
> massive, uncomplaining.

—

> As if from an ancient glacier
> it emerges, the head of this young goat
> crystals of ice defrosting on eyelashes
> and falling as tears.

>   Suede stubs of horns are not yet full-grown
>   but surely that implacable gaze
>   waits only for the final thaw's
>   long regeneration.

These short poems refer to the goods for sale on the butchers' stalls in the market. Ox tongue, cows' feet and goats' heads all become the subject of poems. In the first poem, cows' feet lie on the glass counter of one of the butchers' stalls. We can identify in Rachel Hu's observational field notes the poem's provenance:

> As I wander round the stalls I am struck by how many 'cows' feet' (3 for £5) are visibly displayed on some stalls. One stall has around thirty of them lined up on top of its very long counter, all with their hooves dyed bright pink, as if the animals' last request was to go to the nail parlour.

The poem is of course more than the field note chopped into short lines. The 'fingernail' transforms the animal to the realm of the human. The end-stopped first line sets the context. The poem segues from a description of the line of pink-dyed hooves to an apparent oxymoron in which worlds of glamour and sacrifice are coexistent. Reliability of perception is called into question here ('toenail, or is it / fingernail'), as connotations run beyond the mundane to the fantastical. But again these are not entirely flights of fancy. The colouring of the cows' hooves does put us in mind of glamorous costume. The painting of the hooves does appear careless. There is a sense that, moments before the sacrifice of the animal, preparations were rushed. The structural framework of the poem is permissive. It indulges its creative impulses, referring to one thing in terms of another, and in so doing finding relationships between them. Here, in Seamus Heaney's (2003) terms, something has been made of something else. As with rhyme, one of the attractions of figures of speech which denote or connote one thing in terms of another is that they prompt originality. The poem expands the meaning of the literal by invoking a comparison with the non-literal. Ethnographic poetry has the potential to evoke open-ended connections between things, thus emphasising the power of possibility. It can touch us as both cognitive and sensual beings. It allows the reader to arrive at their own understanding, or to receive multiple interpretations, without excessive researcher influence. As a result, it potentially allows us to come to more complex, nuanced and thoughtful conclusions than might otherwise be the case.

The second poem cited above also relies on Rachel Hu's field notes as a source of material. It describes a regular customer at a stall selling offal:

> An old Chinese man loudly says hello to the assistant butcher, BJ, who smiles at him. He's one of the regulars, and the only thing he will buy is

pig's heart. This time is no exception. He taps on the window cover above the tray containing the hearts. Knowing that BJ knows him, he doesn't even bother to tell him what he wants. BJ doesn't need to ask either, but picks up ten pig's hearts for the old man, and wraps them up in a plastic bag. The man talks to Mei in Cantonese for a minute, and departs with the bag of hearts, leaving a five pound note on the counter.

The sense of a service interaction conducted almost entirely through embodied action is evident in both the field note and the poem. In the field note the customer taps the window cover. In the poem he nods, and holds up fingers and thumbs to indicate how many hearts he requires. In the second half of the poem the butcher holds one of the hearts up to the light, perhaps to show the customer, and it 'shimmers like a creature washed up / still wet from the sea'. The comparison perhaps acknowledges that the heart is organic, still part of life, almost alive.

The third poem is prompted by a display of ox tongue. The first line is structured by the repetition of vowel and consonant sounds. It is also characterised by the repetition of 'not', emphasising that the tongues, set on the butcher's counter, have no purpose other than as offal. They do not speak, and of course they never did speak, 'not ever'. The assertion that they will not speak draws attention to the distinction between the world of the ox and the human world. The simile is striking: the tongues are like new-born babies lying side by side, and 'you can almost hear them breathe'. The distinction between human and animal worlds seems to narrow. Perhaps we are more alike than we realised. End-stopped at the stanza break, the poem pauses to take stock. White space is filled with contemplation. Now the tongues are red, heavy as stone. The caesura introduces a further pause, following which a shift of focus takes us away from the market. The juxtaposition of 'heavy', 'heave' and 'massive' performs a bass melody against which the ox is once again living, somewhere at labour. The ox does not complain. Things are what they are.

The last of these poems describes the severed head of a young goat. Again, the poem is reliant on transformation through imaginative leaps based on visual comparison. The young goat is not merely the product of butchery; rather, it emerges 'from an ancient glacier', still in thaw, 'crystals of ice defrosting on eyelashes / and falling as tears'. As was the case with the ox tongues, death is transfigured as life. The goat not only lives, but it becomes human, shedding tears of sorrow for itself, and for the world. If there is hope for the goat as it waits for 'the final thaw's / long regeneration', there is perhaps hope for humankind. The comparison reveals the metaphoric engine by which language revivifies itself, and the metonymic nature of all human naming (Paterson, 2018). One idea turns into another, and in doing so, creates an original expression to reflect this new thought, and new expression. We are simultaneously able to perceive both the depth and surface, the strangeness and accuracy of the trope.

The comparison is close to the visual world of the market, drawing on hard-earned field notes, yet distant enough to arrest the reader with its felicity and originality. This is what the poem can do in ethnography.

A further leap, perhaps a further liberty, is taken in *Voices of a City Market: An Ethnography*, in a poem which transcends the boundaries of the strictly empirical.

> We first used to come when we were courting.
> We'd be out of the office at lunchtime
> and order half a dozen oysters.
>
> They'd shuck them there and then, dress them
> put it all on a plate, lemon, vinegar,
> salt if you wanted it, Tabasco sauce.
>
> We'd stand there in the middle of the market
> like Lord and Lady Muck
> sucking fresh oysters out of the shell.

Ethnographic poetic representation is always looking for the poetry implicit in speech. Consequently, poetics from testimony demands constant awareness of the raw material of the speaker's voice, in order to uphold the integrity of the dialogue, and search for a speaker's true vocal timbre and rhythm (Rapport & Harthill, 2012). The poem may exaggerate or at least call attention to the rhythms of everyday speech. Poetry emerges from speech as the immediate consequence of emotional urgency, and a desire to communicate this urgency by organising and intensifying those natural features of language which best carry it (Paterson, 2018). In empirical research we are more or less comfortable with the notion that the truth, or at least *a* truth, or at least an authenticity, may be represented through verbatim transcription of the spoken word. In poetic speech, sound and meaning rise like a tide out of language to carry individual utterance away on a current stronger and deeper than the individual could have anticipated (Heaney, 1989). There is much scope for poetry to do service in the representation of voice.

This poem is not a verbatim transcription of 'data'. Rather, it is a response to the research environment, not based on a specific interview, audio-recording or field note. Poems are often imaginative responses to their environment. There is no reason to suppose that the experiences of the poem are a representation of the experiences of the poet. The poem is a text produced as a creative act, and as such should not be constrained by adherence to facts. In the voice of a customer in the market, the poem does not represent the voice of an identifiable research participant. Rather, it represents a constructed voice, an imagined narrative, and a response to the environment in which the research is done. Like other poems, it does not come from nowhere. This market sold oysters from the shell, which customers would purchase and eat there and then, standing at the counter, where they could add lemon, vinegar, salt and Tabasco sauce. The setting, then, is one observed during ethnographic fieldwork. The 'voice' of the poem is a creative non-fiction, or perhaps a construction, an act of imagination which serves to represent an experience of the market hall. The poem is carried forward through the repetition of sound. It has its own music: 'lunch', 'shuck', 'Muck', 'sucking'. From the second line of the poem to the final line, the poem plays a consistent tune. It makes what Heaney (2003) calls 'articulate noise'.

Another poem in *Voices of a City Market: An Ethnography* relies less on constructed voice, but is closely based on field notes written during observation in the market, and on video-recorded material. Now observation is not of the butchers' stall, or the shellfish stall, but the stall which doubles as nail parlour and tattoo studio:

> A pair of blue rubber gloves heavy on clear plastic storage boxes.
> Inside the boxes hundreds of false nails like razor shells
> washed up on a beach and stripped clean.
>
> On the shelf above, bottles of nail polish and nail lacquer.
> Aquamarine, bronze, old gold, copper sunset, pearlescent,
> satin black, Prussian blue, mandarin, indigo.
>
> On the top shelf a display box. In each cell of the display box
> a brightly coloured nail, each one like a butterfly,
> or a bird's egg collected from a remote expedition.
>
> On the lowest shelf, a prosthetic hand, the sort that can be
> screwed into an artificial arm. It is flesh-coloured.
> Each finger of the hand wears a long, curved nail.
>
> The nail on the little finger is crimson, ring finger vermilion,
> middle finger mauve, index finger scarlet, thumb metallic pink.
> Inscribed in large letters across the knuckles of the hand,
>
> in permanent black marker pen, DONT TOUCH ME ... PLEASE.

The form of the poem, deploying both repetition and lists, contributes to the claustrophobic atmosphere of the tiny stall at which a couple make their living. Repeated iterations of similar items ('storage boxes' ... 'Inside the boxes' ... 'shelf a display box' ... 'cell of the display box'; 'On the shelf' ... 'On the top shelf' ... 'On the lowest shelf') suggest boxes stacked on top of each other, on multiple shelves, making use of every cubic centimetre of available space. A list of colours of nail polish and nail lacquer further points to multiplicity. The nails are the detritus of the natural world ('razor shells / washed up on a beach and stripped clean'). At the same time, they are precious items, museum exhibits meticulously collected and displayed, 'like a butterfly, / or a bird's egg'. The image of a prosthetic hand, pressed into service as a display mannequin, brings together repetition ('little finger' ... 'ring finger' ... 'middle finger' ... 'index finger') and another list of colours: crimson, vermilion, mauve, scarlet, pink. The oppressive atmosphere of the crowded stall continues to build. The final image, in the last line of the poem, is both humorous, as the prosthetic hand acquires a voice, and resonant with other discourses circulating beyond the nail parlour. It might be argued that the poem, based on field notes and video-recording, is more 'true' (and therefore more 'ethnographic') than the poem which relies on constructed voice. However, both poems represent their own truth of the market hall experience.

A category of poem which straightforwardly presents itself to the ethnographer is the 'found poem'. The market hall is replete with texts, both written and spoken. They are the stuff of the commercial world, and the stuff of poetry. But how do they become poetry? Paterson (2018) suggests that when text is presented *as* a poem it is read in a way that is different from the way it is read if it remains in another form. That is, if text looks like a poem, with an unusual amount of white space surrounding it, and if it incorporates some of the technical features normally associated with poems, it is reframed by the reader as 'a poem', and read with greater sensitivity to signification. Here is a poem 'found' at the African foods stall in the market:

STRAWBERRY CORDIAL
ACKEE
FUFU FLOUR
DALGETY HONEY & GINGER
SUPERMALT
CARNATION EVAPORATED MILK
FOSKA OATS
TATE+LYLE GRANULATED SUGAR
COCONUT PEANUTS
FISH TEA
CREAM WHEAT
SMOKED CATFISH FILLET
SMALL IWISA
GRACE SYRUP
GLENRYCK PILCHARDS
NESTLÉ MILO INSTANT MALT CHOCOLATE DRINK
COCONUT OIL
PUMPKIN SOUP MIX
CALLALOO
NIDO MILK POWDER
BUTTER BEANS

MCDOUGALL'S SELF-RAISING FLOUR
BONELESS SALT FISH
ABODI
HONEYCOMB BEEF TRIPE
PLANTAIN CHIPS
GIZZARD
COW FOOT
BIBLE (ENGLISH/YORUBA)

The poem is no more than a list of items available for purchase at the stall. Yet at the same time it *is* more than this. In what Paterson (2018) calls the cultural contract between reader and writer, the list is written as a poem, presented as a poem and read as a poem. More than a list of items for sale, the reader takes the poem as synecdoche, in which the list 'stands for' something greater than itself, of which it is a part. Many of the items on the list index the multi-ethnic, superdiverse city ('ACKEE / FUFU FLOUR' ... 'BONELESS SALT FISH' ... 'PLANTAIN CHIPS'). They also index distant localities. The salience of detail is enough to declare the items symbolic, or evidential. That is, if these items are presented as being-in-a-poem, they must *signify* something. The poem represents the superdiversity of the market. Every line other than the ultimate line refers to a food or drink. That final line, however, introduces two additional aspects of the superdiverse city: religion and bilingualism/biliteracy. The positioning of these referents in the final line opens out the poem beyond its concern with the epicurean, to wider implications of the superdiverse world. In Paterson's (2018) terms, the final line invokes a larger state by positioning itself as an interpretable object.

Another found poem, which is also another 'list poem', represents the world of the hardware stall in the market. Here rhythm and rhyme are paramount in turning a list of mundane items into a poem with energy and drive:

watch straps	rat traps
whites booster	feather duster
fly paper	ice scraper
barbeque set	mosquito net
sewing machine oil	aluminium foil
wallpaper paste	turkey baster
sugar soap	towing rope
wasp killer	wine chiller
picture hooks	plaster ducks
fix & grout	insect powder
Elvis clock	sink unblocker
birthday candles	door handles
USB cable	folding table
measuring jug	bath plug

magnetic catch	gate latch
exterior filler	ant killer
reading lamp	workbench clamp

The white space in the middle of each line plays its part, introducing the slightest pause between phrases. The structure of the poem becomes almost a call-and-response, each response rhyming with its call. The rhythmic, rhyming structure of the poem – its urgent engine (Paterson, 2018) – injects energy and excitement in what is at first glance merely a list of items of hardware. The poem's music is the technical means, the more or less describable language and form, by which its tonality is effected and maintained.

Poetry can be found in the mundane written texts of everyday commerce. It can also be found in the noise of the market hall. Poetry reveals the underlying metrical and intonational regularity of language, and asserts its tendency to pattern sounds. In this sense, the poem is noise ordered in particular ways. What matters most in a poem is its music, which mere denotation all too often curtails. The poem reinterprets the noise of time and makes of it a kind of music. It transforms the cacophony into new and more inclusive music – and in doing so creates new harmonies, new forms, new ways of seeing and new ways of saying (Burnside, 2019). The shout-outs of a team of young butchers is nothing if not music:

ERE Y'ARE DARLIN
ERE Y'ARE
ALL THAT FOR TEN POUND
THAT WHOLE TRAY FOR TEN POUND
ALL THAT CHICKEN HALF PRICE TODAY
TRAY OF CHICKEN HALF PRICE TODAY
WHEN IT'S GONE IT'S GONE
BUY ONE GET A FREE ONE
TEN POUND YOUR CHICKEN THIGHS
TEN POUND DRUMSTICKS AND THIGHS
A WHOLE TRAY ONLY A TENNER
GET THE MOST FROM YOUR TENNER
THAT WHOLE TRAY ONLY TEN POUND
COME ON DARLIN HOW DOES THAT SOUND?
THAT TRAY HALF PRICE TODAY
ALL THAT HALF PRICE TODAY
ONLY TODAY DARLIN
COME ON DARLIN
YOU WON'T DO BETTER THAN THAT
YOU WON'T FIND CHEAPER THAN THAT
TEN POUND A TRAY YOUR CHICKEN
TEN POUND A TRAY YOUR CHICKEN
TEN POUND A TRAY

> TEN POUND A TRAY
> HALF PRICE TODAY
> HALF PRICE TODAY

As with the list of written text at the African foods stall, the presentation of the traders' call as a poem influences the way the reader reads. The poem exaggerates and makes manifest features already present in the butchers' discourse. The poem's energy is constituted in repetition, rhyme, non-standard spelling and capitalised text. The form is a way of making textual a sense of noise, of giving noise order, of giving a meaningful order to lived time. Little has to be done to make music from this particular material – the butchers' shout-outs are song-like in themselves. But the butchers' calls, deploying end-rhyme ('DARLIN / ARE', 'GONE / ONE', 'POUND / SOUND') and unremitting repetition, drive the musical beat, transforming the cacophony of the market into a new and more inclusive music (Burnside, 2019). It is a poem which is fundamentally a matter of sound, and must be spoken aloud. It is the sound of the poem that carries the utterance on a current stronger and deeper than the individual could have anticipated (Heaney, 1989). The music of the poem is dependent on its structure and beat, its play of metre and rhythm. The poet Linton Kwesi Johnson puts this succinctly:

> When you write a new poem, you know, it's the saying of it. Although it's a finished poem it's not really finished until you hear it properly. When you can hear it properly, all the nuances of inflection, of breathing, of pauses – because that's all a part of it you know, it's not just simple words strung together – it's the saying of the poem. And for me, poetry doesn't come alive anyway unless it's read aloud. It's just dead words on the page … the hearing of the poem is important. (Quoted in O'Reilly, 2020)

For Linton Kwesi Johnson, the beat, the rhythm, the metre are fundamental to the poem *as* a poem.

Summary

When we force ourselves to venture outside our usual approach to writing ethnography, poetry can help us to reach beyond the data. It pushes us to be self-conscious about what we are saying, whom we are including or omitting from the picture, how we describe or explain what is going on. It helps us take less for granted (Maynard, 2009). Ethnographic poetic representation can lead to powerful outcomes, interpretive freedom and an economic communication of findings. Poetry has the potential to be dramatic, in ways quite different from other methods. It has the potential to enable us to crack open academic restrictions. Ethnographic poetry is powerful in recontextualising social data. It can expand and enhance those data, understanding social practice through comparison beyond itself. In *Voices of a City Market: An Ethnography* poems contribute to making audible the cacophony of the market hall, through rhythm and through rhyme. The poems evoke the music of time. They reveal what is happening, and propose a means by which the noise of time can be re-experienced as the music of what happens (Burnside, 2019). The poem has considerable potential as a way of seeing, and a way of saying, in ethnography.

Essay 5. Ethnographic Drama

Introduction

As part of the TLANG project we conducted ethnographic observations in an advice and advocacy service in a Chinese community centre. We were interested in people's communicative practices in a context where clients needed help to negotiate bureaucratic systems related to welfare benefits, health, education, insurance, immigration status and more. Following comprehensive analysis of data, conducted collaboratively over several months, we produced a detailed research report. However, we recognised a need to reach beyond the limitations of written ethnography. With this in mind, in addition to publishing the outcomes of the research as a conventional ethnographic research report, we represented the life of the advice and advocacy service as dramatic performance. *Interpretations – An Ethnographic Drama* (Blackledge & Creese, 2021a) takes a creative approach to the representation of research outcomes. In this essay we explore the potential of dramatic approaches to linguistic ethnography to expand knowledge, to heighten the representation of social life and to bring linguistic ethnography to new audiences.

Advice and Advocacy

Our colleague in the TLANG research team, Rachel Hu, was well known to the Chinese community centre, having served as a member of the management committee and before that as a member of staff. She was therefore very well placed to gain access to the site, and to negotiate with potential research participants. The chief executive officer of the organisation was interested in the TLANG research project, and agreed that the community centre would participate in the ethnographic work, and that our focus would be an advice and advocacy service located in the community centre. Whereas in other phases of the research project we had collected data as a team, we decided that the space in which the advice and advocacy service operated was too small to accommodate more than one researcher. Furthermore, the presence of a non-Chinese, male researcher might be intrusive, especially when sensitive issues were raised by clients. For these reasons ethnographic observations in the advice and advocacy service were conducted by Rachel Hu. Adrian Blackledge also regularly visited the Chinese community centre, but did not focus on the advice and advocacy service, instead developing an understanding of the institution's broader activities. As the Principal Investigator of the overall research project, Angela Creese also made visits to the community centre on several occasions, and observed one of the advice and advocacy sessions.

Most of the sessions with clients in the advice and advocacy service were conducted largely or entirely in Mandarin, Cantonese or other varieties of Chinese. Most of the clients required support in negotiating administrative processes at least partly because their English proficiency was limited. First and foremost, however, the advisors were translators of the complex bureaucratic systems with which their clients were faced. Rachel formally observed advice and advocacy sessions two days a week, noting her observations as field notes. After working in this way for five weeks she began also to audio-record the sessions, while continuing to observe and write field notes. In all cases, the research project was explained to the clients, and they were asked to sign a consent form giving permission for observation, audio-recording and subsequent public use of linguistic material. They were also offered the option not to give consent. Where they refused or hesitated to provide consent, Rachel did not audio-record the interaction or write field notes. Working with a filmmaker, we video-recorded a range of activities in the Chinese community centre, but outside the advice and advocacy service. We took the decision that video-recording would be intrusive in the relatively intimate space of the advice and advocacy service.

We met as a research team (Blackledge, Creese and Hu) weekly for two hours to discuss field notes, reading and discussing the texts, having each independently conducted preliminary annotation of the field notes before the meeting. These meetings generated initial analysis. During and beyond the data-collection period, Rachel transcribed the audio-recorded material. We held weekly meetings to discuss the transcripts and recordings. This activity continued for some months, as the transcripts ran to hundreds of pages. We collated analysis of ethnographic material in an extensive research report, *Translating the City* (Blackledge *et al.*, 2018). Having completed the research report, we wanted to go further. We sought a means of representation to enact the multiple voices we had heard, a medium that was true to the ethical and aesthetic world we had observed, and a form that resisted the urge to straightforwardly explain and endow with meaning the lives of others. We looked to the potential of ethnographic drama as a means to represent, interpret and make audible the voices of those we had encountered in the advice and advocacy service. The result was *Interpretations – An Ethnographic Drama*.

Representation

The performative turn in the social sciences offers new ways of representing social practice. We no longer have only textual ethnographies, but also performative ethnographies. Performative ways of enacting observed social practice challenge existing means of representing the world (Denzin & Lincoln, 2005). Ethnographic drama employs techniques of theatre production to present a live performance event of research participants' experiences and/or the researchers' interpretations. It is constructed as dramatic presentation of a selection of field notes, audio-recordings, video-recordings, digital messages and interviews. It does not replace the academic report or monograph. Nor is it produced for novelty value. It is a legitimate and credible form of research documentation. Theatre can be a powerful and popular medium through which to present ethnographic materials to a public audience (Long, 2015). Ethnographic drama maintains close allegiance to the social practices of real people, while presenting their stories through an artistic medium. Norman Denzin (1997) suggests that it has become the single most powerful way for ethnography to recover yet interrogate the meanings of lived experience. Theatre offers possibilities for changing audience members' conceptions, leading to a deeper understanding of the ethnographic materials presented (Long, 2015). Live performance has the power to heighten the representation of social life, and at the same time to capture and document the realities of people participating in the research. The purpose of ethnographic drama is to lay out in performance for an audience social practice as it is observed in research. It has the ability to move audiences to reflective, critical action (Denzin, 2003). It is for these reasons that we chose to add ethnographic drama to the more conventional format of the research monograph.

The research report *Translating the City* is more or less traditional in its approach to reporting academic research. *Interpretations – An Ethnographic Drama* does not replace, or stand in for, the report. Instead, the two texts are complementary. The report was written first; the ethnographic drama came later. The ethnographic drama could not have been written without the detailed analysis which was the foundation of the research report. Much of the analysis may not be readily visible in the ethnographic drama script, but it is there as surely as the artist's first sketch remains beneath the surface of the eventual oil painting, or the finger-marks of the sculptor are discernible in the finished work of art. *Translating the City* offers detailed analysis of six of the 79 client–advisor interactions we recorded in the Chinese community centre. *Interpretations – An Ethnographic Drama* is constituted as 29 scenes. Fourteen of these enact advice sessions between advisors and their clients, and are based on transcripts of audio-recordings and field notes written during these sessions. The other 15 scenes represent interactions between advisors, in the cracks and seams of working life, as they wait for clients to arrive, or take tea breaks. These scenes are based on Rachel Hu's observational field notes, written as she spent time with the team of advisors in the community centre over several months, and also on transcripts of interviews with staff and volunteers.

Making Drama from Ethnography

Whereas researchers are often taught not to let data speak for themselves, ethnographic drama allows research participants to speak on their own behalf, without interpretive intervention. Playwrights of ethnographic drama are storytellers, and story *re*tellers. Rachel Hu collected a vast amount of material in the advice and advocacy service. The 79 advice sessions she observed and audio-recorded were often more than one hour in duration. Not all of the audio-recordings and field notes of those 79 advice sessions, or the transcripts of every interview, could be included in the ethnographic drama script. There was necessarily a process of selection to render the ethnographic data more manageable. And the life of the advice and advocacy service was not only constituted in the interactions between advisors and clients, but also in the discourse of the women who worked there. As we developed the ethnographic drama, two distinct scene types began to emerge – scenes that were representations of advice sessions between advisors and their clients, and scenes that represented dialogue between the advisors, at times when there were no clients present. The two distinct scene types proposed a rhythm in which scenes without clients alternated with scenes based on client advice sessions.

We can give a flavour of the process with which ethnographic material was recontextualised as drama. The following example is an excerpt from a transcript of an audio-recording of a client/advisor session. A client, 'X', is sitting in the office of one of the advisors, 'K'. X has come to the advice and advocacy centre for assistance with her husband's claim for disability benefits. K seeks to establish the nature and extent of the husband's needs by asking X questions from a government questionnaire, which is available on her computer. The questions are in English, and K translates them as she puts them to the client. The interaction takes place in Mandarin. We join the interaction as K asks X questions from the government questionnaire.

K 拿自己穿衣服，脱衣服呢 这方面有没有问题
这是要看他的手指是不是灵活 能不能系鞋带或者类似的事情
<How about putting on and taking off clothes? Any problems with that?
This is to see whether or not his fingers are flexible, like doing his shoe laces, and things like that.>

X 鞋带儿 他现在老是丢东西 昨天我们出去买东西
他吧我让他拿的东西全都丢掉了 哦医生第一次查出来他有高血压的时候
就说他以后会是这个样子的 因为他的病他的手指是不灵活的
<Shoe laces. Nowadays he tends to lose things. Yesterday we went out shopping and he just lost whatever I asked him to carry.
The doctor said, when he was first diagnosed with high blood pressure, the doctor said he would be like this, his fingers are not flexible because of his condition.>

K 所以他的手指不灵活 那他能系鞋带么?
  <So his fingers are not flexible. Can he do his shoe laces?>
X 他能但要好长时间
  <He can, but it takes ages.>
K 所以他可以但要好长时间 那系扣子呢
  <So he can, just it takes longer. How about doing buttons?>
X 系扣子，像昨天 我们去给他买了一条裤子他不会系扣子的
  你知道那种圆的扣子你得这样让扣子平着钻过去
  可他不会这样他让我教他怎么系
  <Buttons ... like yesterday we went to buy him a pair of new trousers and he didn't know how to do the buttons.
  You know those round buttons, you have to do the top button up, but he doesn't know how to do it. He asked me to teach him how to do it.>
K 所以你得教他怎么系扣子那解扣子呢 他会解口子吗?
  <So you have to teach him to do the buttons. How about unbuttoning?
  Does he know how to undo his buttons?>
X 他会就是
  <He does, but just...>
K 很慢?
  <Very slow?>
X 很慢的 所以这是为什么他让我给他买带拉链的裤子
  <Very slow. That's why he asked me to buy him clothes with zips.>
K 哦他会拉拉链, zipper 没有问题的
  <Oh, he knows the zip, he can handle that.>
X 有拉链的裤子就可以要是系扣子的裤子他就不穿
  <If the trousers have a zip that will do for him, but he won't wear them if they have buttons instead.>
K 好那我就写我不喜欢系扣子的衣服
  <Okay, so I just wrote I don't like clothes with buttons.>

K types at the computer, entering answers to questions given by X on behalf of her husband. She types the answers in English, before verbally translating them into Mandarin for her client. This interaction is similar to many others observed in the advice and advocacy service, as advisors asked their clients questions in Mandarin, completed computer-based forms in English, and translated back and forth throughout the session. The interaction between K and X runs for 71 minutes. The transcript of the session is 16 pages long. The session forms the basis of the much shorter Scene 6 of *Interpretations – An Ethnographic Drama*. In the section of the ethnographic drama which represents the discussion about inflexible fingers, buttons and zips, 'X' is now 'Min', while 'K' has been renamed 'Meili'. In the ethnographic drama script Mandarin speech is translated into English. In the following interaction the advice and advocacy worker, Meili, speaks in the voice of her client's husband as she completes the computer-based form. She tells Min that what she has typed on behalf of Min's husband reports his difficulties with shoelaces and buttons:

MIN   It takes him ages to tie his shoelaces. They said his fingers are not flexible because of his blood pressure. And he can't do buttons. He has to have trousers with a zip. He loses everything if you don't watch him. Yesterday he lost the shopping I gave him to carry.
MEILI I have said, I have trouble tying my shoelaces and I cannot wear clothes with buttons.

The editing of field notes, transcripts and other material in making the ethnographic drama can seem to be a process of reduction, as many hours of observations are shaped into dramatic form. Here, recontextualisation renders in more concise form the essence of the original dialogue. If this process is a reduction, it is not necessarily reductive. It is, rather, an intensification, a clarification.

Recontextualisation of original research data includes the rearrangement, substitution, deletion or addition of text. In the following original audio transcript of another advice session, the advisor, 'K', has telephoned a representative at an insurance company on behalf of her client, 'T', who is awaiting the outcome of an insurance claim. The claim has been turned down, and T does not understand why. K hangs up the phone and speaks to T, who is in her office.

K   首先，就是刚才跟你们讲的，她已经跟你们联络Staffordshire警察有在沟通,等他们的回复。
    <First, she said they've contacted Staffordshire Police and are waiting for their response.>
T   Mm.
K   然后这个同时 这个叫做 disclosure，呃就是说看你在有没有犯过罪。
    <At the same time you will need to fill out the form called 'disclosure', to see if you've ever committed a crime.>
T   Mm.
K   这个申请费是25磅，然后她告诉我上网去申请。再告诉我最快的时间出来要14天才能出来。这是一个 disclosure form。所以这个就是 disclosure 表格。然后另外还有一个 application form 是她刚重新发过来的。有没有 email 进来你看一下。
    <You need to fill in this form. Once it is sent back they can see if you have a criminal record. The application fee is twenty-five pounds. She says apply online, and she told me it will take at least fourteen days before you get the result. So this is the disclosure form. Then there's another form, which she just sent you. Have you got an email coming in?>
T   让我看看哈。
    <Let me have a look>
K   你有这个这样的记录吗?
    <Do you have a record?>

T   Hm?
K   有这样的记录吗?
    <Do you have such a record?>
T   有什么记录呢?
    <What record?>
K   叫 conviction, 属于犯罪记录, 什么都算, 包括, 呃, 刑事的上的, 也有民事上的, 还有经济上的。我…但是她要, 你必须都要给她。
    <It's called a conviction, it includes everything, whether it's criminal law, civil law, or economic law. It's compulsory, you have to be honest in disclosing the information.>
T   为什么给她?
    <Why should I tell them?>
K   你不给她她可能不会…这是他们的做事情的程序。 没有这个可能会影响你的索赔。她要求了你不做…如果你不做的话, 她不会给你继续处理下去。
    <It's their procedure for dealing with these things. If you don't comply it might affect your claim. You have to do as they ask, or they won't process your case.>
T   就是说一定要犯罪?
    <So I have to commit a crime?>
K: 不是要犯罪, 因为这个叫 disclosure, 就是把你的这些东西有记录, 是干净还是不干净的, 你把资料填上去, 它就有记录, 有底出来了就可以反馈给他。有, 像我假如说我去申请一份工作, 有的公司要求我, 虽然说我是清清白白的, 它也让我做这个, 因为这才是, 叫什么, 清白的一个证明。
    <No, it's not that you have to commit a crime, this is called disclosure. Once you have filled it in they can track down any criminal record if you have one, or see if you have a clean record. You fill in the document, and it has your record, you get feedback. For me, if I apply for certain jobs, it's possible that the company may ask me to fill in a form like this to prove that I don't have a record. This is called proof of innocence.>

A version of this dialogue is played out as Scene 2 of *Interpretations – An Ethnographic Drama*, 'K' is renamed 'Lifan' and 'T' is 'Chang'. As before, the scene is translated into English. Speech originally in Mandarin is in the serif font; speech originally in English (when Lifan speaks to the insurance representative on the telephone) is in the sans serif font. Lifan is still on the telephone as she speaks to her client.

LIFAN   She said they have contacted the police and they are still waiting for a response.
CHANG   The police?
LIFAN   There's this form called disclosure, it's to see if you have ever committed a crime.
CHANG   I have never committed a crime.
LIFAN   She says your claim is not valid.
CHANG   Why is it not valid?
LIFAN   [*To IR, on phone*] He says why is his claim not valid.

	She says when you took out the policy you failed to complete the disclosure. She says you should have completed the disclosure.
CHANG	What is the disclosure?
LIFAN	He says what is the disclosure. She means the criminal disclosure. Do you mean the criminal disclosure? She says yes, the criminal disclosure.
CHANG	I haven't made a disclosure.
LIFAN	He says he hasn't made a disclosure. She says you failed to complete the basic criminal disclosure check, it shows your convictions.
CHANG	I have no convictions.
LIFAN	He says he has no convictions. She says you don't have to have convictions.
CHANG	I have no convictions.
LIFAN	He says he has no convictions. She says you failed to complete a disclosure.
CHANG	They didn't ask me to complete a disclosure.
LIFAN	He says you didn't ask him to complete a disclosure. She says they did.
CHANG	I have never heard of it before.
LIFAN	He says he has never heard of it before. She says it is standard procedure. You have to send your ID, like a credit card or driving licence, and twenty-five pounds. You have to pay for the disclosure. Do you have a record?
CHANG	What record?
LIFAN	It's called a conviction. It includes everything, criminal law, civil law, economic, any kind of conviction has to be disclosed. It's compulsory, you have to disclose your convictions.
CHANG	Why should I tell them?
LIFAN	It's the procedure. It's their way of dealing with things. There are things they need to know. If you don't comply, it might affect your insurance claim. You have to do as they say, disclose any convictions, or they won't process your claim.
CHANG	So I have to commit a crime?
LIFAN	You don't have to commit a crime. It's called disclosure. Once you fill it in, they can track down any criminal record, if you have one, or they can see if you have a clean record.
CHANG	I have never heard of it.
LIFAN	He says he has never heard of it. She says without the disclosure your claim is not valid.
CHANG	But I have the insurance certificate.
LIFAN	He has his insurance certificate. How does he have the insurance certificate if he had to provide the disclosure? She says without the disclosure the certificate is not valid.
CHANG	How did I take out the insurance without the disclosure?
LIFAN	How did he take out the insurance without the disclosure? She says without the disclosure it is not valid.

	Was he told that when he took out the insurance?
	Were you told that when you took out the insurance?
Chang	They never mentioned the disclosure. I have never heard of it.
Lifan	He was not told about the disclosure when he took out the insurance. She says you would not have been able to take out the insurance without providing the disclosure.
Chang	I have been paying for the insurance.
Lifan	He says he has been paying for the insurance. She says without the disclosure it is not valid.
Chang	But I have not committed a crime.
Lifan	He says he has not committed a crime. She says it does not matter whether you have committed a crime. It does not matter whether he has committed a crime? Oh, it does matter whether he has committed a crime. She says whether or not you have committed a crime you must provide the disclosure. Disclosure of the crime he did not commit? She says you would have been asked to provide the disclosure.
Chang	I have never heard of it.
Lifan	He says he has never heard of it. She says it is standard procedure.
Chang	I have never heard of it.
Lifan	He says he has never heard of it. She says you would have been asked to provide the disclosure.
Chang	I have not committed a crime.
Lifan	He has not committed a crime. She says without the disclosure your claim is not valid.

Recontextualisation transforms the text, not least through the addition of rhythm. The effect of this is most evident in performance. Quick-fire dialogue, repetition, successive question-and-answer sequences, ventriloquation of the present-yet-absent voice of the insurance representative, humour, movement between languages, and making explicit the *ad hoc* translation and interpretation process, all contribute to the representation of communication and miscommunication at the heart of the original interaction. In performance the audience has access to voices they would not normally hear.

Creativity and Truth

Field notes, audio-recordings, interview transcripts, social media messaging, video-recordings, linguistic landscapes, are all material for recontextualisation and representation in performance as ethnographic drama. The performative turn has been taken in ethnography. At the same time, the ethnographic turn has been taken in theatre. Playwrights including Alecky Blythe and David Hare have adapted ethnographic monographs, audio-recordings and interview transcripts, and recontextualised them as theatre. The representation of social practice on stage can lend it not a reductive but an exponential quality, opening out interpretive potential. Ethnographic drama provides opportunities for artists and audiences to examine more closely how we and others experience life, and to shape those moments into new aesthetic forms. In both ethnography and theatre, the combination of creative artistry and ethnographic method has already reaped rich rewards, and has huge potential for the future. However, in both domains there is potential for tension between ethical and aesthetic responsibilities. This tension arises in the ethical obligation to re-create an authentic representation of reality at the same time as producing an aesthetic interpretation of that reality. Dialogue in ethnographic drama is often a plausible reconstruction of research data. What the characters say may be approximate versions, rather than 'true' representations, of research participants' discourse. At the same time, ethnographic dramatists have an ethical obligation to balance creativity with accuracy, credibility and trustworthiness. Ethnographic drama can create a validity, authenticity and integrity which goes beyond the scope of the academic report. This is achieved through ethical rigour and unstinting attention to the aesthetic, rooted in the representation not of realism, but reality.

The ethnographic dramatist does not so much compose participants' voices as creatively and strategically edit field notes and transcripts (Saldaña, 2005). Ethnographic playwrights do not 'write' dramas, they adapt them from research –in terms of both content and theatricality. Ethnographic dramas are not playscripts in the traditional sense, but fieldwork reformatted as performative data displays. Having said this, most dialogue in ethnographic drama is creative non-fiction. Not every empirical source provides the necessary detail for authentic dialogue in the theatre. There are times when we rely on the author's imagination to reconstruct the discourse and events portrayed on stage (Saldaña, 2011). The characters in *Interpretations – An Ethnographic Drama* are not faithful or realistic representations of the community centre staff, or their clients, or the researcher. We might say that they are 'versions' of the individuals who participated in the fieldwork. But even this is inaccurate. The characters are themselves. Their discourse, and their actions, represent a truth and a reality. They are drawn from life, but they have lives of their own. The 29 scenes of *Interpretations – An Ethnographic Drama* represent the social practices of people observed in the community centre. But they also constitute the internal reality of the drama. In Scene 3, a group of advisors, Lifan, Meili, Qi and Xia, are chatting (in Mandarin) about education and about family. A researcher, Jin, is also present.

> QI   After all the sacrifice, all the work, all the driving across the city in the rain and dark three nights a week, all the money, for God's sake, thirty pounds a lesson, ninety pounds a week for a year, for the best part of a year. I daren't even count it up. I daren't.

Xia	And what, you're saying she got a place but she doesn't want to go? She passed the exam and they offered her a place?
Meili	What is it then? Her friends are going somewhere else?
Xia	Or it's a boy, is it? Her boyfriend's going to the local school. That can happen. I knew a family once.
Qi	You wouldn't believe it if I told you.
Jin	Four thousand six hundred and eighty.
Meili	Four thousand?
Jin	Based on fifty-two weeks.
Xia	What is?
Qi	You wouldn't believe it if I told you.
Xia	What?
Qi	After all the studying, the verbal reasoning and non-verbal reasoning, the quadratic equations and simultaneous equations.
Jin	What?
Qi	The Latin declensions and English comprehensions.
Xia	Wouldn't believe what?
Qi	That, after all that, she's decided she's discovered her social conscience.
Jin	Her social conscience? What has her social conscience got to do with which school she goes to?
Xia	Oh, you mean like that girl who protested outside parliament every Friday. What's her name? The one from Finland, or Norway. What's her name? I know her name.
Qi	No, not exactly.
Meili	No, I know who you mean.
Xia	I think she's very brave. She gets a bad press at times.
Lifan	Greta something.
Qi	That wasn't about schools.
Jin	Sweden.
Xia	What is?
Jin	Sweden, she's from Sweden.
Xia	Okay.
Qi	What I'm saying is, she's not yet eleven years old. Three months short of her eleventh birthday and she's decided that selective education is the cause of all the world's inequality.
Jin	That's ridiculous.
Qi	She's not even talking about private school. I mean it's grammar school.
Xia	Where does she get that from?
Qi	Seriously, the money and effort I have had to put into getting her through that exam. The time.
Meili	I know.
Qi	I had to learn it all myself, everything, all the grammar, syntax, that was the worst, the maths, algebra, mental arithmetic, problem solving, all of it, like I haven't got anything else to do with my life, Bought the books. They're not cheap. The hours of revision, and she gets through, passes the exam and then, after all the sacrifices.

Jin	What does she mean inequality?
Qi	She says because they're selective.
Jin	That's the point though isn't it? Isn't that the point?
Qi	She says that's how they cause inequality.
Xia	Grammar schools are the very opposite, aren't they? They are the ladder up for so many people, working people, migrants like us, people who aren't born with all the privileges. A way of levelling the playing field, levelling up for people who aren't born to it.
Jin	They allow the cream to rise to the top.
Qi	That's what I said.
Xia	You have to have a way of rewarding talent. You have to put the brightest and the best together and let them fly. Let them reach their potential. Let them learn together.
Qi	That's what I said, but she won't have it.
Xia	What did she say?
Qi	She says no one ever asked her if she wanted to go to grammar school, we took it for granted.
Xia	That's ridiculous. You are only doing it for her. You want what's best for her. That's the end of it.
Qi	She says the whole grammar school system is about elitism.
Xia	Elitism?
Qi	She says it's about creating an elite at the expense of everyone else. She says the system is designed so that the majority lose and the minority win.
Xia	Who loses?
Qi	She says it's about creating failure, creating failure for most people and allowing a few to succeed.
Lifan	It's the opposite though, isn't it? It's about success.
Xia	It's not about creating failure, is it? You just want to do the best for your own child. Everyone does.
Qi	That's it, that's the bottom line. Everyone wants the best for their own child. We'll all fight for that.
Xia	Exactly.
Qi	But she says it's discriminatory. She says you have to invest in everyone, not the few who can afford the extra lessons and the expensive tutors. She says selection is unfair.
Xia	It's not like we're rich though, it really isn't. We make the sacrifice for our children. We work hard for them because it's their future. Where would they be if they had to go to the same schools as everyone else?
Qi	That's what I said.
Xia	So what did she say?
Qi	She says everyone should learn together. It teaches fairness and equality. She says everyone should have the same chance.
Jin	It's not just the academic side though, is it? There's the music lessons, the trips overseas, the sport, the skiing, visits to the theatre, Shakespeare, the things you can't get just anywhere. You can't give that up and let everyone in, you can't.
Xia	And you have to think, who do you want your children to spend

	time with? Who are going to be their friends? It's about making the right connections. You don't want, well, you know.
Qi	I worked so hard for this. It's the golden ticket. It's what you plan for. It's everything, and she tears it up, says it's against a fair society. I don't know, she throws it back in my face.
Meili	My daughter went to the grammar school. She had all the tutors, we bought all the books, did all the practice papers, she took the test. Maybe it wasn't so tough back then. She got in. She found it hard. She didn't really fit. I used to find her crying in her bedroom at night. I used to hear her sobbing. It broke my heart. I didn't understand. It turned out she was being called all sorts of names. She didn't make friends. She told me she was never happy there. It did, it broke my heart.
Xia	But it isn't always about happiness, is it? You have to look after the future. It's more than happiness.

Partly based on interviews with staff and volunteers, and on conversations heard in everyday life at the community centre, the scene is both fact and fiction, both reality and constructed reality. This scene is not a verbatim representation of a single audio-recorded conversation between five women in the advice and advocacy service. But the discourse of the characters is both true to the world of the drama, and testimony to debates that were in circulation in the Chinese community centre at the time of our observations.

In addition to enacting interactions in the advice sessions, and conversations between advisors, *Interpretations – An Ethnographic Drama* draws on interviews with staff, volunteers and committee members. In the following excerpt, from Scene 23, Meili, a long-term member of staff, is talking to the researcher, Jin, about the history of the community centre. The discussion is in Mandarin.

Meili	I came nearly forty years ago, thirty-eight years ago this month, almost to the day, and thirty-eight years later I am still here.
Jin	You just get on with it.
Meili	I got a job that was supposed to be temporary, but it's just amazing, after all these years, I am still working in the same place.
Jin	Did you come on your own?
Meili	No, I came with my two sisters to study. Three girls together. We were companions for each other, we looked out for each other, it wasn't that bad. It was bad, but not that bad.
Jin	It's easier to stay here when you have a job, you have something that you can commit to.
Meili	It's a commitment because of the job, family, husband, but to be honest I don't intend to stay here when I retire, not at all.
Jin	Retirement? You've got a long way to go before you talk about retirement, you're not old enough.
Meili	Yes, retirement soon. I was trained as a social worker, juvenile

JIN   community worker in the eighties. After I got my qualification I was offered this job by the community centre. I loved the job.
JIN   What was it like back then?
MEILI What was it like? There was nothing for the Chinese community at that time. People lived and worked in silence.
JIN   In silence?
MEILI There was no voice for them, nothing for the Chinese community. It was hard, it was difficult.
JIN   But you came to work here?
MEILI Luckily we won some funding from the council back in the early eighties. It was a challenge. Most people we dealt with, young families, they came on work permits in the seventies and eighties, brought their families. It was a struggle for them, a struggle.
JIN   What were the difficulties?
MEILI They lived in the city with little help. They struggled because of the language. They were mainly from Hong Kong, from the New Territories. They spoke Hakka. They had no English, so it was hard, it was very hard. They didn't even have the basics. They knew nothing.
JIN   So they couldn't access resources because they didn't speak English?
MEILI Yes, but it wasn't only the language. Chinese families lived in small houses. They shared with three or four other families. There was overcrowding. Facilities were really limited.
JIN   In the same house?
MEILI We helped the families, helped them to settle, to get the kids into education, find them a school, help with better accommodation, help them apply for benefits.
JIN   Were you funded at that time?
MEILI Eventually the city council gave us some funding. That's how we managed to employ staff to work with the families. It was hard, it was a really hard time. People needed that bit of support.
JIN   Yes.
MEILI Gradually, we were able to take people to hospital, to translate for them at health appointments, to negotiate with social services, to attend parents' evenings in school. Things started gradually getting on track.

The people we interviewed at the community centre were often willing to talk about their migration histories. While we were conducting the fieldwork, the community centre celebrated its 40th anniversary. Narratives about the history of the organisation, and the history of Chinese people in the city, were regularly on people's lips.

Exegesis

As linguistic ethnographers we observe, listen, ask questions, perhaps participate in and aim to make sense of the social practices (the 'cultures') of people or groups from the point of view of those we study. In order to make sense of people's lives from their perspective, we analyse and we write. At this point (if not before), our own perspective collides, rubs up against or sometimes integrates with the perspective of those we study. When we have completed our analysis we provide explanations which may link our study to other research and to theoretical ideas about the meaning of social practices. But explanation which seeks to make transparent the culture of others almost inevitably becomes a process of diminution. Underlying the urge to explain the lives of people from the perspective of Western thought is a desire for transparency. In order to be clear in our understanding of other cultures, we make comparisons and, perhaps, judgements. We diminish them. However, depreciation may not be inevitable in the representation of observed social practice. Instead of seeking to endow the lives of others with meaning, we could resist trying to distil human behaviour as simple explanation. Rather than seeking to make the cultural practices of others transparent, we might allow them to remain opaque. If the other remains opaque, if we do not grasp the other, or seek to explain the other, we can still stand in solidarity. Opacity is the force that drives every community, the thing that would bring us together:

> Widespread consent to specific opacities is the most straightforward equivalent of non-barbarism. We clamor for the right to opacity for everyone. (Glissant, 1997: 194)

For Glissant, the ethnographic impetus for explanation of cultures is the opposite of accepting difference. To accept opacity is to accept people's differences as they are.

The impetus towards exegesis, the imperative for explanation of other cultures, remains the overriding purpose and principle of ethnography. Contemporary ethnography may be as concerned with gang rivalry in London or New York as with ritual practices to invoke the gods in an Iban longhouse in Sarawak, but the purpose of ethnographic research is normally still to explain the culture of the other. We are by no means opposed to the generation of new knowledge through participation in, and observation of, cultural practices. However, with Glissant, we are willing to resist the urge to make too readily transparent the lives of others. Instead, we are inclined to consent to some things remaining opaque. Ethnographic drama enables us to lay before an audience social practice, to enact what we have seen and heard, and invite the audience to engage in critical reflection. Rather than endowing others' cultural practices with meaning, even meaning as we believe it to be perceived by those others, it may be that ethnographic theatre offers the opportunity to make visible the drama in the mundane of contemporary lives, without the need for explanation (Saldaña, 2011).

Summary

We chose to represent the life of the Chinese community centre as ethnographic drama because it is a form which by definition resists the urge for explanation. That is not to say, of course, that it is free of our own world views, ideologies, prejudices and idiosyncratic orientations. The process of representation is certainly suffused with our biographies. Enacting observed practice involves a combination of curation and creation. It was not our intention to explain or endow with meaning the practices of Chinese or Chinese-heritage people in the UK. The advice and advocacy service in the community centre proved to be a rich site at which to observe the communicative practices of disenfranchised people as they sought advice and support, and the linguistic means by which advice workers rendered the world more just for their clients. It was also a window into the everyday language of work. We looked into hidden spaces where, day after day, advisors' skills of translation and interpretation offered support to people whose linguistic capital was of a kind that would not enable them to access resources to which they were entitled.

Ethnographic drama enables us to show the complexities of interactions in which advice and advocacy workers are essential figures in keeping the city moving. They are mediators, intermediaries, shifters, connecting agents and dispatchers, 'anonymous heroes of communication' (Simon, 2012: 6). Beyond making social space more habitable, they have the potential to make life better for those who come to them for help. In our observation of the advisors' practice, more than anything we see people concerned to improve the lives of their clients. They deploy a wide-ranging semiotic repertoire in which they reword, translate, invent, create, contest, re-semiotise, recontextualise, ventriloquate and much besides. In doing so they oil the wheels of the superdiverse city. In ethnographic drama we can make visible quotidian practice which otherwise remains hidden from sight.

Essay 6. Performance

The structure and rhythm of the practice is almost hypnotic. It is difficult to take your eyes off the action, even though there are no serious points to be won, and this is only training. The repetition of action as the ball is served and returned is a metaphor for social life: each instance a recontextualisation of another, yet unique in itself; each instance similar but different; each iteration commented upon by participants and onlookers; each interaction subject to evaluation; each action the subject of approval, delight, disappointment, frustration, congratulation, apology, explanation. It is more than metaphor: it is social life itself.

(Adrian Blackledge, field notes)

Volleyball

Three researchers watch a men's volleyball team over four months on Friday evenings and Sunday afternoons in a sports hall. The team is coached by Joe Ng, originally from Hong Kong, with players from France, Germany, Indonesia, Iran, Malaysia, the Philippines, Romania, Rwanda, Spain, Taiwan and the UK. Observational field notes record what the researchers see and hear (and smell, and taste, and touch) as they follow the communicative practices of men who come together to play. They record the voices of the players as they joke, laugh, tease, complain, criticise, support, encourage, exclaim, celebrate and so on. But the voices are not all. Integral to the communicative repertoires of the players is the body. The researchers also record how the body is put to work in the game. They see that communication in volleyball requires going beyond 'language' and 'languages' to include repertoires in which embodied interaction is integral.

What we observed over four months with the coach and his team was the rhythm and ritual of social life, played out on the volleyball court, whether in training or on match day. The social practice of the volleyball team is not only polyphonic and polyrhythmic, but also polysemiotic. The researchers observe the players as they become a team, as they develop their knowledge and understanding of each other through a rhythm of becoming. They focus also on the coach, on his repetitive structures of teaching and learning, encouragement and reward, organisation and instruction, evaluation and sympathy. They look at the social relations of the players, their banter and laughter, their cursing and complaining, their convivial interaction. They analyse the rhythm of movement as the players jump and dive, block and retrieve, raise arms aloft in celebration and shrug with disappointment. They notice the repetition of small rituals and ceremonies. They record the players' and coaches' commentaries on themselves, and on each other, as they praise and reward, encourage and chastise, support and tease.

Coaching sessions were scheduled on Friday evenings and Sunday afternoons. During the sessions the coach, Joe, wore a lapel microphone attached to a digital voice recorder. The microphone was clipped to his sports attire at the neck. We advised him that he had the right to switch off the recorder whenever he wished to do so. We decided not to ask players to wear digital voice recorders, as the small machine might be a hazard, and cause them injury when they were diving and sliding as they played the game. A first listen to the audio-recorded material was discouraging: the sound of a dozen volleyballs smashed around a brick-built gymnasium with a wooden floor just about drowned out the human voice. However, on subsequent occasions the speech of the coach was quite clear, even if the players' verbal communication was sometimes indistinct. At this point we decided that video-recording would be an important method to record our observations, as physical action was fundamental to what was happening on the volleyball court. If we couldn't hear everything clearly, we wanted to be able to see, and to be able to look again at what we had seen. We explained the research project to the players, and they read and signed consent forms. Over 16 weeks we wrote around 75,000 words of observational field notes, made 30 hours of audio-recordings and video-recordings, took more than 200 photographs, collected online, digital and social media material, and conducted interviews with the coach and the players. In addition to observing Joe in his role as a volleyball coach, we observed him at work in his business, a city centre hair and beauty salon. We regularly shared data from the volleyball sessions, and emergent research outcomes, with Joe, for his comments and feedback. In more than one of these meetings he reported that the experience of viewing the video material had caused him to revise his approach to coaching. We commissioned a professional filmmaker to make a short documentary film which focused on Joe's role as a volleyball coach, and as manager of the salon. The film is available at https://tlang.org.uk/digital-stories.

In the process of analysing the empirical material collected in the four months observing the volleyball players, we shared field notes with each other on a weekly basis. Rachel Hu transcribed audio and video material, together with audio files of interviews with players and coaches. Towards the end of the fieldwork period we would meet weekly as a research team (Blackledge, Creese and Hu) to discuss excerpts from the data sets, beginning with field notes. These meetings began to shape the interpretive process, as all three researchers annotated field notes and transcripts. We made a substantial investment of time in viewing together excerpts from video-recordings. We each commented in detail on the video-recordings, not only in relation to audible verbal communication, but in terms of observable embodied action. These analytic meetings continued for two months, with comprehensive note-taking and writing of summaries. Following this we began a process of further annotation, returning first to field notes, and then to audio and video transcripts, and then to interview transcripts, looking across all data sets for patterns and thematic resonances. A 129-page report, *Translanguaging, Volleyball, and Social Life* (Blackledge *et al.*, 2017), brings together the analysis.

Enacting Linguistic Ethnography

As we saw in Essay 5, in recent times ethnographic drama (also known as ethnodrama and ethnotheatre) has gained purchase in the United States. At the forefront of this work has been Jonny Saldaña (2011), who proposes that live performance has the power to heighten the representation and presentation of social life, and at the same time to capture and document the realities of people participating in the research. Ethnographic drama, he says, provides opportunities for artists and audiences to more closely examine how we and others experience life, and to shape those moments into new aesthetic forms that bring us closer to notions of what is real and what is true. Denzin (2003) argues that performance ethnography can refocus the gaze of the ethnographer and open the audience to new ways of seeing research participants as characters presented on stage. Anna Deavere Smith, a pioneer of ethnographic drama, focuses on the external life of her characters: she builds connections through a process of physical approximation and appropriation of voice, inflection and gesture. She does not attempt to relate to her characters through an exploration of their internal life, or seek to naturalise the text by making it psychologically plausible. In her ethnographic drama practice Smith draws on the radical theatre of Bertolt Brecht.

For Brecht, theatre consists in producing living representations of reported or invented events involving human beings, for the purpose of entertainment. At the same time, Brecht redefines the role of the theatre audience, so that it is questioning and analytical. In Brecht's theatre the audience should link socially critical drama to a type of theatrical representation that does not simply 'reproduce' reality in a neutral and self-evident manner. Brecht brought together in the theatre historians, sociologists, playwrights and actors as a collective to convey aspects of social, political and historical life. Sometimes known as 'epic theatre', or 'epic drama', Brecht's theatre insists that the audience should not be swept away by the action before it. The audience should not be persuaded to engage emotionally with the characters on stage. By means of a range of dramatic techniques, a distance, or alienation, or estrangement is created and maintained between the action on stage and the audience, allowing the spectator to become a critical observer of the life represented in the drama. In what follows in this essay we consider how such techniques are employed in *Volleyball – An Ethnographic Drama* (Blackledge & Creese, 2021b), which is a dramatic representation of our observations of the volleyball coach and his team.

An Ethnographic Drama

Volleyball – An Ethnographic Drama is based on the research we conducted in the volleyball club. It is structured as four acts:

Act I A meeting room at the House of Commons
Act II A sports hall at South England University, in use by South England Thunder Volleyball Club
Act III A meeting room at South England University
Act IV A sports hall at South England University, in use by South England Thunder Volleyball Club.

In Act I the action takes place in a room in the House of Commons. A team of researchers, Amy, Ben and Wendy, is meeting with the government Minister for Sport, Tourism and Heritage, to report on their research. The coach of the volleyball team, Al, and one of his most experienced players, Ryan, accompany the researchers in the meeting. The minister's Assistant Private Secretary, Sarah Maugham, is also present, as is an interested party, Ed Powey, of Exercise UK. The question of whether such a meeting actually occurred between these people is not the most important. The characters are not naturalistic, but they represent the kind of people at the sort of meetings in which academic researchers regularly participate when reporting research to authoritative bodies. The action is presented at one remove from the audience. That is, the actors are not in any real sense the characters they perform. They are instead quoting them, showing the audience what this type of person does and says, in these conditions, at this time. In Brecht's terms, the actor's every sentence is offered for the verdict of the audience, every gesture submitted for the public's approval or disapproval.

Gestus

The action of Act I takes place six months later than the action of the other three Acts. It is separate from the other Acts, almost a play-within-a-play, with its own internal structure. Act I does not set up a significant plot line, a tension or problem to be played out in Act II and Act III, before being happily (or unhappily) resolved in a dénouement in the final Act. In conventional theatre we would expect characters introduced in Act I to reappear later, and contribute to the progress and resolution of a dramatic

94　Part 2. Enacting Linguistic Ethnography

issue. Neither the government minister, her assistant, nor Ed Powey of Exercise UK reappears after the end of Act I. Having served their purpose, they are consigned to history. However, they are far from insignificant in the drama. By means of what Brecht termed *gestus*, the physical and verbal actions of the characters show specific attitudes the characters assume towards each other. In Act I Scene 1 the researchers, Ben, Amy and Wendy, begin their presentation to the government minister, Sally Letwin, MP. Characteristic of the play throughout is overlapping speech. The start of overlapping speech is indicated with [/].

BEN	Minister, thank you for making time to see us this afternoon. We are here to report outcomes of a research project funded by the Arts and Humanities Research Council, in which we investigated how people communicate in cities which are increasingly superdiverse.
SALLY	[*Whispers to Sarah.*]
SARAH	[*Whispers to Sally.*]
BEN	Increasingly, increasingly superdiverse.
SALLY	[*Coughs.*]
BEN	Super, superdiverse, particularly when people with different backgrounds, different languages, different experiences come into contact, / and …
SALLY	Quite so, quite so.
SARAH	The minister was wondering, the minister has read your report, has read the executive summary of your report, and was wondering, what is, well, so super about superdiversity?
AMY	The term was introduced to characterise the diversification of diversity, say in a city like London, where people who live side by side are different not only in terms of ethnicity, but also in terms of education, employment history, nationality, migration route, legal status, linguistic / background.
SALLY	Legal status? / I …
WENDY	And you could say that the term defines not only those multiple differences, but also the ways in which people get along with each other in such contexts.
ED	Sorry, sorry, this is about sport, is it?
WENDY	We spent four months observing in sports clubs in four cities.
SALLY	Legal status?

Everything about the minister should display a lack of interest in the research. Attendance at the meeting is for her a chore to be tolerated. Throughout the scene (and throughout the Act) the actor shows the minister as one who is typical of her privileged social class. The way she speaks is crucial to the representation of the minister. And more than this, every movement of her body contributes to the audience's interpretation. Brecht referred to the *gestus* to denote the complex of gestures and utterances, the overall embodied attitude of those taking part in an interaction.

How someone moves and holds themselves on stage has a bearing on how the character is engaged with by the audience (Long, 2015). The minister's speech is peremptory, and should be portrayed as such, in clipped, uninterested intonation: she whispers to her assistant, she coughs, she deploys a discourse marker designed to hasten the end of the researchers' presentation ('Quite so, quite so'). The two iterations of 'Legal status?' should have a different character from her general indifference: the minister's ears prick up. She is alert to this. If there is some question of the (il)legal status of immigrants, she is interested. This contrast in interest should be performed physically as well as verbally, through facial expression, tilt of the head, eye-gaze, even an actual pricking-up of the ears. At all times it should be clear that in performing the minister, the actor is showing this kind of character to the audience.

The physical and verbal action of the minister should be powerful enough to create uncertainty in the researcher, Ben, who is stopped in his tracks by her whispering, then her coughing, and finally by her staccato 'Quite so, quite so'. She closes him down and he must be rescued by his colleagues. The character of Ben should not be presented in a way that encourages or permits the audience to empathise with him. He should be played in a way that prompts the opposite of empathy. The actor playing Ben does not *become* Ben on the stage. In Brecht's theatre, the idea of the actors' total transformation into their character is abandoned, so the actors speak their parts not as if they were improvising it themselves, but like a quotation. When Ben is interrupted his response should not be emotional, but uncaring. He is interrupted by a senior politician who is too self-important to listen to the findings of academic researchers. Presented almost as a tableau to that effect, the first scene does not prompt the emotional involvement of the audience, but instead their critical reflection.

Brecht proposed that certain incidents in the play should be treated as self-contained scenes, raised above the level of the obvious and expected. That is, although there need not be stylisation or extreme exaggeration, the actors should step outside the naturalistic, forcing the audience to look at the situation from such an angle that it becomes subject to criticism. The actors have not transformed into their characters – they are merely showing them to the audience. Techniques for the estrangement of physical and verbal action are nuanced. In Act I Scene 2 the setting is the same as the previous scene, as the researchers continue in the meeting with the Minister for Sport, Tourism and Heritage. Here is the end of the scene:

  AMY Volleyball requires the organisation of a specific place and time.
  BEN On a beach, in a park.
  AMY The dirt courts of Kigali.
  BEN The streets of Lima, Peru.
  WENDY We watch the game unfold, point by point.
  BEN It is emotionally involving.

AMY	Transformative.
SARAH	The minister.
ED	Transformative?
BEN	Transcendent. The game changes things, changes people.
WENDY	The emotional charge.
AMY	Contained within set time and space.
BEN	Prescribed actions, themselves defined by rules established over time.
ED	Yes, yes, I see that.
SARAH	I wonder whether…
BEN	In volleyball each rally, each point played is a communicative event.
WENDY	Within each communicative event, three identifiable elements – social practice before the ball is served, social practice during play, social practice after the point has been played.
AMY	That social practice is ritualised as recognisable action – expression of intent, determination, engagement, celebration, disappointment, joy, frustration, despair.
BEN	Each point subject to comment and reflection.
ED	I see that, yes, I see that in, yes, in other sports, tennis, badminton, even basketball, yes.
WENDY	It runs through different sports, but beyond sport.
BEN	Ceremonial, ritual behaviour, sets of actions which follow compulsory patterns, agreed rules.
SALLY	I really…
WENDY	Runs through social life.
SARAH	The minister.

In contrast to Scene 1, the researchers are confident and fluent in their presentation. Once again, though, the actors are not transformed into their characters. The researchers, Amy, Ben and Wendy, could certainly be performed in a naturalistic way. They are enthusiastic about their research, and they are making the most of the opportunity to communicate their findings to the government, in the person of the minister. But the scene should not be performed naturalistically. In order to maintain an estrangement, the scene is performed with rhythmic speech which goes beyond anything that would be normal in a meeting with a government minister. This emphasis on rhythmic speech also goes beyond anything that would normally be done to bring the theatre audience into close proximity with the action. The scene therefore may be entertaining, but it would be difficult for an audience to empathise with the characters of the researchers. There is something a little too surprising, a little too strange, for the audience to become emotionally involved. In contrast to the previous scene, now both the minister and her assistant are ignored as they attempt to intervene. Attention should be paid to body position, and to the positioning of characters in relation to each other. Scene 2 should mirror Scene 1, but now the boot is on the other foot. In this scene it is worth noting the character of Ed. At first struggling to keep up with the arguments of the academic researchers ('Transformative?'), he clings on, and appears to (or wants to appear to) come to new understandings ('Yes, yes, I see that'; 'I see that, yes, I see that'). Neither remote politician nor ivory tower academic, he is perhaps an Everyman, a touchstone against which the audience is able to measure its own response. If Ed gets it, the audience does too. The character of Ed should be played in just this way – not as a 'real' person, but as a barometer with which to take a common-sense reading. His character is not to be empathised with but to be viewed from a distance.

In Act I Scene 3 the estrangement techniques in Act I Scene 2 are expanded. The characters pick up the rhythm. In this scene one of the volleyball players, Ryan, and the team coach, Al, join in the dialogue:

RYAN   The corporeal rhythm of each player and each coach.
AL   The warm-up routine, repeated action, taking turns, leaps and falls, synchrony and disharmony, all are rhythmic.
ED   Different measures and beats coexist with each other, overlap.
SARAH   The minister.
RYAN   Rhythm of learning.
SARAH   The minister.
AL   Rhythms intertwined, complex.
SARAH   The minister. [*Looks at watch; points to watch.*]
RYAN   Rhythm of banter and laughter.
SARAH   [*Louder*] I am afraid the minister.
AL   The clown, the carnival, the dancer, the dance.
     Sarah whispers to Sally. They both collect their papers, and leave the room; Ryan, Al, Ed, Amy, Ben and Wendy continue.
RYAN   Heart, breath.
AL   Birth, death.
RYAN   Being.
AL   Becoming.
RYAN   Serve, pass, set, spike, block.
AL   People need the game, we need the game.
RYAN   What we find, what we find is that all of life is the game, the game is all of life.
AL   The playful and the serious.
RYAN   The rational and the irrational.
AL   The social and the convivial.
RYAN   That's what we find, that all of life is the game.
AL   The game is all of life.
RYAN   The game, the game, without the game, without the…

In the closing stages of Act I Scene 2 the academic researchers present their arguments in rhythmic speech which stands outside the norms of naturalism. Here, in the closing stages of Scene 3, the rhythm of speech mirrors the rhythmic speech of Scene 2, but there has been a role reversal. Whereas the research findings were presented in Scene 2 by the three academic researchers, now it falls to the coach, Al, and his senior player, Ryan, to speak. At all times the actors presenting Al and Ryan are aware that they are performing. There is nothing naturalistic about the dialogue. Internal rhyme and end-rhyme ('Heart, breath / Birth, death') suggest that the piece may belong in the genre of performance poetry. Content becomes form, and form becomes content. Again Ed joins the performance, if only ephemerally. As before, the minister's assistant attempts to intervene but goes unheard. The minister, for her part, also goes unheard, and the two of them leave in silence. Undeterred by the lack of audience, Ryan and Al press on with their performance. The government may no longer be present, but the theatre audience remains, and the volleyball player and coach keep going. Ultimately they finish their poetic performance in mid-air, unfinalised, unfinished, looking both to the future, which the actors inhabit, and the past, which is where the characters are headed in Act II.

The *Verfremdungseffekt*

In Brecht's theatre the *Verfremdungseffekt* alienates the audience by taking the self-evident, familiar and obvious, and making it unfamiliar and strange. In doing so it creates a critical distance between performed action and audience. The *Verfremdungseffekt*, or V-effect, means that plays are not dependent on empathy, but are directed in such a way that the audience does not identify itself with the characters. Acceptance or rejection of their actions and utterances takes place on a rational, conscious plane, instead of at an emotional or subconscious level (Brecht, 1978). In terms which resonate with ethnographic research, Brecht proposes that in its representations of the way people live together, the theatre must make the familiar strange.

Before the start of Act II, a placard is presented, with the words 'Six months earlier' (if preferred, a projection of the same may be presented). In this there is no pretence, no artifice. The audience does not have the illusion of being the unseen spectator at an event that is really taking place, in real time. The placard makes visible the machinery of the theatre. It demystifies traditional dramatic devices, drawing attention to the fact of being in the theatre rather than the 'real world'. Making the devices of the theatre visible contributes to the V-effect. Five scenes in *Volleyball – An Ethnographic Drama* are preceded by titles on placards or screens which refer to time shifts. Something happened six months ago, implies the title at the start of Act II. Now we will show it to you, and you will give it your critical attention.

Act II Scene 1 invites the players (in both senses of dramatic and sporting players) to briefly introduce themselves. The researchers tell the coach and players that they will watch them while they train and play during the forthcoming months. Some of the players do not appear to be completely comfortable with being put under the research team's microscope ('I'm not so sure about it all'). From this moment the actors are aware that they are being watched by the researchers. They are also aware that they are being watched by the audience. Each of these layers of estrangement should be evident in the actors' performance. But the audience's empathy is not entirely rejected. The audience identifies itself with the researcher as an observer, and accordingly develops an attitude of looking on. In Act II Scene 1 we find conventional stage directions (e.g. *'The players continue their warm-up activity'*). After this scene there are few identifiable stage directions in the text. Instead, stage directions, or what can appear to be stage directions, are spoken by the three researchers, Amy, Ben and Wendy. Brecht (1978) referred to the speaking aloud of stage directions as an alienation technique, resulting in a clash between two tones of voice, estranging the text proper. In *Volleyball – An Ethnographic Drama* the researchers, always on stage, speak aloud their observations, their field notes, which in the theatre are also spoken stage directions. A typical example is the opening of Act II Scene 2:

> WENDY   Al demonstrates the movement he wants the players to copy. He takes nimble sideways steps on his toes, before jumping vertically, arms raised, fingers extended. He lands softly, feet together.
> AL   One, two, jump! One, two, jump!
> BEN   Each word corresponds to a step, as if Al were a choreographer rehearsing a Broadway musical.
> AMY   Al needs a volunteer to demonstrate the move.
> AL   We need wing blockers. Finn, can you show us? Come on, wing blockers, wing blockers.
> BEN   Finn is joined by Toby. They perform the blocking drill, leaping together on each side of the net, touching fingers above the net. Two steps to the side and they jump again.

In all instances in which they speak stage directions, or field note observations, it should be clear that Amy, Ben and Wendy are speaking directly to the audience. When the actors turn to the audience, it is a whole-hearted turn rather than an aside. The actors have one eye on the action being described and one eye on the audience. The actors are *showing* the audience apparently natural, familiar characters and incidents from ordinary life. This is achieved partly by the researchers describing the action as it is performed, introducing a layer of estrangement. In some instances the action should be described immediately *before* it is performed:

> WENDY   Lukas finds it difficult to get off the ground. Ryan is opposite Hubert. Their timing goes awry, and they get their jump wrong. Ryan is not happy. He shouts across the net to Hubert.
> RYAN   What was that? How was that a block?

BEN	Ryan has a smile on his face. Constant peer evaluation goes on during the practice. There seems to be a fine line here between supportive feedback and mockery.
AMY	Al waves his hands above his head, shouts to the players to stop, then demonstrates the moves again, talking them through the sequence.
AL	You block in the middle first, block in the middle first....

The action seems particularly alien when it takes place after having already been announced by the researchers. Ryan shouts after Wendy has announced that he will shout. Al talks the players through the sequence of movement after Amy has announced that Al talks them through the sequence of movement. It is as if the actors presenting the players and coach are exemplifying the observations of the researchers. Here, you see – the actors say to the audience – this is what life is like. Only through *Verfremdung* is this possible in the theatre.

Dance, like music, offers a further degree of estrangement. Act II Scene 2 is dependent on choreography. Here the actors must do more than run through volleyball training drills. Their purpose is not merely to demonstrate how players learn to block the ball at the volleyball net. The players not only practise their defensive drills, but they do so with the rhythm and poise of dancers. Coach and players coexist with characters from a Broadway musical chorus line, or a ballet troupe. The audience is not dependent on empathy with the emotional lives, or the inner being, of the characters as coach and players. That is, if the actors step outside of their role as participants in volleyball and become dancers, nothing is lost. The actors should play the whole scene in a way that represents both the volleyball player and the dancer. Both are present at all times, and neither ever absent. Brecht (1978) suggests that in the history of the theatre it is a relatively recent error to suppose that choreography has nothing to do with the representation of people as they really are. Theatre, he argues, cannot dispense with choreography. The mere elegance of a movement, and gracefulness of a pose, can produce *Verfremdung*. Act II Scene 2, which takes place on a volleyball court and not in a dance studio, let alone on Broadway, is nevertheless suffused with opportunities to demonstrate the elegance of a movement and the gracefulness of a pose.

As we have seen, Brecht proposes that the performance of the social *gestus* corresponds to making social realities visible. *Gestus* is not a matter of explanatory or emphatic movements of the hands, but of overall embodied attitudes. The attitudes adopted by the characters are manifested physically as well as verbally. In Act II Scene 2 the typical (in sporting contexts) action of the 'low five' becomes significant. The low five, an action in which two players slap each other's hands with arms extended at or below waist level, is a physical manifestation of celebration, consolation, solidarity, encouragement, greeting and so on. In Act II

Scene 2 it also becomes a contested action. Actors show the audience their drill as they practise blocking at the net. In one group the players have been finding it difficult to coordinate with each other as they jump:

    AMY   When their turn comes round again, Ryan, Dan, Hubert and Justin finally jump together in unison, and touch fingers over the net. Ryan nods approvingly to Hubert and laughs loudly.
    RYAN   Ha ha ha ha! Better!!
    WENDY   Hubert makes a gesture towards Ryan, attempting a low five to resolve the tension. But Ryan turns away, ignoring Hubert's outstretched hand. Al comes onto court and stops the players.

The action performed here should be deliberate, and precise, so that nothing of its significance is lost. The attempted and rejected low five constitutes a gestural expression of the social relationship between Hubert, a new player, and Ryan, an old hand and former coach. The offered hand should be clearly visible to the audience, almost in slow motion. Hubert need not be presented as offended or otherwise disappointed. Ryan, for his part, is indifferent to any offence he may have caused. The actors should take up a position in which they are showing the audience the action of this sort of person in relation to that sort of person. It is the showing that is key. The first condition for the achievement of the V-effect is that the actors must invest in a definite *gestus* of showing (Brecht, 1978). In order to do this it is necessary to drop the assumption that there is a 'fourth wall' cutting the audience off from the stage, and the consequent illusion that the stage action is taking place in reality and without an audience. Once this is achieved, it is possible for the actor to address the audience directly.

In Act II and Act IV, both played out on the volleyball court, the researchers, Amy, Ben and Wendy, sometimes speak simultaneously with the character of the player or coach they are observing. Simultaneous speech normally occurs at the end of an utterance spoken by a player or coach, so examples are short. In the following extract from Act II Scene 2, the point at which two or more characters begin to speak the same words simultaneously is indicated with [//]:

    BEN   Al wants them to work on body position.
    AL   It starts with your // footwork.
    BEN   Footwork.
    AMY   His speech is rhythmic, matching his movement.
    AL   Step, step, // jump, turn!
    AMY   Jump, turn!
    WENDY   Al embodies the rhythm he is trying to instil in the team. Finn and Runi copy his steps.
    AL   That's it! Good! Step, step, // jump, turn!
    WENDY   Jump, turn!
    BEN   The players are attentive to Al's commands.

AL   Step, step, // jump, turn!
BEN   Jump, turn!
WENDY   The activity continues rhythmically, each leap, touch, land, sideways step, leap again, touch again, land again, producing and produced by rhythm. It is mesmerising.
AL   Step, step, // jump, turn!
WENDY   Jump, turn!
AMY   The drill has a clear functional role as the players practise the blocking technique. At the same time, it is almost like art, a dance which is aesthetic as well as practical.
AL   Good, Runi! Good, Finn! // Good, Hubert!
AMY   Good, Hubert!
AL   Step, step, jump, turn! Step, step, // jump, turn!
BEN   Jump, turn!

The researchers are able to speak simultaneously with the coach because they have been observing him. Now they know him well enough not only to be able to speak with and for him, but to show him with confidence to the audience. None of this simultaneous dialogue should be naturalistic. It is a way of drawing the attention of the audience to questions of observing, watching and seeing. The audience becomes aware not only that the researchers are watching the coach and players, and showing them and their action to the audience, but also that the players and coach are aware of being watched by the researchers, and that all of the actors are aware of being watched by the audience. However familiar it may be, the social practice of volleyball, its rituals and rhythms, becomes something unusual. Simultaneous speech acts as an estrangement technique which permits the audience to view action with a critical eye.

In Act II and Act IV of *Volleyball – An Ethnographic Drama*, researchers Amy, Ben and Wendy not only complete utterances of players and coach in simultaneous speech, they also complete the actions of players and coach in simultaneous movement. That is, when they speak synchronously with the other character, the researchers physically shadow the character, and address the character's addressee. They also adopt the intonation of the character whose speech they share. As with simultaneous speech, the actions of the researchers give every impression that they know precisely how the player or coach is about to move. There should not be the slightest time lag between the movement of the player or coach and the movement of the researcher. There is nothing magical or imaginative about the shadowing of physical action. It is part of the process of the researcher showing to the audience the embodied life of the player or coach. At the same time there is nothing naturalistic about the process. There is no illusion that what is being played out on stage might be played out in the real world. It is a process of showing, of making strange the action of ordinary life. The *Verfremdungseffekt* takes human action and labels it as something striking, something that is not to be taken for granted. It allows the spectator to constructively evaluate the action on stage from a social point of view.

Act III begins not with a volleyball match but with another time shift, to a meeting between the researchers and the coach, Al, to look at video clips of the match filmed by the research team. Here the researchers should speak directly to the audience, sharply aware that they are being watched. In this scene the 'low five' motif is picked up from Act II, and becomes a point of contestation among the research team. They debate whether Ryan's selectivity about giving low fives to fellow players is because he discriminates against players of certain backgrounds. This scene is played without the need for resolution. The matter may remain unfinalised. It has been raised, and offered to the audience for scrutiny, evaluation and judgement. While we have taken up Brecht's proposal that the actors detach themselves from the characters portrayed, and the audience consequently need not invest emotionally in the lives of the characters, empathy will nevertheless occur. In reality, both empathy and a more estranged exemplification almost inevitably coexist. Brecht (1978) characterises empathy and estrangement as two mutually hostile processes combined in the actors' work. Actors derive their true effectiveness from the tussle and tension of the two opposite positions. This is the dialectic of the theatre. The emphasis in Act III, as elsewhere, is on observing, watching and seeing. Al comments on what he can see in the performance of his team. The researchers show to the audience the reflections of the coach and their own contested arguments. The action on stage is multilayered and multifaceted, confronting the audience with a variety of points of view, so as to provoke critical reflection.

In Act IV Scene 2 the coach, Al, insists that the players improve their team chant, which is designed to inspire motivation in the team. The scene picks up on the theme of Act II Scene 4, which is also a brief, self-contained scene in which the coach insists on the rehearsal of coordinated, collective action. In both scenes the players go through some difficulties before their collective efforts are rewarded. In each case they finally achieve improvement, and the coach is pleased. These scenes, which have little or no bearing on the overall plot or storyline, nevertheless show the audience something of the potential of collective action. As before, the actors maintain an attitude of 'showing' throughout these scenes. There is no sense that they are scenes from real life, viewed by the audience as a 'fly on the wall'.

In Act IV Scene 3 time shifts forwards again, to the crucial end-of-season relegation match. The team, South England Thunder, must win to avoid relegation, which would mean playing in the second division next year. As before, *Verfremdung* techniques resist the illusion that the audience are unseen spectators at an event that is really taking place. The actors show that they are aware of being observed, and of observing themselves. Again, the researchers speak aloud observations which have the character both of field notes and stage directions. The researchers engage in simultaneous speech and action, shadowing the players physically and linguistically. The researchers also join in with the team chant. Here they participate in Al's team talk. As before, the beginning of simultaneous speech is marked in the text with [//].

AL   We need to play with rhythm. We are not playing with any kind of // rhythm at all.
AMY   Rhythm at all.
AL   You are chasing the ball instead of controlling the game. We need to // take control.
AMY   Take control.
AL   We are not doing anything at the moment. When we are defending, we are not // in the right position.
AMY   In the right position.
AL   Everybody is defending the tip. You don't need to defend the tip. You can // let the tip drop.
AMY   Let the tip drop.
AL   We need to do our own job, play to // our own rhythm.
AMY   Our own rhythm.
AL   Every point you win, can you get together // and celebrate?
WENDY   And celebrate?
AL   You are really, really quiet on court. You are like strangers. Come on! You have to // play as a team!
BEN   Play as a team!

Here everything about the actors' posture, movement, gesture, speech, rhythm and intonation constitute an attitude of showing.

In Act IV Scene 4 the match moves towards its conclusion. The scene is set in the final timeout, with scores level. Players have come together to give each other encouragement:

AMY   Voices become increasingly loud now.
RYAN   When the spike comes in there's not one of you getting into a defensive position. // That's piss poor!
WENDY   That's piss poor!
JUSTIN What's going on? We're all // looking at the floor.
WENDY   Looking at the floor.
TOBY   We have to come together! We have to push ourselves! We have to fight for each other. We // need each other!
BEN   Need each other!
NAT   We know // our mistakes.
WENDY   Our mistakes.
LUKAS   Guys, it's up to us, // not up to them!
BEN   Not up to them!
RYAN   Come on, // two more points!
WENDY   Two more points!

JUSTIN	You need to serve flat, okay? Don't let them volley. If they volley, they will // win the point.
BEN	Win the point.
DAN	Let's do it. We have got ourselves back into it twice already. We can // push from here!
AMY	Push from here!
RUNI	No lazy points. No sitting on our hands. Every point, // every point!
WENDY	Every point!
DAN	If we can get one, we can get two. Come on! It's // only two points!
BEN	Only two points!
FINN	You need to set // the ball high.
WENDY	The ball high.
BEN	Watch the spin serve, watch the // spin on the serve!
AMY	Spin on the serve!
	The players and researchers come together and place their hands on top of each other's hands.
WENDY	Guys, there's no room for error now, // no more mistakes!
AMY	No more mistakes!
BEN	On our serve, on our serve, serve // away from the body.
WENDY	Away from the body.
AMY	Don't serve directly at them, // they can volley.
BEN	They can volley.
AMY	Come on, let's go!!

The players and researchers move their joined hands in an upward and downward motion in time with the chant.

WENDY BEN AMY PLAYERS	3 – 2 – Thunder!

Lights dim.

The researchers take over the team talk, graduating from speaking in synchrony with the players to effectively speaking the lines of the players in synchrony with each other. Here the actors show the life of the field worker and research analyst, at the same time as the life of the player and team member. Team work, team spirit, mutual endeavour and observation, and analysis of the same, all are made available to the audience.

Act IV Scene 5 is the final scene. The team has won the relegation match by the smallest margin. But all is still not completely well in the team, as the captain and coach are unable to persuade the younger players to attend a victory celebration. In this part of the final scene actors presenting the younger players show with bodily posture and stance their complex and ambivalent attitudes to the game, and to the team. Finally, the 'low five' motif recurs, as the players are leaving the sports hall:

AL	Well played.
JUSTIN	All right, see you.
AMY	Justin starts to walk towards the exit, stops and turns round.
JUSTIN	We won! Ha ha ha! We won!
AMY	Justin and Al embrace. Ryan takes three steps towards Justin and holds out his hand towards him. Justin slaps Ryan's hand in a low five. They gaze at each other for a few seconds. Justin turns away and leaves.

Justin was one of the players Ryan refused to engage with in an earlier scene. Here the actors presenting Ryan and Justin show that they are profoundly aware of being watched, and that they are at the same time observing themselves. The action is not unchangeable, closed off to influence, the characters helplessly resigned to their fate. The audience sees that the world may be changed rather than accepted as it is. The performance does not seek to intoxicate the audience, supply them with illusions, help them forget the world, or reconcile them with fate. In Brecht's terms, the theatre spreads the world before the audience to grasp for their own purposes.

Summary

People go to the theatre to escape the world, to be emotionally elevated, to be intellectually challenged, to be transported to another time and place, to be diverted from the mundane, to be enchanted, to be hypnotised, and for many more reasons. The magical experience of traditional theatre requires that the audience becomes invested in the characters on stage, empathising with their lives. The audience is complicit in the illusion that there is a fourth wall to the theatre, and that the action on stage is happening in the real world. Brecht, however, developed a theatre which was interested in showing the behaviour of people towards one another. He wanted to remove the illusion of the audience as the unseen spectator at an event that is really taking place. He devised techniques which allow the action and characters on stage to become estranged, so that the audience is aware that it is being shown aspects of human relationships and practices, and takes a critical position in relation to them. In considering the most appropriate means of showing the multifaceted social action of a volleyball team, a Brechtian approach to theatre offers a way of showing social practice that can do more than the conventional ethnographic monograph. Brechtian theatre suggests a creative and critical means of representing the outcomes of ethnographic research. In ethnographic drama we place before the audience a version of observed social action, as if to say 'Look, this is the kind of thing that sometimes happens, this is how people sometimes are. What do you think?'

Essay 7. Politics

Introduction

One of the sites in which we observed communicative practices in the TLANG project was the state-of-the-art Library of Birmingham. Audunson (2005) pointed out that in their original conception, public libraries were linked to the rational project of enlightenment. Enlightenment, in turn, was based on the conviction that in the fields of culture, literature and knowledge, we can distinguish between products of high value, which the library should promote, and products of mediocre or low value, which the library should not promote. That is, public libraries are conceived as a force for good in the community, and in the city. In their study of library space and place in Norway, Aabø and Audunson (2012) identified heterogeneous ways in which libraries are meeting places for their users. They are places where people accidentally bump into friends and acquaintances, places where people are exposed to the diversity of the city, places where people live out their role as citizens, sites of joint activity between family and friends, 'meta-meeting places' which provide a channel to identify other social arenas and organisations in the community, and virtual meeting places. Aabø and Audunson also found that libraries play an important social role as sites which relieve isolation, and as places which invest in fostering imagination, creativity and personal development, strengthening local culture and identity, social cohesion and community empowerment. Furthermore, they concluded, libraries contribute to community development by providing free social space, technological resources, connection to the local economy, a sense of ownership by community and a high level of trust. They also have a role in the development of confidence in individuals and communities. Audunson *et al.* (2011) focused on the role of libraries in relation to immigrants, and found that they have the potential to provide them with the information they need to adapt to their new circumstances as well as with opportunities to keep in touch with their place of origin. They found that the public library offered a meeting place that facilitates communication, and offers bridges between minority cultures and the majority culture.

Following her research on libraries in the United States, Johnson (2012) concluded that interactions that take place every day between staff members and library patrons provide a human connection that results not only in instrumental help in gaining access to useful information resources, but also in emotional help that contributes to a sense of individual well-being. These interactions, therefore, may be an important source of social capital that has a positive effect on both individuals and communities. Johnson (2012) found that the library is a positive place, a place people visit without having to provide a reason for being there. It is a neutral place where people can come and go as they please, an inclusive place open to all, and a comfortable, welcoming place that is separate from home or work. Audunson (2005) proposes an agenda for the future of public libraries, arguing that they are meeting places that can promote cross-cultural contact and communication, and physical spaces in which people of different backgrounds are exposed to one another.

The Library of Birmingham opened in 2013, at a cost of £189 million. It was a flagship project for the redevelopment of the UK's second most populous city. It was the largest public library in the UK and the largest regional library in Europe. The brand new, ultra-modern, high-tech building was a far cry from the traditional image of a library characterised by whispered conversations and oak-panelled walls. Coca-Cola machines, mobile phones, computers, a job club, an immigration advice centre, and much besides, were now the order of the day. The library attracted a diverse constituency of users, including not only local people from the city but visitors from all over the world. Nearly two and a half million people went through the doors of the library in the year after it opened, making it the tenth most popular visitor attraction in the UK. It was clear that this was an ideal site at which to investigate communication in the superdiverse city. We approached the director of the library, who was happy to give us access to conduct ethnographic research over a period of four months. One of the library staff, Millie (a pseudonym), agreed to be a key participant in the research. Millie worked as a customer experience assistant, providing information and support to library users in a range of different departments. Originally from Hong Kong, Millie had worked in the city's library service for 18 years.

When we first negotiated access to conduct the research, the library was a beacon of civic pride for the city. But by the time we started our fieldwork, six months later, the government had made cuts to local authority funding. The city's finances were hit hard. The new library's opening hours were significantly reduced. The library announced that it would have to make more than 50% of its staff redundant. To this end, library workers were required to reapply for their own jobs, or to apply for voluntary redundancy. In spite of the news of funding cuts, the library staff were more than willing to accommodate the research team. Researchers Adrian Blackledge and Rachel Hu were introduced to staff in the different departments of the library. In all cases, and notwithstanding the uncertainty surrounding people's future employment, the library extended a cheerful and warm welcome.

The research design for our investigations in the Library of Birmingham was consistent with the methods adopted across the 16 case study sites in the research project. Over the course of four months we conducted observations, wrote field notes, made audio-recordings of Millie's interactions with library users and colleagues, collected online and digital communications from Millie, gathered institutional documentation, took photographs and made video-recordings in the library. Rachel Hu shadowed Millie two days each week, participating in her work routines, at the same time recording her observations as field notes. Rachel shadowed Millie as she moved between different work spaces, across several floors, in a number of different departments, front-stage and back-stage, and in the kitchen and the lunch room. Rachel's relationship with Millie changed over time. We provide a more detailed discussion of the development of their relationship during the research process in Essay 10. Adrian Blackledge also observed Millie once a week, always while Rachel was shadowing. Angela Creese observed in the library on several occasions, and also wrote observational field notes. In all we wrote 29 sets of field notes, amounting to 101,225 words. The field notes describe as much as possible of what we could see and hear as we observed Millie at work and in her break time. Our field notes also describe the institutional discourses of the Library of Birmingham.

After writing field notes for five weeks we asked Millie to audio-record herself while we continued to observe her at work. We continued to write field notes throughout the data-collection period. Millie audio-recorded herself with a small digital voice recorder, which she kept in her pocket. A tie-clip microphone was secured to her clothing close to her throat. This meant that we were able to audio-record Millie's speech and, in most cases, the speech of those with whom she interacted. Rachel similarly wore a digital voice recorder. Millie's colleagues had been told that audio-recording was going on and we also regularly reminded them in person. They were told that they had the right to avoid participation in the research project if that was their preference. It was impractical for us to gain the written, informed consent of all members of the public who interacted with Millie at the information desk. We therefore created a highly visible sign which informed members of the public that if they did not want their voice recorded they could inform Millie, and she would let the research team know. Millie recorded herself at work in the Library of Birmingham for 42 hours, including in the staff room during lunch and tea breaks.

We asked Millie to send us examples of her online, digital and social media communication. Although she was not an enthusiastic participant in social media, she used WhatsApp, and she also used email at work. Millie copied and sent to the research team 500 WhatsApp messages (40 screenshots) and 50 emails. The research team took 300 photographs in and around the library, and also at Millie's home. We asked Millie to audio-record herself either in domestic or in friendship group settings (or both). She did both, and these audio-recordings, many of them at the family dinner table, amounted to 16 hours of interaction. Millie also audio-recorded Skype conversations with her (adult) daughter, who was living in South Africa at the time of our data collection. We collected around 200 leaflets and documents associated with the library. Rachel interviewed Millie on two occasions, and frequently recorded conversations with her while shadowing her at the work station and in the lunch room. Finally, we video-recorded Millie at work in the library for a total of two and a half hours. We had also planned to interview senior members of staff at the library. However, the scheduled period for interviews coincided with the library's announcement of cuts to staffing and to opening hours. The library management was wary of increased media attention at this time, and told us that they did not want us to interview staff. We therefore did not go ahead with the scheduled interviews.

During and beyond the data collection period Rachel listened to all of the audio-recordings and selected interactions for transcription. She then sent the transcripts to Adrian and Angela, together with a reference to the audio file, which was commonly available to them. Each of us listened separately to the audio-recording, while reading and annotating the transcript. We held weekly meetings to discuss the transcripts. These meetings were themselves audio-recorded for future reference. This activity continued for some months, as the transcripts ran to hundreds of pages of text. During and after this period we wrote thematic summaries, which formed the basis of a research report. This report (Blackledge *et al.*, 2016), which was over 90,000 words in length, subsequently became a valuable resource as we wrote research articles and book chapters. Other publications based on the research in the Library of Birmingham include Creese and Blackledge (2019a, 2019b).

In exchanges between library staff and their clients, and also in interactions between colleagues, language in use reflected the fluidity and flux characteristic of superdiversity. In communicative practices in the public space we largely observed a positive orientation to linguistic, cultural, ethnic and national differences. The Library of Birmingham was a convivial place where a multitude of histories, trajectories and expressions converged, and people got on with the business of communication. However, as we observed everyday talk in the library it became clear that politics was taking centre stage.

A Political Turn

In approaching the library to conduct linguistic ethnographic research, it was not our intention to engage with politics. As it happened, during the period of our observations a general election was held in the UK, to elect a new national government. This event elicited a good deal of discussion between colleagues in the library, as it would in many a workplace. As we observed everyday social practice, it was clear that both national and local politics were on people's minds. In the following example from a transcript of an audio-recording, Millie is talking to a male colleague, Saj, in the days leading up to the election. Ed Miliband was the leader of the opposition Labour Party:

Millie You vote? Do you vote?
Saj I will vote on Thursday.
Millie Oh, who you vote for? Which party?
Saj I will vote Labour as it is, hehe, what about you?
Millie I don't talk to you any more, hehe, you vote Labour.
Saj Haha! Are you Tory?
Millie Hehe. No, no, no, no, I have nobody. But I don't like Ed Miliband, he's not sharp enough.
Saj He's not sharp, but the only problem is I like the party. But I don't, I ... I ... I agree that Ed Miliband is not very sharp but....
Millie Mm.
Saj But I don't like, I don't like the Tories.
Millie Well all, all the U.K. politics, nobody good anyway, isn't it?
Saj Yeah, yeah, one thing really is, the thing is I don't like the idea of not voting, I have to vote.
Millie Yea, you vote, yea yea.
Saj And, and it's just about, you know....
Millie You are part of it, isn't it?
Saj That's right. The both parties are ... the both parties are pretty much, it's a big decision.
Millie I vote UKIP.
Saj You vote UKIP?
Millie Yea! To stop the immigrants. Stop immi.... Maybe I have to go, everybody have to go. But no, no, I am just joking.
Saj I don't like UKIP, they are just trying to cause, cause, like fear.
Millie The thing is, funny thing is that UKIP is no good, but it's a good job to have UKIP there, you know why, to constrain the two party, otherwise they can say anything, because no opposition party, you know.
Saj I don't....
Millie Yea but UKIP may be too racist you know, yea, isn't it?

In this ordinary encounter between colleagues during a quiet moment at the information desk, Millie and her workmate Saj talk about politics. The conversation moves across a range of views about leadership, voting behaviour, democracy and party politics, until Millie wrong-foots her colleague, joking that she plans to vote for the anti-immigration United Kingdom Independence Party (UKIP). Millie jokes that if UKIP is successful in the election, 'Maybe I have to go, everybody have to go'. It is relevant that Saj was British Asian and therefore, like Millie, potentially threatened by a rise in the popularity of the anti-immigration party. Despite the fact that she says she is 'just joking', Millie nevertheless pursues her point, offering a rationale for supporting the ultra-right party. Finally, almost debating with herself, or rehearsing circulating political discourses, she concludes that 'UKIP may be too racist'.

Debate about the general election was evident at almost every turn during this period of our time observing in the library. We recorded another example, as Millie engaged in conversation with a male colleague, John, on the day after the general election, when the Labour Party had been defeated by the Conservative Party, and the Labour leader, Ed Miliband, had resigned:

Millie   Yea, because Ed Miliband has been five, four, five years, and once people has criticise, not criticise, people are saying there is no charisma, he's no plan, so bored.
John   The thing with Ed Miliband is his speech.
Millie   Mm, he's not strong enough.
John   His haircut, I know it's ... but it's all about his voice really, you need to be a presenter, you don't want somebody who puts you off before he's even spoken yet, you know what I mean? That's ... tha ... that's the harsh reality of the ... world.
Millie   Yea, the image, that's why ... why I said his brother is good, his brother David Miliband.
John   Yea, he won't come back.
Millie   Too late.
John   Yvette Cooper will make a good leader, but who's us to say, we are not ...
Millie   Wha ... whatever happens it's another four years.
John   Five.
Millie   Five years, it's long years, five years.
John   Five long years.
Millie   And David Cameron said he won't try again after five years, he's he's he's already officially said it.
John   Yes, you'll see Boris Johnson take over.
Millie   Really? I don't really like him, he's ...
John   He's an eejit. Well, sometimes. My mates studied England, said he's like some comic eejit, it's evil underneath.
Millie   Hehe, really?
John   I don't, I don't, I don't like ...
Millie   Be fair, if between David Cameron and Johnson, Boris Johnson, I think I like Cameron more. Between these two, whatever he is, he's slimy or what, he's firm, he tell you what message was, he play very well politics, yea I must say.
John   Ed Miliband comes across not firm enough.
Millie   That's it, that's the problem, image. Be firm and cruel.
John   What I want is a firm woman in charge, really.
Millie   Yvette ...

John	They want a woman in charge, they attract women voters door to door … but you recognise who I talk about.
Millie	Yea, yea.
John	Yvette …
Millie	Cooper, yea, she's very sharp, fit, intelligent, tick all the boxes, hm?
John	She'll tell it straight, yea … I think she's quite short, but that's nothing, you know, put her on a podium. She's always on the stage on television anyway.
Millie	Like me, ha hee hee! People hear the voice, uh?
John	It's all about voices, isn't it?
Millie	No, no, the voice and the policy comes out spot on.
John	Yea, the problem with Ed Miliband, he puts you off when his voice starts doesn't it?
Millie	Tha … tha … that's right.
John	It doesn't work like that, the world doesn't work like that.
Millie	It's not fair to him.
John	I know it's not fair to him, but you've got to control it, people won't just …
Millie	You know what I mean?

The two colleagues engage in evaluative commentary on a number of high-profile politicians (Ed Miliband, outgoing leader of the opposition Labour Party; David Miliband, former candidate for the leadership of the Labour Party; Yvette Cooper, member of the Labour opposition shadow cabinet; David Cameron, Conservative Prime Minister; Boris Johnson, Conservative Mayor of London and future Prime Minister). Ed Miliband is 'not firm enough', David Miliband 'won't come back', Boris Johnson is a 'comic eejit' [idiot], 'evil underneath'; David Cameron is 'slimy' and 'firm'; Yvette Cooper is 'sharp, fit, intelligent' (if 'quite short'). Running through the exchange is commentary on appearance and, particularly, on sound. Millie says 'the problem' is 'image'. But she concludes that what sets Yvette Cooper apart as a politician of the future is that 'People hear the voice'. John agrees, 'It's all about voices'. Millie says 'the voice and the policy comes out spot on', and John returns to Ed Miliband, saying 'he puts you off when his voice starts doesn't it'. Millie and John acknowledge that it's 'not fair' that politicians are judged by the sound of their voice. Nevertheless, they too appear to judge politicians on the way they sound. The interaction is both light-hearted gossip and thoughtful political discussion. It is a means both of passing the time of day at work and of engaging with national issues. As we observed and listened in to the people who worked in the library, politics was frequently at the forefront of discussion. When we came to represent the communicative life of the library it was almost inevitable that the narrative would be dominated by political concerns.

Ode to the City – An Ethnographic Drama

The discourses in circulation in the library during our period of observational research are represented as a research-based play, *Ode to the City – An Ethnographic Drama* (Blackledge & Creese, 2022). The play represents a moment of local and national political tension. The action focuses on the staff room in the library, where the fictionalised characters of four customer experience assistants take their lunch and tea breaks. The ethnographic drama is not a verbatim account of research data. It is a creative curation of field notes, transcripts, audio-recordings, video-recordings, conversations and observations. It is creative non-fiction. It lays the observed social world before an audience for critical engagement. It is based on observation, but at the same time the drama is constructed in a way that may interest an audience. In making the drama it was not enough to merely transcribe the voices we had recorded or to reproduce extracts from field notes. We created the four characters in the staff room as a means to articulate, or ventriloquate, the discourses evident in and around the public institution. In the drama, these four fictional characters are given the option to apply for their own jobs, with no guarantee of success, or they can apply for voluntary redundancy, again with no guarantee of success. This is a story based on what we observed was happening when we started our fieldwork. The ethnographic drama takes that moment of tension as a starting point and follows each of the four characters as their future prospects play out. They are the only characters on stage and they are all on stage throughout the production. In their interactions the voices of others are heard, as they ventriloquate the positions and points of view of multiple stakeholders.

The context of the research almost inevitably proposes an account which takes sides. Battle lines were drawn: national government, local government, trade unions, protest groups, lobbyists, workers threatened with redundancy, all protagonists. We were conscious that for reasons both ethnographic and aesthetic we needed to keep our balance. The playwright David Hare put this well:

> There is an awful lot of pious theatre at the moment, where you go to have what you already believe reinforced. You are simply told that gay people are people just like everyone else, that racism or misogyny is a terrible thing. You are confirmed in your own righteousness. (*The Guardian*, 2022)

We were concerned that the ethnographic drama should represent multiple voices to articulate the truth of what we observed in the library. In order to represent that truth we may need to incorporate fiction. In order to represent that truth we also need to steer clear of piety and righteousness. In creating, or curating, ethnographic drama, decisions have to be made about what to include and what to leave out. The huge amount of material we collected as audio-recordings, video-recordings, field notes, online communications, Skype meetings and interviews had to be artfully edited into a play which could be performed on stage in little more than 90 minutes. In the process of editing, additional material may be included, which was not originally collected as 'data'. In *Ode to the City – An Ethnographic Drama* we wanted to show what we saw, and what we heard, during our time in the library. In linguistic ethnography we seek to represent the perspective of those we observe and those with whom we collaborate. In deciding what story to tell in the ethnographic drama we were driven by the emic perspective of the library staff. Politics was on everyone's mind and on everyone's lips. What we saw and heard during the months we spent in the library caused us to focus our gaze on the political. The play's narrative shows how political decisions affect people's lives. The four characters in the play do not mimic the people who worked in the library, or pretend to directly represent people who participated in the research. However, they articulate the discourses in circulation in that time and place. *Ode to the City – An Ethnographic Drama* is an artistic representation of knowledge earned through scientific investigation. The ethnographic drama was written after the fieldwork, analysis and academic writing had been completed. It was a primary outcome of labour-intensive research which took a number of years to complete. The fieldwork was done in 2015. *Ode to the City – An Ethnographic Drama* was published in 2022.

A Starting Point

In the course of ethnographic observation in the library we audio-recorded a conversation between Millie and her colleague Mark as they drank tea on their break in the staff room. They are discussing employment options in the light of a management instruction that all staff must either apply for their own jobs or apply for voluntary redundancy (VR). Mark asks Millie whether she has applied for voluntary redundancy:

Mark   Have you gone for the VR thing?
Millie   I haven't decided.
Mark   Yea, but yea, you've applied, you've done the application of interest?
Millie   Expression of interest to see, hehe.
Mark   How, how long have you been here?
Millie   Uh?
Mark   How long have you been with the council?
Millie   Eighteen years.
Mark   Full-time? You'll get, whatever your weekly wages are, times that by eighteen. That's what your, that's what your figure will be.
Millie   Eighteen.
Mark   So you will get eighteen, eighteen weeks' pay.
Millie   I thought they said that, er, P-I-R-O-N? Three months. P-I …

Mark   Yea PIRON, pay in lieu of notice. But that, that, that, doesn't affect that, because all the pay in lieu of notice means is, say for instance you get six weeks' pay in lieu of notice, it just means instead of having to work six weeks, your last six weeks, they'll just pay you off.
Millie   Oh pay me off, yea.
Mark   So you can go straight away.
Millie   We'll see. But meantime I lost, I lost, I lost the job forever.

In Act I Scene 1 of *Ode to the City – An Ethnographic Drama* we meet the four characters, Abbi, Angel, Joe and Raj, in the staff room for the first time. They are on their tea break, discussing a directive recently received from the management of a large, new, city-centre library, where they work as customer experience assistants:

Raj   They said either you go for VR or you have to apply for your own job.
Angel   VR? What's VR?
Abbi   Voluntary redundancy.
Joe   They pay you off and that's it, you're finished.
Angel   Why would you apply for that?
Joe   If you don't, you could end up with nothing.
Abbi   Some of us will end up with nothing either way.
Angel   Why's that?
Abbi   If you've been working for the council for less than two years you don't qualify for redundancy pay.
Angel   So what's the point of going for VR then?
Abbi   Exactly.
Angel   Wait. You either apply for VR or end up with no job?
Abbi   Or you apply for your own job and you might still end up with nothing.
Joe   They've got you either way.
Abbi   But if you've been working here a while, you do get redundancy pay.
Raj   A week's pay for every year.
Abbi   How long have you worked for the library service?
Angel   Me? Eighteen years.
Joe   So it would be your weekly wage times eighteen.

The attitude of the actors in this first scene should show confusion and indignation, resignation and resistance; it should show fight, and it should show defeat. The apparent choice for the library workers establishes a central dilemma for the four characters and for the entire workforce: apply for redundancy pay and leave, or apply for your own job, with no guarantee of success. The way each character responds to the dilemma will shape the progress of the play. Which of the four will leave? Which will stay? Are there other possible options, other avenues? In Act I Scene

1 potential trajectories and courses of action become visible and hint at possible futures. The choice offered to the library staff during our field observations is re-created as a starting point for the ethnographic drama.

As the action moves forwards, the workers talk about attending protest rallies and about going to meetings with management and trade union representatives. The characters become narrators of their own fate, tellers of their own tale. Abbi is not able to get a mortgage, due to the uncertainty of the future. Angel wants to move to part-time working and study for a degree, but such an option does not appear to be available. Joe is ready to leave employment at the library, but his talk of a job in the theatre may be little more than a pipe dream. Raj, required by her bosses to attend an interview to explain why she has not applied to keep her own job, is disillusioned and defiant. For each of them the possibility of transformation and change is mooted. For each of them that possibility may as easily be crushed. Not one of them feels that positive change is securely within their compass. In Act III Scene 3 the four characters gather in the staff room following a meeting with management and trade unions to discuss redundancies.

ANGEL   I'm none the wiser.
RAJ   It was a talking shop.
JOE   They go round in circles.
ABBI   Back to square one.
ANGEL   So what they're saying now is the union....
ABBI   The union won concessions.
RAJ   Concessions.
JOE   Concessions that mean there will be no compulsory redundancies.
ABBI   Unless the number of voluntary redundancies is insufficient to stabilise the financial situation.
RAJ   Which means?
ABBI   We're still in the same position.
JOE   We're still in the same position we were in before the meeting.
ABBI   What was she saying about applying for re-employment?
RAJ   About applying for your own job?
ANGEL   When you apply for your own job....
JOE   There are new criteria.
RAJ   If you don't meet the criteria.
ABBI   You've been doing your job all this time, doing a decent job, no one ever said anything about....
ANGEL   No, it's new. You have to meet....
JOE   You have to meet the new criteria.

The circular discourse of the four characters implies the inevitability of their destiny and the futility of protest. The performance here should emphasise repetition, speech interrupted and perhaps overlapping, as the characters share an increasing frustration. The attitude of the actors should show resignation, but also irritation. There should be suggestion of a skirmish lost and a struggle still to be won.

Political Discourse

Act I Scene 5 of *Ode to the City – An Ethnographic Drama* is set on the day of the general election in 2015. During their lunch break the four customer experience assistants, Abbi, Angel, Joe and Raj, discuss the political situation:

ANGEL   Ed Miliband, I can't get on with him, his voice.
ABBI   My family always votes Labour.
JOE   It's true, he doesn't come across well in the media.
RAJ   His policies are all right.
ANGEL   Did you see that picture of him with the bacon sandwich?
JOE   You want someone to look prime ministerial.
RAJ   It's when he speaks.
ABBI   It's about the policies though, isn't it?
JOE   No, you're right.
ABBI   You can't vote against him because someone put a bacon sandwich in his hand and started snapping away with a camera.
JOE   No.
ANGEL   Cameron has already said this will be his last time.
RAJ   Then who will we have?
ABBI   He'll hand over to Osborne.
RAJ   Like Blair and Brown.
JOE   Watch out for Boris.
ANGEL   He's done a good job as Mayor of London.
JOE   Has he?
ABBI   They won't allow him to be leader. Will they?
RAJ   You don't know. He plays the clown, but I've heard he's ruthless underneath.
ANGEL   You might need that. A good leader has to be tough.
RAJ   Is he standing in the election?
JOE   Uxbridge and South Ruislip.
ABBI   Safe seat.
RAJ   I didn't know he was even standing again.
ABBI   If you vote Tory you'll get a referendum.
ANGEL   Referendum?
JOE   On Europe.
ABBI   Cameron promised it.
JOE   They made him promise.
ABBI   Backed him into a corner.
JOE   Backed himself into a corner.
RAJ   Come on, there's no way people would support leaving Europe.
ABBI   You've got UKIP pushing for it.

This scene resonates with Millie's conversations about the general election, audio-recorded during observations in the library. However, this is not Millie, but an artistic representation of political discourse. The action does not reproduce the 'original' interaction precisely as it was recorded. The characters on stage stand for themselves and stand on their own feet. They are not participants in the research. They show everyday political discourse to the audience, in all its complexity.

Act II Scene 1 of *Ode to the City – An Ethnographic Drama* is set on the day after the general election. The Conservative Party has won power. The four customer experience assistants are again on their break in the staff room. There is a sense of predictable, and predicted, disappointment.

> RAJ   Miliband's resigned.
> JOE   And Clegg.
> ANGEL   And Farage.
> JOE   It's going to be last man standing.
> RAJ   Labour needs a woman leader.
> ANGEL   Who?
> RAJ   The one married to Jack Dromey, what's her name?
> ANGEL   Who?
> RAJ   Labour woman.
> JOE   I know who you mean.
> RAJ   She was on a lot during the election.
> JOE   Or the one married to Ed Balls.
> ABBI   He lost his seat.
> RAJ   You mean Yvette.
> JOE   Cooper, that's it, Yvette Cooper. She's good.
> ANGEL   She's not very tall.
> ABBI   We need someone who will put a more radical agenda to the people.
> JOE   But who?
> ABBI   I agree we need a woman, but Yvette Cooper and Harriet Harman are both too close to Miliband.
> RAJ   Harriet Harman, that's who I was thinking of.
> JOE   There will be a leadership election.
> ABBI   We need a more radical voice, a radical agenda.

As the characters reflect on the result of the general election, their thoughts shortly turn to a change of leadership for the main opposition party, Labour. In the actors' performance there should be both a sense of history in the making and at the same time a sense of the mundane passing of time during a break in work. In their attitude there should be both an understanding that the result of the general election brings little possibility of change, and an acknowledgement that it promises harder days ahead for some. At the same time, there are new possibilities on or just beyond the horizon. All of this should be available to the audience in the actors' performance.

Power

In Act IV Scene 1, Angel is quizzed by her colleagues about her interview for her current job. The questions of Abbi, Joe and Raj are staccato, and rapid fire, so fervent is their curiosity about the interview. This scene is played not naturalistically but with something of the character of a benign interrogation. As the cross-examination comes to an end, Angel's colleagues in turn ask her how she feels. She responds at length.

> ANGEL After eighteen years in the library they don't know me. As if all this time I've been invisible. It's like starting from scratch. Eighteen years of dealing with the public. Whoever comes to the desk, you listen, you engage, you find common ground. They can't speak English too well, but you find something in common. You go from there. Something. They speak Spanish, you try that out. They speak French, you give it a try. You find that common ground. People with no confidence, no self-esteem, don't know what to do with themselves, want to get on. People think nothing of themselves. People want a qualification. People want a job. People don't know what they want. People think they don't deserve anything. You pick them up. You point them in the right direction. You walk with them. You lead them by the hand. You help them navigate. You smile. You ask them. You listen. Sometimes they come because they're angry. They come because they need to be angry. You let them. You listen. You try to understand. You try. You don't always understand. You can't. You do your best. You always do your best. You're polite. You're courteous. You're convivial. You try. You make a difference. The slightest difference. Give people the help they need. They don't know. You try. You turn things round. They appreciate it. Day in, day out. Eighteen years. Thousands of people.
>
> ABBI But what?
>
> ANGEL You walk into an interview in the place you have worked for eighteen years, and they don't know you. You're invisible. They don't know what you've been doing all that time. They don't know the difference you make. They don't know how you turn things around. You can't tell them. You try. You can't. They would have to be there. You can't tell them. They don't know. So you say nothing. You answer their questions. You say nothing.

Angel's speech is delivered directly to the audience. The actor moves towards them, looking directly at them as she speaks. Her attitude is no longer that of one answering the questions of her workmates. Instead, she turns to the audience, not to offer moral instruction, but to tell them this is how things are, this is how things have been. This is what it is like to be invisible. This is what it is like to be subject to unequal relations of power. Rhythmic and repetitive, her monologue has a force of its own. For all her eloquence, however, she concedes that rather than telling truth to power, 'You say nothing'.

In Act IV Scene 5, the outcome of Abbi's application for her own job becomes known. She receives the news by email.

RAJ	What does it say?
ABBI	I can't even speak.
RAJ	Is it…?
ABBI	I can't.
JOE	What does it say?
ABBI	I….
RAJ	Do you want me to read it?
ABBI	Mm.
RAJ	'It is with regret I must inform you that your application for the post of customer experience assistant does not meet the prescribed criteria.'
JOE	Oh no. What else?
RAJ	'I wish you every success in your future endeavours.'
JOE	What? That's it?
ANGEL	It's like you never worked here.

The email does the work of the institution, coldly and clinically delivering unwanted news. The attitude of the actors here is not so much one of emotional response as of showing to the audience an effect of the collapse of global capitalism and of the ruthlessness of government policy. Their attitude is one which asks questions of the audience: Should the library service be saved? Should Abbi's job be saved? If so, what should not be saved? What should be sacrificed? It is a story bound up with recent history, with global economics and with inequalities of power. The actors present social action and in doing so ask the audience to have an opinion. Abbi's colleagues close ranks and offer her support. But consolation is only consolation, and her job has gone.

Hope

Rather than closing on injustice and despair, however, the play finally offers possibility and hope. Later in Act IV Scene 5 Abbi considers an alternative future.

ABBI	I'm going to do it.
RAJ	You?
ABBI	I'm going to do it.
JOE	To do?
ANGEL	Teaching?
ABBI	The library might not want me.
RAJ	Well, the….

ABBI	But teaching.
JOE	Go for it.
ABBI	I'll make myself a teacher.
ANGEL	Are you sure?
ABBI	I'll be a teacher.
RAJ	You will.
ABBI	Jenny says I'm a natural.
JOE	You are.
ABBI	She says I need to be braver.
JOE	I don't know.
ABBI	Today I got braver.
RAJ	You'll be a great teacher.
JOE	You definitely will.
ANGEL	You'll be an inspiration.
ABBI	I don't know about that.
JOE	You will. You'll show them.
ABBI	An ordinary teacher.
JOE	You will.
RAJ	You will.
ABBI	I don't know.
ANGEL	You will.
ABBI	I'm going to try.

As one door closes, another one opens. Abbi decides to become a teacher. In the context of what has gone before, her decision comes as a surprise. Abbi's narrative had not indicated that teaching was an ideal solution for her. The thought that teaching might be a career option is introduced in the indirectly reported voice of Abbi's partner, Jenny, who says she is 'a natural' and 'should think about school teaching'. But Abbi is not convinced and has said in Act III Scene 5, 'I don't know whether I fancy teaching really'. The question is debated by Angel and Raj (Act III Scene 5), citing as a witness their colleague in the Archives department, an ex-teacher who 'hated' the 'constant pressure' of teaching in schools which were 'exam factories'. They say, 'You ask yourself, is it worth it?' and 'You wonder why you do it'. Joe, in his turn (Act IV, Scene 5), quotes a negative cliché from his sister, a teacher herself: 'Those that can, do; those that can't, teach'. The weight of evidence seems to be against choosing teaching as a profession. But Abbi does so. Her about-face raises for the audience the question of whether such solutions would be available outside the storytelling world of the theatre. Abbi's trajectory, like the lives of her colleagues, is subject to political and economic factors. However, against the odds, she is capable of overcoming these structural forces and looking towards a brighter future. The task of theatre is to show the world as it changes, and also how it may be changed (Brecht, 1978: 79). Abbi's story shows the coercive power of iniquitous structures, but also shows the possibility of transformation. Theatre is, of course, primarily for entertainment. The ending of *Ode to the City – An Ethnographic Drama* does not aim to 'send the audience out of the theatre confirmed in their wonderfulness' (*The Guardian*, 2022) but it might leave people with ambiguous feelings about what can be done to address the ills of the world.

Summary

In *Ode to the City – An Ethnographic Drama* four characters show the social world to the audience through the performance of discourse. The world they show is one which is at the mercy of global economics, institutional power, and local and national politics. It is a world weighed down by immovable forces of oppression, yet open to the possibility of transformation. The world they show is one of individual action and collective action. It is a world steeped in the mundane, narrated in the staff room. It is a world which 'shows characters and events as historical and alterable, and as contradictory' (Brecht, 1978: 269). Throughout the play there is a tension between the inevitable fate of those at the lower reaches of power and the possibility of overcoming adversity for a better future. The library staff room becomes a nexus of discourses which include the global financial crisis, the great recession, the election of a Conservative government, city council politics, and institutional decision-making, all of which impact on the lives of the four library workers. It is also a nexus of discourses which include a young couple's desire for a new home, aspiration to develop a love of literature through study, dreams of employment in the theatre, and a nascent ambition to become a teacher. Played out in a moment of political, economic and institutional tension, the four characters show the audience the world as it is, and invite critical comment.

Part 3
Relations in Linguistic Ethnography

Essay 8. Relational Ethics

Introduction

In the essays which make up Part 3 we pay attention to researcher subjectivity, focusing on listening in field relations. We approach the relationship between the researcher and the participant as central to the analyses we have produced, attending not only to encounters between participant and researcher, but also to encounters between researcher and researcher in team relations. We are aware that a team approach to linguistic ethnography introduces complicating factors, as identified by Behar:

> A recent trend among some anthropologists is to work as overseers of large teams of assistants on big research projects.... The tendency is to depersonalize one's connection to the field, to treat ethnographic work (only a small part of which is done personally by the principal investigator) as that which is 'other' to the 'self,' and to accumulate masses of data that can be compared, contrasted, chartered, and serve as a basis for policy recommendations, or at least as a critique of existing practices. (Behar, 1996: 25)

Through experience we have become aware of the dangers highlighted by Behar, including the potential for hierarchies within teams, distance from the field, othering of research participants and research team members, and the over-production of large, impersonal data sets. However, funding regimes have changed, and working in teams of researchers across disciplinary boundaries is more common, at least in the social sciences in the UK. And this shift requires that we engage with these issues by attending to the voices, values, thoughts and feelings (Appiah, 2007) of a linguistically, ethnically and socially diverse research team.

We have adopted a particular strategy for listening to individual researchers' voices in the team, which we have come to call the 'research vignette'. In the essays in Part 3 we present examples of this kind of writing. Neither field note nor diary, we might say the research vignette is a mini auto-ethnography. The vignette highlights researcher–researched as well as researcher–researcher relations, producing accounts of 'feelings, desires, needs, aesthetic reactions, and moral dispositions' (Hamilton *et al.*, 2008: 20). The research vignette has come to play a specific function within teams of researchers, serving to bring back the ethnographic moment of individual fieldwork observations, while making those moments available to the larger group. Research vignettes describe what it feels like to work in a team in which there are pre-existing hierarchies. They document what happens when the researcher walks into the world of complete strangers and is faced with the task of subjecting them to intense scrutiny. They deal with the tensions, anxieties, missteps, recoveries and small victories of that process. Research vignettes are intended as a space for researchers to address these tensions and for the team to pay attention to them. They navigate the interface of private and public ethnographic scholarship.

In the TLANG project, research vignettes were written after researchers had ended a phase of research and had departed from the field. They were intended as reflexive pieces which allowed researchers to dwell on relations in the field and relations in the team. The form the vignette took was left open to the researcher, although a length restriction was suggested at 500–1000 words. Over the four years of funding, 45 research vignettes were written by members of the research team, with some researchers writing four each. Adrian, co-investigator for the Birmingham case study, wrote four vignettes over the course of the TLANG project. However, Angela wrote none. As principal investigator, and project director, she visited all 16 research sites across the four cities, but did not engage in ethnographic fieldwork, or build direct relations with key participants. In the essays which follow we present eight of the vignettes. The eight are selected for their representation of relational ethics, but also to exemplify reflections on different phases of research across the four cities. Our orientation to the eight research vignettes is as listening subject, in which we attend to the polyphony of our colleagues' voices, values and views, acknowledging our responsibility for them as they generously reveal their vulnerabilities and provide us with an opportunity to learn from them. We suggest that the research vignette is a primary means of listening to researchers as they listen to themselves listening to the participant.

An Interdisciplinary Approach to the Human Subject

Across the essays in Part 3 we navigate between two theorisations of the human subject, broadly described as sociological and philosophical. Sociological orientations propose that individuals come to occupy the position of the subject through discourse. That is to say, we come to understand the 'subject' through the power of language. Here, subjectivity is constructed through the ability of discourse to define and know. Sociolinguistic accounts have contributed significantly to understanding how social processes come to name the subject, often through objectifying accounts of 'othering' which simultaneously categorise and subjugate the other. A sociological orientation conceives of the 'other' as 'a being' whose identities may be multiple and constantly evolving, but whose 'difference from' the other always relies on the self's distinctiveness as unique.

The sociological perspective leads to a conceptualisation of difference as instrumental, meaning we can only understand what is meant by the 'subject' if we can point towards someone (or something) who is not a subject. 'Difference from' is an effect of discourse in which people become categorised, and knowable to themselves and others (Biesta, 2016).

Philosophical orientations propose that we approach subjectivity beyond discourse, arguing that humans have the capacity to forge connections relationally, in ways which transcend signification through language. Here, we approach subjectivity in terms of the 'ethical subject' (Critchley, 2013) and the 'resonant subject' (Nancy, 2007), attending to meaning as a sense, an echo and a reverberation. The resonant subject does not approach the other as already determined in discourse, but instead as accessible through perception and indeterminacy. Focused less on processes of asymmetrical power production, the resonant subject attends to 'the other in me' (Alford, 2004: 162). Here, the subject claims not to comprehend or know the other but, rather, to exist 'in difference' (Williams, 2021) with and for the other. Drawing specifically on the 'humanism of the other' (Levinas, 1985), we approach signification in terms of the ethical subject's propensity to listen to the address of the other and be responsive to that call. Levinas proposes that in the face of a hierarchising society, we can make a difference to the way we encounter one another as individuals beyond the social and linguistic categories which name us. The 'Other' is said by Levinas to be the beginning of a more responsive self.

While sociological orientations to 'difference from' were familiar to us as linguistic ethnographers when we commenced the TLANG project, the philosophical writings of Levinas, and his relational perspective to 'in difference', were new. Indeed, we came to Levinas's 'humanism of the other' only after the funded period of the TLANG project had ended. However, while Levinas was unknown to us during data collection, a new imperative was beginning to form during fieldwork, which prompted us to ask why and how people bind themselves interactionally to ethical relations, or, as Critchley puts it, 'to some conception of the good' (Critchley, 2013: no page number). 'Goodness', Ochs and Capps (2001: 7) explain, is not a readymade set of moral tenets, but the pursuit of sense-making, 'to air, probe, and otherwise attempt to reconstruct and make sense of actual and possible life experiences'. That is to say, as the TLANG research project progressed we were in search of theories to explain the subject's willingness to cleave to ethical behaviour in their relations with others. In the TLANG project we were constantly surprised by the positive way in which strangers engaged with each other, including in relations between researchers and key participants who were unknown to one another at the beginning of fieldwork. People showed a disposition towards social engagement, and a desire for participation and connection. Although there were occasional examples of conflict, cruelty, malice and hostility in the encounters we observed, much more common were compassion, humanity, empathy and understanding. We noticed that people sought contact and involvement with one another. Relational ethics provided a point of entry into understanding human engagement in everyday encounters. While indexical analysis was able to point to and reveal ideological complicities and asymmetrical power relations, we needed other ways to understand the subject's compulsion to trust and be responsive to the other.

As the TLANG research project came to an end, we had the good fortune to be introduced to Levinas's work on relational ethics by colleague and friend Maggie Kubanyiova. Her leadership of the ETHER[1] (Ethics and Aesthetics of Encountering the Other) project created a dynamic international research network, which asked the question, 'How do people of conflicting world views, memories and future visions encounter each other?' Over 18 months the ETHER network brought together artists, linguists and philosophers to inquire how a relational ethical-aesthetic framework could serve as the basis for the political achievement of a just society (https://ether.leeds.ac.uk). We gained hugely from the insights of these conversations, particularly in relation to the concept of the ethical and listening subject in research processes, prompting us to ask ourselves, in line with Richardson (1997: 57):

> How does our writing ... reproduce a system of domination, and how does it challenge that system? For whom do we speak, and to whom, with what voice, to what end, using what criteria?

Individualism and the Human Subject

Rosine Kelz signposts her discomfort with a view of the human subject as self-contained: 'Defining the human primarily as consciousness, as the solipsist thinking self ... provides an impoverished understanding of (human) existence' (Kelz, 2016: 5). Kelz moves towards the development of a relational perspective which emphasises the 'non-sovereignty' of human beings. Following Levinas, she proposes a thesis which constructs individuality in relational terms. Kelz calls for an 'exodus' from neoliberal forms of governmentality which cast the individual as engaged in a continuous cycle of competition, rivalry, self-celebration and self-obsession. She constructs the individual as interconnected through relations with others, rather than as isolated in their own consciousness or being.

Critiques of neoliberalism in applied linguistics and sociolinguistics express concern that a shift in focus to individual agency devalues collective movements. A shift away from emphasis on social structures may lead to an inability to bring about change across institutions. Kubota

---

(1) Ethics and Aesthetics of Encountering the Other: New Frameworks for Engaging with Difference AHRC Seminar Series. 1 November 2020 – 31 May 2022. Maggie Kubanyiova (PI), University of Leeds. Angela Creese Co-Investigator (AH/T005637/1).

(2016: 476) warns of 'ideological complicities', in which foregrounding individual subjectivity over the collective needs of minoritised and marginalised people risks buying into 'a neoliberal capitalist academic culture of incessant knowledge production and competition for economic and symbolic capital' (Kubota, 2016: 475). Sucked into competing for neoliberal accolades such as prestige, prizes, ratings and research funding awards, the individual researcher is under constant pressure to shine, be better and achieve ever greater praise. Pavlenko (2019) critiques academic branding in an entrepreneurial climate. Jaspers (2018: 1) speaks of 'popular new concepts' with 'chameleonic capacity' that cover too much but say very little. Kubota and Miller (2017) point to fetishising concepts in the academy. Reyes (2014: 367) worries that the 'super-new-big' agenda is put forward by 'capitalist industries that set the conditions under which we are expected—or allowed—to study', rather than developing as a response to the needs of those we research. Block (2017: 42) is stark in his warning: 'this move from the collective to the individual, from human beings as social beings to human beings as individuals, leads to a pessimistic view of human existence'. Certainly, we are similarly concerned that neoliberal forms of governmentality reproduce the individual as self-interested and free from any ethical concern or responsibility towards others. However, in this essay we will explore conceptualisations of individuality which articulate alternative values. To do so requires an understanding of the individual in relational rather than solipsistic terms.

Butler (2005) proposes that individuals come to occupy the position of the subject through language. The subject is discursively constructed and emerges as agentic through interactional relations with others. Butler points out that to be named in a socially significant way is to become a recognisable subject. However, the human subject is not fixed, but a structure in formation (Butler, 2005). While subjects are constituted through norms, there is a flexible and reciprocal relationship between the individual and the norm. This flexibility comes through the manner in which language is repeated across settings and by different players. By re-accenting others' voices, narrators and ordinary speakers establish positions for themselves (Wortham, 2001). Butler locates agency in the struggle between the self and the norm, where the self formulates itself in reference to, but at a certain distance from, the norm. As Butler puts it:

> The norm does not produce the subject as its necessary effect, nor is the subject fully free to disregard the norm that inaugurates its reflexivity. If there is an operation of agency or, indeed, freedom in ... this struggle, it takes place in the context of an enabling and limiting field of constraint. (Butler, 2005: 19)

The dynamic between individual agency and social structure is set out by Butler here in ways which are recognisable to linguistic ethnographers.

Linguistic ethnography plays a role in unpicking the discourses which construct subjectivity. It is worth illustrating the agency–structure relationship with two examples from linguistic anthropology. The first example is from Rosa's (2019) research into the construction of Latinidad in the United States. Rosa identifies emblems of difference that come to form subjectivities which are perceivable, recognisable, taken up and resisted. Carefully avoiding what he calls the romantic portrayal of triumphant individuals, Rosa allows us into the lives of several young adults who manage social categories to establish positions of ambiguity. In his analysis Rosa speaks of race and language becoming 'intertwined in countless, indeterminate ways' (2019: 212). A second example is Inoue's (2003) study of a male researcher's account of schoolgirl voices in 19th-century Japan. Inoue illustrates the historical, political and economic contingency of metacommentaries which emerge in the male researcher's perspective. According to Inoue such perspectives were widely circulated, and created the 'speaking subject' of the Japanese schoolgirl, despite having little to do with the reality of schoolgirls' ways of speaking. Rosa and Inoue are both concerned with the listening subject. They reconfigure the balance away from speaker subjectivity to listener subjectivity. Both are concerned with othering processes which fail to pay proper attention to the perspective of the marginalised. Rosa and Inoue both refer to 'indexical inversion'. In his study, Rosa speaks of 'inverted Spanglish', through which Latinx people invoke stereotypes about White Americans' stereotypes about Latinx. Both studies interrogate the way particular iterations of language performatively produce particular subject positions. Both Rosa and Inoue investigate how subject positions are socially constructed through powerful discourses of 'othering'.

In sociolinguistics, alterity, or otherness, describes the social process by which elites objectify others as different, and usually inferior to themselves. Rosa explains:

> I approach race and language ... as rooted in the rearticulation of colonial distinctions between normative Europeanness and Othered non-Europeanness that emerged through the contested production of modernity as an ideology and power formation that is global in its scope. (Rosa, 2019: 3)

Rosa argues that semiotic ideologies recruit signs of difference to homogenise Latinx people as 'racial Others'. 'Inversion' is an important concept for both Rosa and Inoue, because it illustrates the interplay between ideology and agency in category making and category contestation. Rosa's capitalisation of the 'Other' serves to reinforce the distance that powerful elites create in separating themselves from those who are not them. Similarly, Inoue emphasises this gap when she notes, 'the schoolgirl's voice was heard in Japan as an echo of an "other" modernity, coming from the margin, and was thus heard as threatening to Japan's (male) modernity'

(Inoue, 2003: 159). Both researchers use punctuation to create a distance between subject positions in relations of power. Capitalisation or inverted commas mark out social difference, pointing to the divide between the formation of the white, male, bourgeois and heterosexual human subject. While the distinction between the other/Other may seem to be a minor point, Butler argues that we should pay attention to such distinctions because they index significant disciplinary differences in the description of human relations.

In work which draws on the philosophy of Levinas, Butler (2005) makes a clear distinction between 'the Other' and 'the other'. Here, Butler foregrounds Levinas's ethical dimension of difference. Following Levinas's philosophy of relational ethics, Butler invokes the capitalised 'Other' specifically to refer to individuals in relations with other individuals. Here she emphasises the timeless moral relationship which underpins the possibility of human relations to acknowledge uniqueness. Butler contrasts this with the lower case 'other' to describe sociological accounts of humans in specific relations in social and cultural contexts. In making the distinction between the Other and the other, Butler helps us to see two different academic traditions: one draws on philosophy and relational ethics, while the other draws on sociology and linguistics, and examines the consequences of social categorisation. The Other and the other index two different understandings of 'difference' as a phenomenon. In relational ethics, the Other is a shared human quality. It is not an 'othering' of one group by another. Rather, it is a recognition that each individual possesses a singularity common to all humanity. That is, we are all located 'in-difference'. In the field of sociology, on the other hand, notions of the 'other' are typically approached as embedded in hierarchical power structures, and reproduced in social and linguistic processes of othering. That is, there is an element of 'different from', as comparisons are made across social categories. We are interested in both interpretations of Other/other, and we retain Butler's distinction in the essays which follow.

Our thinking in these essays is also informed by the work of Stuart Hall, who argued for the retention of a sense of difference in accounts of social life:

> I come to the present, to who I am, by a different route from yours; and therefore, our conversation has to recognise that different histories have produced us, different histories have made this conversation possible. I can't pretend to be you. I don't know your experience. I can't live life from inside your head. So, our living together must depend on a trade-off, a conversation, a process of translation. Translations are never total or complete, but they don't leave the elements exactly as they started. I don't want to be you. I don't want you to be me. I don't want to insist that you give up being who you are and become me. Well, how are we to proceed? Questions of democracy, questions of equality, questions of difference, all have to be resolved. (Hall, 2007:148)

Questions of democracy, equality and difference are at the forefront of Levinas's engagement with relational ethics.

Relational Ethics

Levinas's philosophy proposes a radical ethics which counters the liberal tradition of indifferent individualism. His philosophy has been described as 'inverted liberalism', because it flips a liberal conceptualisation of individuality on its head by retaining singularity but losing autonomy (Alford, 2004). For Levinas, individuals no longer serve themselves but are bound to the Other relationally. Alford argues that Levinas provides a non-liberal justification of the supreme value of the individual, a key assumption of liberalism. This is what Butler refers to when she speaks of the Other as a timeless moral relationship (Butler, 2005). It is to consider the relationships between self and alterity not in terms of ego, identity and freedom, but in terms of responsibility and unfreedom. Butler, following Levinas, argues that we are unfree because our responsibility to the other was not chosen, but is nonetheless required if we are to retain our humanity.

Summarising Levinas, Alford (2004) emphasises the centrality of the individual. The concept of the individual is necessary because the apparatus of the state too often fails to see the tears of individual suffering. Alford points out that,

> Someone must be there to see the tears. 'The I alone can perceive the "secret tears" of the Other, which are caused by the functioning – albeit reasonable – of the hierarchy' (Levinas, 1996: 23). This is Levinas' non-liberal defence of liberal individualism. The individual is the greatest value, but only because he or she can see the tears of the other. (Alford, 2004: 155)

The complexity of Levinas's philosophy can be daunting, and various analogies have been developed to ease comprehension. Alford (2004) offers the metaphor of an apartment door bell ringing, which when opened reveals an 'other'. The ringing bell is not at first welcomed by the owner of the apartment. In fact, it is an interruption. But the bell rings persistently and is difficult to ignore. There you are, explains Alford, getting on with your own daily business and routines, in your own home, shut off from the rest of the world, happy with this state, and suddenly somebody is on your doormat requiring attention. You find yourself in a quandary. You've been living a satisfying enough existence in your own home. Indeed, you don't mind the isolation or the solitude, at least not too much. But the appearance of the other at the door starts something off. This something niggles away at you. You come to the realisation that something is missing from your life. And your encounter with the face at the door reminds you of what it is – it's 'the rest of the world' (Alford, 2004: 151).

You become aware of the limits of your own life-world. While you have banished hospitality from your home, the person at the door reminds you of the possibility of generosity and welcome. Suddenly the knock at the door stands for a different kind of life. In fact, the other at the door is actually your 'saving grace' and your route out of the trap of narcissism. This person on your doorstep is your chance to address 'the other in me' (Alford, 2004: 162). The neighbour on the doorstep is the opportunity for affinity with another human being and with the humanity that they bring with them. The relevance of this analogy to the TLANG project relates to our observations of people's willingness, and even desire, to go beyond the transactional and instrumental exchange. In the efforts of a library assistant to understand the needs of a client, and to meet those needs, is an investment in the stranger which goes beyond what is required. The client leaves the library happier, and with a new direction in life, for now at least. In the thousands of brief encounters between people observed in the TLANG project, we saw that attachment had little to do with defined identities and more to do with the possibilities of relating to others.

Another analogy for approaching the thinking of Levinas comes from Critchley (2015), who speaks of Levinas in terms of drama. Drama has the capacity for showing moral responsibility to be complex and contradictory, as people struggle to be just in their relations with others. Critiquing moral philosophy for its non-contradictory accounts and moralising discourse, Critchley presents Levinas as locating ethics in human relations, where dilemmas are never straightforward but offer the only hope of reconciliation. Critchley argues that tragic drama in particular offers access to the experience of ambiguity, where often justice appears to be on both sides, and the audience is swayed back and forth as the tragedy unfolds. As Critchley (2015: 10) puts it, 'the experience of tragedy is watching one conception of justice turn into its opposite, and then turn inside out'. This means that justice is not one, but at least two positions. Justice is conflict, and to understand the other demands viewing justice through the eyes of the other, a perspective which resonates with the pursuit of emic accounts in linguistic ethnography. Critchley (2020) further dwells on relations with the other, describing one of the most salient features of Greek tragedy as negotiation with the other, especially the 'foreign other'. Critchley argues that what drama invites is

> neither the blind impulsiveness of action, nor some retreat into a solitary life of contemplation, but the difficulty and uncertainty of action in a world defined by ambiguity, where right always seems to be on both sides.... (Critchley, 2020: 5)

Drama offers an invitation to look at disjunction, without immediately seeking a unifying ground, or looking to a higher power for reconciliation. Ethically, the responsibility is local and requires actors to look for a range of different human possibilities. Aesthetically, drama is a way of holding onto the complexity of shifting dynamics, as justice swings this way and that. Drama challenges particular rationalities as different points of view are explored and performed.

Levinas insisted that a starting point for conversations about morality cannot be the question 'Why should I be moral?' If anything, for Levinas such a question signals the demise of moral conduct. People face moral dilemmas daily. Certainly, in recording interactions in the TLANG research project we observed people regularly handling ethical predicaments. Moral ambivalence and ethical relations were in constant tension as people invested or disinvested in one another. For example, library assistants generously gave time to many older people struggling with new technologies, and listened carefully to them in the course of mundane problem-solving. One option for library assistants was to move visitors quickly along, but this rarely happened. Another example was in local community hubs, where advice workers gave guidance about welfare benefits claims, asylum applications, citizenship law and much more, often going the extra mile to ensure that their clients gained access to resources to which they were entitled. We observed kindness and support which went far beyond the exchange of instrumental information. We saw evidence of empathetic listening to complex life stories. Time and time again we observed that attachment grew out of responsibility for others and that this developed through mundane transactional exchanges.

What is so important about Levinas's philosophy is that he redefines the notions of freedom and sovereignty. That is, while he retains attention to the singularity of individuals, insisting that we resist categorising people because of the damage it does, he simultaneously argues that an ethical vacuum is created by viewing individuals as sovereign. 'Being' and 'consciousness' are inadequate concepts to explain the propensity to care or not. Morality and ethics exceed consciousness. As Kulick (2005: 618) points out, there are elements in a person's self which are not underpinned by 'conscious allegiance to a particular social position'. For Rapport (2015: 257), summarising Levinas's philosophy of humanism of the other,

> A humanistic approach not only recognises in the language-speaker and the culture-member the social being so designated and 'produced', but also recognises that there is more to conscious and self-conscious individuality than cultural construals of personhood.

Levinas argues that we become individuals only through our relations with others. It is through encountering the Other that we become ethical, and therefore individual. Kelz (2016) adopts Levinas's thinking to develop her concept of the 'non-sovereign' individual, emphasising agency not in terms of autonomy but, rather, in terms of connectivity. Kelz argues,

> If we understand humans as non-sovereign, relational and singular beings, this can inspire a positive normative evaluation of more fluid practices of political association, which are not based on shared social identities. (Kelz, 2016: 136)

As we have suggested, for Levinas ethics is located in relations between people. The individual comes into being through a responsibility to the Other. It is this dynamic which needs better representation in linguistic ethnography and in the analysis of relationships observed in research. In the essays which follow, we will explore discourse as not only social but also ethical. This concern stems from observation of convivial interactions, in which people bother to get involved with others when they do not need to. It is also driven by a methodological concern with investigation of research relationships forged in the field. In shifting our focus to the relationship between the researcher and the researched, we approach ethics through the lens of alterity, and examine the possibilities and challenges of ethical relations in linguistic ethnographic research practice.

Signification and the Ethical Subject

What we also take from Levinas is the centrality of the body, and the senses, in signification processes. For Levinas, the ability to respond to the proximity of the Other offers the promise of signification. Levinas proposes that,

> The beginning of language is in the face. In a certain way, in its silence, it calls you. Your reaction to the face is a response. Not just a response, but a responsibility.... Language does not begin with the signs that one gives, with words. Language is above all the fact of being addressed ... which means the saying much more than the said. (Levinas *et al.*, 1988: 169)

For Levinas, the Other can be grasped primarily through the proximity of the human face and through the possibilities of human relations. The face 'is a notion through which man comes to me via a human act different from knowing' (Levinas *et al.*, 1988: 174). The face is not a literal face but the possibility for ethical justice to repair the world (Tahmasebi-Birgani, 2014: 34). To come into contact with another's face is not to observe eye or skin colour, nose or mouth shapes, but to face up to the rights and freedoms of another. The face is not a vision or an object of knowledge. Rather, it is a 'generosity' and a 'moment of faith' (Levinas *et al.*, 1988: 175). Levinas pushes back against semiosis as 'sign' in the linguistic sense. His concern is not with what we know through language or other modalities but, rather, the signification gained through being in contact with others. The face therefore provides the possibility of ethical kinship, but also political action, because observing the face of the Other is a call to address injustice.

The concept of proximity is also relevant in the philosophy of Jean Luc Nancy (2007), who emphasises meaning as 'a coming into presence' (Nancy, 2007; Biesta, 2016). Nancy, a philosopher of music, focuses on the senses associated with listening. To listen, Nancy suggests, is to be inclined towards the opening of meaning in which the senses resonate and rebound, fold and unfold, echo and vibrate. Listening is an 'intensification and a concern, a curiosity or an anxiety' (Nancy, 2007: 5), in which the self enters an attentive state. In this perceptible realm, listening becomes a sensibility towards sound. To listen to the voice of the other is to attend not only to the message but also to the tone, timbre, rhythm and vibration of how something is said. The 'sonorous body' amplifies and brings density to the interpretation of sound beyond perceived meaning. Nancy builds the concept of the 'resonant subject' as opposed to the 'phenomenological subject', posed already in its point of view. Instead, the resonant subject is attentive to the sonorous present in which the voice echoes, reverberates and rebounds. It is a subjectivity in which the body senses what is outside and inside the self, in which listening is 'to be open from without and from within, hence from one to the other and from one in the other' (Nancy, 2007: 14). Nancy suggests that listening is a process of both self-discovery and a willingness to be open to another's story. It is an opportunity to connect with and share the moment. The listening or the resonant subject strains towards sense rather than towards intentionality. As Nancy (2007: 13) puts it,

> Sonorous time takes place ... in waves on a swell, not in a point on a line; it is a time that opens up, that is hollowed out, that is enlarged or ramified, that envelops or separates, that becomes or is turned into a loop, that stretches out or contracts, and so on.

Signification happens primarily through sensory proximity, which brings with it the potential to remain open to others. This is ethical time, according to Levinas, because it pushes past the synchrony of real time to make us all responsible for the past.

> In ethical time, the past of the other – or of all humanity – is not my present, and I have not participated in it. Yet it concerns me. Although the past of the other is incommensurable with mine, I am nonetheless implicated in that past. (Levinas, in Tahmasebi-Birgani, 2014: 103)

What we might take from both Levinas and Nancy in terms of signification theory is their insistence on the openness and indeterminacy of meaning. Both philosophers are concerned with critiquing a mode of signification which fails to acknowledge 'a mode of sensibility' (Nancy, 2007: 57). In sociolinguistic terminology, we are already familiar with such a shift, made evident in conversations about 'languaging' (Becker, 1995) and 'translanguaging' (García, 2009); it has also long been observed in the call to attend not only to what is said but also to how it is said (e.g. Hymes, 1972). Because Levinas is concerned with the ethical possibilities of human contact, he steps away from language as predominantly symbolic and referential, and appears more concerned with the phatic and the poetic. The problem with language for Levinas is its capacity for totalisation, that is, its representational ability to name, and its indexical ability to determine. As he puts it, 'men can be synthesised. Men can easily be treated as objects' (Levinas *et al.*, 1988: 179). He strives to describe significance in ways which 'speak to the other who is not encompassed'. Levinas views interaction as fundamentally an address, or an opening, in which people enter a possible state of involvement and attachment. Signification is a response to the call of the Other – not a response to signs, which carries the danger of the reproduction of social categories. The distinction that Levinas makes between saying and said is central to his work:

> 'Saying' is 'dedication to the other' [Levinas, 1998a]. It is a form of language that does not reduce the other to known categories, and hence does not turn otherness into sameness. (Herzog, 2020: 21)

Levinas proposes that language should be conceived as face, proximity, sense and touch. The 'saying' is about connection, affect and involvement, which goes beyond the passing on of representational knowledge. Levinas is interested in a different kind of knowing. Rapport (2015) characterises it as 'pretextual' or 'nontextual' knowing, which exists in a sphere beyond the conventions of culture or language. It is a knowledge which transcends 'taken-for-granted symbolic, conceptual, textual, and doctrinal language-world[s]' (Rapport, 2015: 256). 'Saying' involves the multiple possibilities gained through contact and perception, rather than representation. Levinas is in search of non-representational ways of knowing and communicating.

However, we cannot dismiss 'the said' out of hand. As Herzog points out, Levinas's philosophical treatise is reliant on 'the said', 'discourse' and 'language' to deliver his academic argument. As Levinas acknowledges,

> In relating the interruption of the discourse or my being ravished from discourse, I re-tie its thread.... Are we not at this very moment in the process of deleting the exit that our whole essay is attempting to take, thus encircling our position from all sides? (Levinas, 1998a, in Herzog, 2020: 21)

In other words, Levinas may wish to reconfigure signification processes, so that they foreground 'sense' and 'affect' in this concept of saying, but he continues to depend on the referential and indexical capacity of the said. In the essays collected in this volume we are similarly interested in how we might interrupt our own 'said', in the course of giving voice to researchers and the researched. But we also understand that our arguments depend on projecting a new set of ideals. We therefore simultaneously rely on both 'difference from' and 'in difference', sociological and philosophical orientations towards subjectivity, the said and the saying, and concepts of the other and Other, in pursuit of the arguments we wish to make.

Relational Ethics and the Political Order

In the TLANG research project we looked at how people communicate in contexts of social and linguistic diversity. This meant we were interested in difference and in language. For the most part, key research participants were migrants, as indeed were many of the researchers. Migration is of course more than a discursive issue. The way a country treats those who are 'newcomers' is an ethical and moral issue. The possibilities for migrants in British society, the difficulties and restrictions they often face, their rights and denials of those rights, provided an important backdrop to our analysis.

Levinas argues that the state should exist for those who are without voice, unable to fight for their own 'being' in ways that more protected groups are already empowered to. He believes that sustainable life must be secured by a political contract designed around the protection of rights. But he also believes that responsibility must be located in daily encounters between people. Levinas comments on an observation by philosopher Paul Ricoeur, published in the French newspaper *Le Monde*, about the then recent 'English' elections:

> Ricoeur, in *Le Monde*, speaking of the recent English elections, expressed his sorrow that, in England, a majority of people, having what they need, vote as landlords, as no one is concerned about the poor. [This is] one of the dangers of democracy: the permanent exclusion of a minority that always exists. (Levinas, 1998b, in Alford, 2004: 165)

For Levinas, a political system which encourages care for the self and not for others will not develop fair and just institutions. So, while treating everyone the same is better than 'invidious discrimination' (Alford, 2004: 155), democracy is guilty of ambivalence towards the individual and violation of human particularity. Herzog summarises Levinas's perspective:

> In our Western society, free and civilised, but without social equality and a rigorous social justice, are we not – asks Levinas – involuntarily but objectively guilty of the suffering and death of so many? Are we not guilty 'by negligence'? Does our society not neglect people without even being conscious of it? Is our wealth not the origin of wars and carnage in many places in the world? (Herzog, 2020: 49)

The category of the migrant is often constructed by a stigmatising media as that of an outsider. As Tahmasebi-Birgani (2014: 144) points out, 'modern politics is based on the fear of the other – the stranger, always constructed as a potential threat whose menace must be controlled by a higher power'. Drawing on Levinas, several scholars (e.g. Herzog, 2020; Kelz, 2016; Tahmasebi-Birgani, 2014) suggest ways forwards which resist these totalising accounts. Each seeks ways to counter the potential for the political right to hijack identity politics for its own cause. Tahmasebi-Birgani (2014: 24) raises provocative questions for the political left:

> Does the right-wing dismissal of social movements as 'special interests' not entail a warning as to the orientation of many recent social movements? Is Levinas not accurate in his criticism of twentieth-century revolutions, that they were merely reactions to, and antitheses of, a liberal capitalism that held on to the 'capital of being'? And as such, that these revolutions were prisoners to that which they aimed to negate?

Tahmasebi-Birgani (2014: 36) suggests that ethical justice in Levinas is the fight for the rights and freedoms of another human, and against the sufferings of the excluded and forgotten. The dangers of identity politics are alluded to here. Kelz (2016: 104) makes the same point and notes the problematic nature of the 'ongoing preoccupation of the self and of the political subject'. Quoting Riley (2000: 5), Kelz suggests,

> We have to ask therefore what a compromise would look like, where we would be able to develop shared political positions without becoming bound to totalising and lasting identifications with fixed identity categories. Such a formulation of political identity would have to 'withstand the misplaced nostalgia for wholeness' which Riley detects in the 'recent turn to collectivised personal identities'. But it would also have to avoid falling into 'a radical individualism to stand against all categorising' which, as she continues, 'only a rabid ahistoricism' would attempt. (Kelz, 2016: 75)

In liberalism and neoliberalism, collectivity becomes weakened through the centrality awarded to the autonomy of the individual. The way we conceptualise individuality in our ethnography is consequential. We take the line that critiquing neoliberalism requires maintaining the centrality of the individual as primary in shaping sociopolitical processes. But this requires a radically different orientation to the individual. We have suggested that the individual is non-sovereign (Kelz, 2016) and unfree (Butler, 2005), and can be constituted only in relations with others. These are philosophical proposals for backgrounding ego, and for highlighting the dangers of the sovereign, autonomous individual. Welten explains:

> What Levinas has in mind is the deconstruction of the Western ego, not the encounter with difficult people in horrible situations. Judith Butler makes this clear when she comments: 'It is important to note here that Levinas is not saying that primary relations are abusive or terrible; he is simply saying that at the most primary level we are acted upon by others

in ways over which we have no say, and that this passivity, susceptibility, and condition of being impinged upon inaugurates who we are.' (Welten, 2020: 358)

Levinas argues for a disruption in the order of the ego. The ethical starting point is not 'I', but the Other. For Levinas, the face of the Other elicits obligation before even the notion of 'being' in the world. Put differently, ethics precedes ontology. This ethical responsibility is an element of everyday living, says Levinas. It is performed as non-indifference. This was a quality of human interaction we noted in our observations of encounters between people.

Openness and Contingency in the Research Vignette

In the essays which follow, we make substantial reference to the 'research vignette' as a means of recording the complexity of sense experience. We argue that the research vignette is a form of empiricism which acknowledges 'the sensuous and affective nature of social life' (Deumert, 2022: 1). In order to move beyond the referential and expand the ethnographic repertoire, we have been working in genres that blur social science and literary writing, and consequently disturb the boundaries between fact and fiction, and between truth and imagination (Richardson & St Pierre, 2005). In our view, personalising, aestheticising and poetising sociolinguistics through forms such as ethnographic drama, ethnographic poetry and research vignettes expand and elaborate social phenomena, rather than reducing them (Blackledge & Creese, 2019, 2021a, 2021b, 2022).

We consider the research vignette to be an example of a 'biographical and speaker-centred approach' (Purkarthofer & Flubacher, 2022) to writing ethnography, which sits on the 'auto-socio-bio-ethnography' continuum (Busch, 2022). Research vignettes are often highly personal and draw upon the experience of the author/researcher, while also incorporating multi-genre approaches such as 'short stories, poetry, novels, photographs, journals, fragmented and layered writing' (Hamilton *et al.*, 2008: 22). The biographical and personal narrative is now a well established form of ethnographic writing, and despite ongoing concerns that it is atheoretical, too subjective, uncritical, solipsistic, interiorised and open to commodification, it is 'here to stay' (Behar, 1996: 32).

As will be evident in the following essays, vignettes provide a unique perspective because they offer accounts of categories constructed, as well as categories contested, as researchers move between immersing themselves in the field and writing up their accounts for a wider audience. In considering the ethical and aesthetic dimensions of the research vignette, we also attend to the researcher's imperative to interrupt their own views, and to deprivilege their powerful, voyeuristic eye (Behar, 1996). Fundamentally, the research vignette is an untidy, incomplete and unresolved voice, not simply of researchers who are authoring themselves, but of researchers who are authoring the other, and who find themselves responsible for this representational process.

Summary

We are aware that, as sociolinguistic ethnographers, we have stepped into unknown territory in this essay. Why bother with a philosophy which appears so idealistic that it is unable to offer practical advice for solving the social and political problems we face? We have persevered because the problems which face us – the economic, ecological, social, legal, linguistic, cultural and political challenges – require responses beyond any single discipline. We have followed the writings of Levinas to reconceptualise the individual away from a self-interested and ego-centred autonomous self, towards a non-sovereign, relational being. We have adopted this stance to find ways to go beyond identity politics, and to reach for communal action which responds to the complexity of human relations and helps explain human interactions. In Levinas we find an argument for the individual to be conceived as a force for developing ethical relations, as a way to look outwards, to others, to acknowledge difference and to address injustice. Levinas provides an explanation for the small but repeated acts of courtesy, kindness and politeness which we observed again and again in our research. The empirical evidence we collected in the TLANG research project demanded that we produce a reasonable explanation of this (on the whole) non-egoistic action, just as we seek an explanation for discrimination, racism and misogyny. We have suggested that the research vignette provides accessible personal narratives which add academic rigour to accounts of human difference in relationships. They are narratives of the observations, listenings and writings of everyday people engaged in banal, quotidian actions that involved small generosities and courtesies. These instances deserve attention and should not be dismissed. We believe an opening up of applied linguistics to strands of philosophy, and to the creative arts, allows us to witness and comprehend the complexity of human experience as we encounter it, and as we encounter one another. And it allows us to document this more fully in our work. To do so requires that we listen to the multiplicity of polyphonic voices involved in research to record a chorus of individual perspectives, each with its own singularity and irreducibility.

Essay 9. Responsibility and Trust

Introduction

Linguistic ethnography is a collaborative activity which depends on a working relationship between researchers and research participants. While some research relationships are effortless, others can be sticky and contentious; while some result in friendships, others remain aloof and cool. As with any relationship, researcher and research participant may experience various and complex feelings and emotions as they encounter one another during the ethnographic research process. In this essay we draw on the vignettes of two researchers on the TLANG project, Agnieszka Lyons and Amal Hallak. At the beginning of the project Agnieszka had just completed a PhD in Linguistics, which focused on digital communication. She was born in Poland, but was now resident in the UK. Amal was born in Aleppo, Syria, and was studying for a PhD in Critical and Cultural Studies during the period of the TLANG project. Both researchers are multilingual. In addition to their research vignettes, we include comments from Agnieszka and Amal on an earlier draft of this essay. In choosing to present the researchers' comments in this way, we illustrate the collaborative but contested nature of knowledge construction in team ethnography.

Responsibility

Relationships developed in research, whether in the field or within teams, depend on sensitivity and understanding. While rationality and logic have their role in this process, it is the empathy of the individual which shapes collaboration. Individuals' emotions, feelings, bodies, gestures, gaze, experience, values, beliefs, attitudes and dispositions all contribute to the relationship and may be read as signs of how things are going. Research relationships are forged in ordinary, everyday moments which are nonetheless consequential for taking the research in multiple directions. The individuals involved regularly face moments of decision-making, requiring particular courses of action. Each moment is a reflection of the moral and ethical self, as performed to the other. The literary critic Gary Saul Morson suggests that lives generally are saved or ruined by innumerable prosaic moments, which together shape the self and all its subsequent actions. If we are honest, we must be so moment by moment; there are no unimportant moments. (Morson, 2013: 22)

While Morson is describing literary characters in the novels of Tolstoy and Dostoevsky, a similar observation can be made about lives lived by researchers. The countless moments played out between researcher and research participant shape their relationship and contribute to its success. The research relationship consists of much more than intention and calculation. Each moment is filled with moral value, as researcher and research participant respond to one another, and draw on their beliefs in ways which they consider appropriate. They are tied to one another ethically and morally, which means they are implicated in one another's lives, as well as in the research programme in which they are participating.

The relationship between researcher and research participant is central to ethnography, not least because it is through this relationship that access to the situated world of the other is revealed. There is therefore a lot riding on it. Ethnography puts significant pressure on the individuals involved in the research relationship, exposing them in ways more fundamental than in other forms of qualitative research. The research site can feel like a charged space when researcher and research participant are initially building their relationship. Responsibility towards one another is far more than a contract. In ethnography, responsibility involves drawing on the moral and ethical self. What might we mean by the word 'responsibility' in the context of relationships between researcher and researched? Agnieszka Lyons asked this question in providing commentary on an earlier draft of this essay:

> I wonder if I would stop at the word 'responsibility' here. I would be tempted to head in the direction of openness to one another. I get that responsibility is an inner here. It feels, though, that responsibility is a feeling that somehow envelops the other, whereas what I would say I felt in the field was a direct openness to another human being, with 'the institutional' progressively more and more stripped from the relationship, more or less consciously distanced from the interpersonal and intersubjective human.

'Responsibility' is a red flag here for Agnieszka. The danger comes from the risk that it 'envelops the other'. Agnieszka's objection to the term 'responsibility' appears to stem from its usual connotations. There are several possible concerns. Responsibility can be said to index power relations in which the institutionally more powerful, here the researcher, 'takes care of' and has oversight of the less powerful and more vulnerable, here the key research participant. Another possible concern is with the concept of atonement that responsibility references. One can be said to be held accountable for harms and wrongs done to others, and to accept responsibility for these harms. Neither of these interpretations describes the developing relationship between Agnieszka and the key research participant. Whatever Agnieszka rejects in the word 'responsibility', she prefers the concept of 'openness'.

'Openness' is what Levinas means when he refers to the concept of responsibility in his philosophical writing. He takes responsibility to be an elemental quality underpinning human relations, meaning an openness to, and willingness to engage with, the otherness of the other. Responsibility for Levinas is a human quality that demands that we address the vulnerabilities of others, whether we have committed an injustice or not. Levinas speaks not to the atonement or absolution of previously committed sins (however important this process may be) but, rather, to humanity's capacity to recognise the injustices others have suffered and respond to them regardless of who committed the crime. As Smith (2017: 157) put it, 'Levinas has us looking outwards into the world, which is itself the source of the demand that we act'. In other words, we behave ethically because we are relational human beings. What drives our ethical behaviour cannot only be explained as duty or obligation set out by societal institutions, but as a recognition that the Other must come before us if we are to retain our humanity. From an applied linguistics perspective, we might argue that this kind of interpretation set out by Levinas is vague, intangible and ephemeral. However, it speaks to the ambitions of the ethnographic researcher in developing field relations. It speaks to an openness to seeing the uniqueness of the key participant, a desire to listen, a willingness to see beyond categories, a refusal to 'envelop', and a striving to form a relationship surpassing professional role demands. Agnieszka describes the necessary step change in relationships between researcher and research participant, moving beyond relations of duty or atonement to something fuller: 'I think the shift in the nature of this relationship is essential for the occurrence of a true ethnography'. As Agnieszka makes clear here, an openness to the other should be a key dimension of the ethnographic relationship. Indeed, the research relationship cannot depend on the academy's protocols for solutions to issues faced in the field. Rather, it depends on people's willingness to engage. In research relationships this means highlighting the importance of human spontaneity. This can be seen in the sympathies and loyalties researcher and research participant develop with one another. While the socially recognised categories of 'researcher' and 'researched' may be useful in the initial stages of ethnographic research, they soon outlive their purpose. More important is the manner in which the pair develop their relations with one another. Rapidly, if not immediately, an acceptance of trust, contingency and openness are required for the relationship to develop and prosper.

We might say that ethnography gains from instituting a weak ontology in field relations (Kelz, 2016). This means creating a discursive and ethical space where we recognise that our deeply held beliefs are contestable, where a stance of generosity and trust means living with ambiguity, and where we accept that not everything is fully comprehensible. Relations between researcher and researched require an escape from the 'stiff armour of artificially instructed ethical codes', in favour of a re-personalised ethics (Bauman, 1993: 34). Here, duty does not manifest itself in formalised relations accorded through social roles or codified ethics. Rather, duty is a form of responsibility which is manifested in a willingness of people to understand one another as human, rather than as defined types. Agnieszka comments, in responding to an earlier draft of this essay,

> This reminds me of what empathy is about in therapeutic understanding – a willingness to give oneself to another person, to soak in their world and be an instrument in a co-construction of understanding of that world.

Agnieszka makes an interdisciplinary comparison here, recognising the value of learning from difference, and the potential of that learning to build trust in difference.

Trust

The philosopher Knud Ejler Løgstrup (1956/1997) suggests that encounters between people presuppose a basic trust, even where mistrust is widespread and endemic. He explains that without trust social life would not exist:

> It is a characteristic of human life that we normally encounter one another with natural trust. This is true not only in the case of persons who are well acquainted with one another, but also in the case of complete strangers. Only because of some special circumstance do we ever distrust a stranger in advance.... Under normal circumstances, however, we accept the stranger's word, and do not mistrust him until we have some particular reason to do so.... This may indeed seem strange, but it is part of what it means to be human. Human life could hardly exist if it were otherwise. (Løgstrup, 1956/1997: 8)

Løgstrup argues that while trust is spontaneous and natural – a starting point – mistrust is learned through social experience. Trust requires no explanation, whereas mistrust does. In Løgstrup's thinking we see similarities to Levinas. Both share a concern with the human situation beyond social immediacy. Both propose that accounts of 'being' are insufficient to account for the human subject, and instead move in the direction of relationality. Both philosophers are concerned with the shared human quality of difference, suggesting that differing beliefs and values can open up ethical behaviour rather than close it down.

Bauman (1993) asks whether the contemporary world conspires against trust. Don't we see the wolf when we open the door, he asks, rather than the neighbour? Bauman proposes that trust and mistrust are related phenomena. As he puts it,

> We trust, and we do not; we are equally afraid of trusting (that will render us easy prey to any confidence man) and mistrusting (regular mistrust would render our life unbearable). Left to our own devices (what would they be?) we are incapable of choosing between trust and mistrust. (Bauman, 1993: 115)

Ethnography deals with trust and mistrust. The moral and ethical relations people build with one another in the field are aspects of the interactional encounters we study. Yet linguistic ethnography has been slow to explore this dimension of moral space in research practice, or to consider how trust and responsibility play out in relationships between researcher and research participant.

Moral Spacing

Bauman (1993) observes that a conceptualisation of space should include dimensions beyond those typically covered in the sociological case study. 'Moral space' requires attention to the stance people take towards one another, which is not easily synthesisable in a linguistic or social analysis of stance. To describe moral spacing is to search for what cannot be presupposed. Rosenthal (2003: 195) describes this as 'beginning again', or 'having another chance'. This means keeping the moment open to what is possible and what it might become. It is a time which is 'oncoming' and a flight from linear time.

Moral spacing is a term that attracts Agnieszka's interest:

> I find this term very interesting. The interpersonal aspect is very clear to me, but I'm also left wondering about the meaning of 'space between', which indicates that the relationship is very clearly between two separate individuals, who perhaps try to negotiate the distance/closeness somehow. It brings to mind something I've read in a book by Robert Hobson [a British psychotherapist], where he says that true understanding takes place only in the condition of *aloneness-togetherness*. He says:
>
>> 'I distinguish aloneness from isolation and loneliness; and togetherness from non-differentiation or fusion.... I can only be alone in so far as I can be together with another. I can only be together in so far as I can stand alone. To be a separate person and also go out to meet another means caring, and it means taking risks. We need trust and we need courage. If we are open to understanding, we are also open to being hurt.' [Hobson, 1985: 194]

In this comment Agnieszka addresses the individual's uniqueness and the togetherness required to take action. The moral and the ethical can be properly addressed only by looking at the way we encounter one another in social context. However, this requires a contingency and uncertainty in the upcoming moment. Morality is spatial because 'the being' of the human is always 'a being' in place (Malpas, 2017). It is 'here' we are human, and responsible for one another. It is 'in this place' where we feel answerable.

In linguistic ethnography we typically consider power to be located in everyday activities and quotidian encounters. Linguistic ethnographers describe how temporalities, spatial environments, ideologies and identity positionings shape the interactional moment. Interaction is embedded in social institutions that are constantly demanding. Little attention has hitherto been paid to the 'moral space' in interactional encounters. Interactions are often described as if they take place in a moral vacuum. One way to address this concern is to examine researcher–researched relationships as they develop. As we have suggested, not only are researcher–researched relationships consequential for the kinds of knowledge constructed in linguistic ethnography but they are also the contexts in which individuals become responsible for one another.

Research Vignettes

In this section we turn to look in more detail at trust and mistrust, and ethics and morality, in relationships between researchers and those who participate in research. We approach this through research vignettes, in which researchers reflect on aspects of the process and experience of research. In this essay we present four research vignettes, two written by Agnieszka (in London) and two by Amal (in Cardiff), and follow each researcher's vignettes with a short commentary.

As we saw in Essay 1, there were four phases of data collection in the TLANG research project. The first focused on business and commercial settings, while the second focused on the cultural heritage sector. These phases were consecutive in the project design. Data were collected over a four-month period in each phase. The third and fourth phases, also each of four months, focused on sports clubs, and on interactions involving legal and welfare advice. New research participants were recruited to join the project at the beginning of each phase, with an offer of £1000 as payment for their contribution to the project. This contribution included providing access for researchers to observe them at work, and make audio- and video-recordings of their interactions with others. We also asked them to audio-record themselves at home, share with us some of their online digital and social media exchanges, take part in interviews and participate in a brief research training programme. In both London and Cardiff the research site for the business phase was a small family grocery store.

Here we refer to the London research participants as Edyta and Tadeusz (pseudonyms). They were originally from Poland, and were now settled in England, with a young daughter. In Cardiff the research participants were Mrs B and Mr B. Originally from Iraq, they were now living in Cardiff with a young family. In London the key participant for the cultural heritage phase was a community artist, referred to here as Marta (a pseudonym). She was also born in Poland, and was now established in London. In Cardiff, the research participant in the cultural heritage phase was a senior librarian from Iraqi Kurdistan, referred to here as Kaja (a pseudonym).

Agnieszka set out her reflections on the research process in the business phase in her vignette.

Agnieszka Lyons, London

When I first started working on the project, I felt both excited and anxious. Excited because I'd be working with Polish language and Polish speakers, and anxious because ... I'd be working with Polish language and Polish speakers! Indeed, I felt the weight of being THE Polish speaker in the team, which meant I would be relied on as an expert on the language and culture, which I didn't necessarily think I was. Working with Polish speakers was fascinating with respect to my exploration of my own Polishness. I worked as an English teacher in London for a number of years, and being Polish felt to me like a disadvantage, because how could I teach English (including teaching native speakers) if English was not my mother tongue?! I felt the need to prove myself, and to give myself more credibility. I even avoided telling students I was Polish (my distinctly Polish name was a bit of a giveaway though). What a change the project made! I was now openly a Polish native speaker, and appreciated for it! I also re-discovered my other foreign languages, especially Russian, which proved very useful. As the project went on, I found myself more and more proud to be Polish, and joined our key participant in singing the praises of Polish food, and actively participated in socialising senior researchers Zhu Hua and Li Wei into the Polish culture during our joint visits to the shop. I also felt right at home in the mixture of languages which surrounded me as we were doing fieldwork.

Thinking back on my relationship with our key participants, I think I worried about it a lot, especially during the preparation stage. Later I eased into it a bit more. The reason for this was that I knew we would be asking a lot of our key participants, and I guess I was expecting them to at some point say they'd had enough, and were now out. I didn't want that, so made sure I listened to all the little noises they made, to tackle any potential problems as soon as possible. It seems that my worries were unnecessary. Both Edyta and Tadeusz seemed very happy to help with the data collection, and didn't seem to think about dropping out at all. In fact, they proved very cooperative, and I soon started feeling at ease with them.

Researching a couple who were shop owners was very interesting. At the beginning, it was Tadeusz I interacted with more, but as the weeks went by, my relationship with Edyta strengthened and developed into a sort of friendship. Edyta wanted me to visit when she, rather than Tadeusz, was around, and was pleased to have someone to talk to when there were no customers in the shop. It's such a small shop that you can't avoid interacting with each other. It's also not very busy in general, so Edyta and I spent a lot of time talking about pretty much everything, bar academic stuff. I knew she thought there was a big divide between me – being quite academic – and her – being not academic at all. She often brought it up, saying she wasn't intelligent or studious. I found myself covering up behind a jokey, down-to-earth manner, and did my best to shed this academic self. I felt very protective of Edyta at the same time, playing down the scariness of the forthcoming visit from the 'big professor' (that would be Angela), and trying to cushion Edyta's interactions in the academic context. In conversations with the key participants, I often asked myself how much I should say or ask to maintain good relationships with them but not cross 'the line' (and what is 'the line' anyway?). In the end, in the emptiness of the shop, I tried to be myself rather than some researcher with a magnifying glass, through which I would 'inspect' participants' lives. After all, I was asking them to record and video-record, and give me insight into their private lives.

The fact that the project team is so large and multidisciplinary has meant working in a mix – of levels of experience, personalities, working patterns, and knowledge. It's a great privilege to observe how these differences are mediated, and positive outcomes negotiated. On the local level, working with two extremely busy co-investigators, I've been my own boss, and taken the lead in getting things done. On a more global project level, I was confused at the beginning as to which decisions are taken centrally, and which are a more local matter. It's also extremely interesting to observe the dynamics in each of the local teams, and speak to other Research Fellows. Although we do the same job, our work and experiences in the field are so different! It's been a learning curve, and I'm really pleased we'll get to run the whole process three more times. By the third one, I should have a tried and tested system in place.

Agnieszka set out her reflections on the research process in the cultural heritage phase in her second vignette.

Agnieszka Lyons, London

The second phase. Surely, after the experience we gained in the first phase of data collection and analysis, we are now much better equipped, and much better prepared. We know our strengths and weaknesses, and we are better able to plan. Or are we?

Working with our second key participant, Marta (a Polish actress, artist and founder of Polish Artists in London), was preceded by a good few months of talks and meetings – Marta always with her black Moleskine notebook, diligently making notes of what we've discussed, and often emailing both (co-investigator) Zhu Hua and me with a summary afterwards. Already during the first meeting, as we were waiting to pay for our coffee at Battersea Arts Centre café, Marta told me in Polish that she'd just accidentally touched some random guy where she shouldn't have. And that, admittedly a slight shock, was an indication of what she would be like. Marta was very confident, forward, and in some ways uninhibited. In contrast, I was quiet, reserved, and trying to match her style. I don't know whether it was a test of how I would fit in, or just a throw-away comment, but during my first research observation Marta's collaborator Nigel said that normally they work stark naked. It was all very cool, daring, arty and ... liberated.

This time round, the meaning of 'research site' had to evolve. 'Site' was not fixed, but rather attached to the key participant like a picnic blanket: Battersea Arts Centre (in its numerous guises: The Bees Knees, the café, Council Chamber), Chats Palace, numerous cafés around East London, a sixth-form college in Newham, Nigel's house.... Difficult to talk about getting to know the site well when the site is so mobile. Planning ahead was also rather tricky. Marta often didn't know until the very last minute where exactly they would be rehearsing. It meant I had weekly conversations (often on Sunday night or Monday morning, often via WhatsApp) to try and agree a plan of observations for the week. It also meant that it was more difficult for my co-researchers Zhu Hua and Li Wei to plan observation sessions. This marked an interesting contrast in styles between the fairly well structured working lives we had and Marta's *ad hoc* arrangements.

Marta was fluent in English, and really interested in language. Her ease with the language, and her general creativity, rekindled my own creative energy, leading to regular language games between us – talking in Polish using calques from English, for example. But there was another important side-effect of Marta's interest in language and academia. She cared about providing us with good data, and ended up thinking a lot about her participation in the project, and her relationship with me. You often read accounts of ethnographers reflecting on their field relationships, but here this was done by the key participant. She was constantly asking herself what status our conversations had, and indicated that she mustn't get too hyped up about the fact that someone was interested in her, as the project would end at some point, and life would go on, as she said, 'only without the audience'.

Working with Marta has made me give a lot of thought to ethics. It seems to me that we have a certain duty of care towards our key participants – to make sure we don't shake up their lives, only to say our profuse thankyous and leave. However, a duty of care applies also to researchers, who can find themselves in the thick of relations between key participants and co-investigators, negotiating relationships. We need to think about the consequences of building strong relationships in research contexts, and the long-term effects they may have.

My role in maintaining relationships in the field in this phase didn't involve much help and guidance for Marta. She knew exactly what she wanted to achieve through her participation in the project, and made it clear when it was inconvenient for us to observe, or for her to record. I was more of a facilitator and a silent witness here. Marta's relationship with me developed differently from her relationship with the co-investigators.

Over the duration of this phase, I found it fascinating talking to other members of the research team, and seeing how perceptions of the key participant differed. I wonder if it's the culture, my uber-sensitivity to people, or purely the amount of time I've spent with her. It wasn't language so much this time, I don't think.

It is immediately evident that the range of topics covered in Agnieszka's two vignettes could take the discussion in many different directions. The complexity of the research relationship speaks for itself in her two short accounts of relationships formed in the field. Each vignette describes a changing relationship with the key participant. We get a sense of how time and place shape their development: moments of shock and surprise which highlight differences between researcher and key participant; routines established, sitting together in a quiet shop, talking about shared histories and similarities, while acknowledging differences; schedules disrupted by changes in the balance of power as researchers scramble to keep up with the key participant's professional and personal practices; current concerns for future lives, and for who holds the responsibility for these. The accounts indicate the moral and ethical weight felt by the researcher in managing relationships with key participants. Through the eyes of the researcher we have a window into the agency of the key participant in the research process. In both accounts, being oneself becomes more important than being a researcher. It becomes impossible to describe the research relationship in terms of social roles, namely 'researcher', 'shop-keeper' or 'artist'. Rather, it is the whole person who is brought to establishing and nurturing relationships. Agnieszka, Edyta, Tadeusz and Marta are of course more than any one social category. Even the most detailed listing of social roles would never account for the emotional and human connections which researcher and research participant build, or do not build. We get a sense of the ethical demands made on everyone, and the tangled sensitivities and vulnerabilities such demands create. The vignettes illustrate working interpretations of the research relationship, along with the instability of those interpretations.

In Agnieszka's accounts, emotions are palatable and fast-moving: unease quickly gives way to confidence; closeness is balanced with distance. Emotions are also evident in the stances played out in the relationship, described as 'jokey' and 'reserved'. As Bauman (1993: 33) argues, it is time to return the emotional to our accounts of ethics:

> Dignity has been returned to emotions; legitimacy to the 'inexplicable', nay *irrational*, sympathies, and loyalties which cannot 'explain themselves' in terms of their usefulness and purpose. Functions, manifest or latent, are no more feverishly sought for everything that people do to each other and to themselves. We learn again to respect ambiguity, to feel regard for human emotions. (Original emphasis)

Through the descriptions of social spaces of the local shop, or the mobile work spaces of Marta's life, we see the ethical responsibility of the individuals involved. Care and compassion go beyond the duty of social role or exchange. Interactions in the shop or in the café are not just social encounters, but moral spaces in which the allegiances and empathies of the research relationship play out.

Amal Hallak set out her reflections on the research process in the business phase in her vignette.

Amal Hallak, Cardiff

When I first joined the TLANG team I did not know much about ethnographic research. The first thing I learned about it was that it is based on fieldwork, during which researchers observe people in certain settings for a period of time, and write about their observations. I also learned that because of the nature of the subject matter of ethnography, certain measures must be taken to ensure that ethnographic research is conducted ethically. Even though I spent all last summer reading and learning about ethnographic research, and about the ethical issues involved, I could not anticipate the extent to which ethical issues would colour my fieldwork experience, including establishing and maintaining a healthy relationship with our key participants.

When we started fieldwork all I thought about was what I was going to be doing, and how I was going to be conducting myself as a researcher in the field. I also wanted to make sure that our key participants, a shopkeeper husband-and-wife team, to whom we are truly grateful for letting us do our fieldwork in their food shop, were fully informed about the nature of our research, and their rights and responsibilities. To me that was all paperwork. Once it was sorted there was no need to think about it anymore. However, the reality of fieldwork proved to be filled with challenges, including the need to remain true to research ethics, while managing relationships with the key participants. On the one hand, we wanted to make sure that all measures were taken to let shoppers know what we were doing in the shop. On the other hand, we wanted to make sure we were not being obstructive to the workflow. That was very difficult because I found myself in a position of having to reassure our research participants that we have their best interests at heart, and that we do not want to cause them any harm. It was quite a challenge that our key participants did not seem to fully grasp the significance of abiding by the ethics of fieldwork, such as letting shoppers know at all times what we were doing. It was frustrating having to explain every week that the customer information sheets had to be displayed and visible to shoppers, and that it was the shoppers' right to know that they were being observed and recorded. Every week I'd have to stress the fact that we must not deceive people, and that we must be honest with them. At times our key participants would behave in a way that revealed a lack of trust in us. It was ironic that the more transparent we were with them, the more distrusting of us they seemed to become. I cannot say that I was not hurt. I became uneasy about the sort of relationship that was growing between me and our key participants. It was both interesting and frustrating that they were willing to participate in our research, but not willing to relinquish control. While they were very welcoming and generous, they always kept us in our place, which made me wonder what we did to make them behave in that way towards us. I believe we were nothing but reassuring, considerate, and fair to them. Even now as I am writing this vignette I am anxious about saying anything that would end up being hurtful, inconsiderate, or unfair to anyone.

On a larger scale of things, I am befuddled by our key participants' attitude towards us, especially because all the while I was in the field I was thinking about my own personal responsibility as a researcher towards the research community, how I represent it in general, and towards the TLANG team in particular. I was very excited when our key participant agreed to go to the research training programme we provided, because I wanted them to get to know the other members of our multi-lingual, multidisciplinary team, and other participants in the research. I was hoping that they would have an insider's perspective on the research, that they would see themselves as part of a research community, that they would feel supported and reassured, and that they would understand the need to work in accordance with what the other teams were doing. It was unfortunate that our key participants seemed really tired on the day of training, and didn't seem able to appreciate the experience fully, and that the training did not seem to leave as deep an impression on them as I would have hoped. In fact, I couldn't help but feel very lonely at times during fieldwork, despite working with a wonderful team, because of the challenge of managing our key participants. I wonder how our fieldwork experience in the next site is going to be, and what kind of relationships we are going to have with our next key participant, a librarian.

Amal set out her reflections on the research process in the cultural heritage phase in her second vignette.

Amal Hallak, Cardiff

We did our fieldwork in a Welsh university library, basing our observation on a key participant who speaks Kurdish, Arabic and English. Her name is Kaja. The whole experience was like a saga. Months before the start of fieldwork in the library, we arranged to meet Kaja to introduce the project to her. I happened to be late for that meeting for various reasons. When I eventually arrived, I was so worried that I had given the wrong impression to Kaja. For a long time after that meeting (the time it took Kaja to consider the matter carefully and make up her mind about participating in our project) I was worried that I had cost us the one potential participant who was best suited to do the job. That is why when we actually started fieldwork I was apprehensive, and not very confident about how it was going to go. I did not know what to expect, especially because fieldwork in the last site was traumatic for me personally when I experienced reverse cultural shock, which I would have expected to experience when I returned home.

As far as I was concerned there was no reason for me to expect things to go well. You can imagine my surprise that things went really swiftly and smoothly in this site. My surprise was brought about for various reasons. First, there is our key participant. Kaja is such a professional. It was a great pleasure indeed to watch her do her job, and on top of that to do what we asked of her. She has a calm, serene presence. She is caring and kind. She is elegant not only when it comes to what she wears, but also in how she comports herself. I look up to her with admiration and respect. Kaja embraced her participation in our project gracefully. From the very start she made sure she got the consent forms of her colleagues signed and returned to us. As for those who were hesitant or uncertain, Kaja made sure she did not put pressure on them, and worked on arranging our visits to the library in a way that would accommodate everybody's needs. As fieldwork progressed, I had an increasing appreciation for Kaja as a key participant. Interestingly, I started to have more appreciation for our key participants from the last site, probably also because I'd gained some healthy distance, which enabled me to have a different perspective on our last fieldwork experience, and to see the challenges we were met with as a blessing in disguise. I started to think about those challenges (from managing the key participants, to managing my relationship with them, to making sure they understood the ethical implications of our work without sabotaging data collection) methodologically, and perceiving them as learning opportunities. As the weeks passed, I grew more confident, more relaxed, and more accepting of, and prepared for, the challenges of doing ethnographic fieldwork.

I started to feel passionate again, and to actually enjoy fieldwork. That is not to say that fieldwork in this site was free of challenges. The first challenge for me was to manage my relationship with our key participant efficiently. This was not a particularly easy task given that Kaja is almost my mother's age. The fact that she's kind and caring always reinforced the mother association for me. I had to make sure I didn't get too personal in my relationship with her, not while we were conducting fieldwork anyway. I felt ambivalent at times when we had chats of a semi-personal nature during Kaja's break, when we would constantly be talking about ideas we have in common, like religious views, or social upbringing, or love, since we both come from the same part of the world. While I always appreciated those conversations and enjoyed getting to know Kaja on a more personal level, I was constantly trying to keep an ethnographer's distance. Luckily Kaja's level of professionalism was a constant reminder for me that I'm a professional first and foremost, which brings me to the second challenge. Kaja's professionalism was indeed helpful for fulfilling duties, but how can you tell a professional who is your mother's age what to do? Luckily my relationship with my mother was a good model for me to follow in this respect. My mother is my best friend, and as such we have the kind of relationship that enables us to constantly advise and enlighten each other while respecting each other's input and different expertise. I simply appropriated the skills I developed from having this friendship with my mother to ask Kaja to do certain tasks in a certain way, and to remind her of other tasks and time frames for those.

The third challenge had to do with issues of ethics and confidentiality. As a professional, Kaja understood very well the ethical implications of doing her job, too well at times. Sometimes during fieldwork, Kaja would restrict our access to certain things to preserve confidentiality, no matter how much we stressed the fact that we will be handling all data confidentially. Furthermore, when it came to sharing social media data, Kaja was resistant for some time, because she thought that she could not share personal emails or messages. We were really fortunate that with the passage of time, Kaja appeared to appreciate our work, and eventually let her guard down. Interestingly, I happened to start writing this vignette last week, and came back to it this morning before I went to interview Kaja about her social media data. In this meeting she was updating me about how recording at home has been going. She said she had recorded an encounter with her husband that could be considered 'inappropriate', where he was teasing her about her dress. She said it was up to me whether I wanted to keep the recording or delete it. I was indeed impressed by how her attitude towards our fieldwork and data collection had evolved over the past few months. Today's encounter was definitely rewarding, and I am very pleased with how fieldwork in this site came to a conclusion.

Amal's vignettes speak for themselves in their complexity. However, on reading an earlier version of this essay Amal made the following observations:

> It was the most challenging thing I have ever done, so much so that when a sort of similar opportunity presented itself for me to do interactive research with Syrian refugees, to record their experiences and stories, I had to turn it down. I had not yet recovered from the ethical and moral repercussions of engaging with other people's lives and experiences intimately. It was very difficult to focus my observation and field notes on the key participants' work, rather than the politics of the work, while maintaining confidentiality, and respecting and protecting their privacy.
>
> I remember Angela and I had a conversation about the financial struggle Mr and Mrs B faced at the time, because of their religious background and the political tensions back at home, and how that tension was reincarnated in a small family shop thousands of miles away. I remember feeling torn between my desire as a researcher to engage in an academic discussion about those politics, and the need to protect our research participants from being exposed any further because of something I observed or wrote.

For Amal, the emotional rollercoaster of conducting ethnographic research was still raw. These sensitivities ranged from 'traumatic' to 'rewarding'. Amal's own experiences as a refugee were evident. What stood out in Amal's vignettes were the pressures of the moral space, and the handling of trust and mistrust. On the one hand, she had to manage the protocols of the university, while drawing on her own sets of values and beliefs to meet the needs of the key research participants. This was complicated by conflicting positions in relation to the ravages of war in Syria. Moreover, when Amal turned to the university for support in maintaining moral standards, she did not find solace. We see that while the university promotes ethically approved solutions to ethical causes, such as putting up notices daily informing the public about research, these prove problematic for her in relation to the research participants. She recognises that she must convey the importance of 'conformity-commanding powers waiting and willing to carry the torch of ethical enlightenment in order to make the world hospitable to morality' (Bauman, 2007: 115), while at the same time she is required to handle the extremely complex needs and concerns of Mr and Mrs B.

Despite Amal's supportive conversations with others in the research team, at times she felt overwhelmed by the relationship with the research participants. This was clearly stressful, and she was disappointed that the long-anticipated field observations were not working out as planned. However, all was not lost. In the second phase of the research, she developed trust in her relationship with Kaja, not through university protocols, but through building on the experience of supportive family relationships. From there she had a new perspective on the previous phase of research. Bauman describes uncertainty (in relation to Løgstrup) as the 'home-ground' learning of the moral person:

> The point is, though, that blunders and right choices arise from the same condition. What I have learned from Løgstrup is that far from being a major threat to morality (and so an abomination to moral philosophers), uncertainty is the home-ground of the moral person, and the only soil on which morality can sprout and flourish. (Bauman, 2007: 126)

Through this 'learning opportunity', Amal grows in confidence, and her trust in herself develops alongside her relationships. Amal later reflected on the ever-changing nature of researcher–researched relationships:

> I do not envy the researcher who is doing this now – when it came to the consequences of the Covid-19 pandemic and lockdowns. Establishing trust is hard enough to achieve in person, let alone online. You might want to mention something about the privilege of doing linguistic ethnography before the pandemic, as opposed to the current situation. I agree that there is a lot to be said about the ethical agency of a researcher managing relationships in the field.

Summary

In this essay we have considered responsibility, ethics, trust and mistrust in the relationship between researcher and researched. Because research is not 'an esoteric pastime conducted at an enormous and non-negotiable distance from the business of daily life' (Bauman, 2007: 115), we have approached the research process as a philosophical act of responsibility, as people are brought together and form relationships. Ethical and moral issues are conceived, born, confronted and resolved in field encounters and negotiations. Ethnographers learn to live with ambiguity and 'indifference', and develop a weak ontology in their field relations. Human togetherness is always uncertain, and moral phenomena are inherently relational. Bauman (1993: 13) argues that 'the social management of morality is a complex and delicate operation, which cannot but precipitate more ambivalence than it manages to eliminate'. And it is for this reason that he suggests moral spacing be added to social and cognitive understandings of time and space.

In the four research vignettes presented in this essay we have seen how both Agnieszka and Amal accounted for relations in the field. While they may have sought institutional assistance, the university offered them little immediate support in terms of relieving everyday tensions. Indeed, if anything, the institutional protocols of the academy may have got in the way of developing trust. It is possible that 'mistrust' found a home in the notion of 'research', with its close scrutiny, rational order and authoritative know-how. Trust, alternatively, developed in emergent self-confidence, built through encounters with others. This is put best by Agnieszka:

> In the end, in the emptiness of the shop, I tried to be myself rather than some researcher with a magnifying glass, through which I would 'inspect' participants' lives.

Essay 10. Strangeness and Proximity

Introduction

In this essay we introduce the voice of another member of the TLANG research team, to illustrate the collaborative, but also contested, nature of producing ethnography. We draw on the vignette and field notes of Rachel Hu, a research team member working on the Birmingham case study. A Mandarin speaker born in China, Rachel had lived in Birmingham for 12 years at the start of the project. At the time of writing this essay, she was undertaking a PhD. As we saw in Essay 7, one of the research sites where we conducted ethnographic research was the Library of Birmingham. In this essay we draw on Rachel's observations about her relationship with Millie (pseudonym). Millie was a customer experience assistant at the library. Originally from Hong Kong, she had been working in public library services in Birmingham for 18 years.

Strangeness, Togetherness and Proximity in the Public Sphere

Biesta (2014) draws on the thinking of philosopher Hannah Arendt to argue for the political significance of the public sphere. Arendt proposes that 'human plurality is the paradoxical plurality of unique beings' (Arendt, 1998: 17) and it is in the public sphere where the potential for political agency is most apparent. She stresses that human togetherness is gained through interaction with others, where difference is acknowledged and uniqueness observed. While the private sphere is where people who resemble each other meet, the public sphere is characterised by plurality, but also by the possibility of common action. In sites such as the public library, the unanticipated consequences of human interaction can create something completely new and unplanned. This is not grounded in any quality of the individual agent but in interaction with others (Kelz, 2016). Biesta (2014: 20) summarises Arendt's conceptualisation of attitudes to public space:

> [Arendt] shows that, as soon as we begin to reduce plurality, as soon as we begin to 'homogenise' and 'purify' public spaces by prescribing and

policing what can be done and said in such spaces, by prescribing and policing what is 'proper' and what is 'deviant,' we begin to eradicate the very conditions under which action is possible, and freedom can appear.

Human togetherness is dependent on interaction in the public realm. But it is an interaction built around debate rather than consensus. Plurality enables us to 'call something into being which did not exist before' (Arendt, 1977: 151). Plurality is not made possible through 'fraternity – a common identity or a cosmopolitan sense of sameness – but relies on the preservation of distance and strangeness' (Biesta, 2014: 21). The public library sits in the public sphere and serves as a meeting place for all kinds of people. It is in this space that Rachel observed Millie. In what follows we consider how plurality and difference are crucial factors in the researcher–researched relationship between Rachel and Millie, as Rachel worked to close down the distance between herself and the key participant.

Familiarity is a well known trope in linguistic ethnography, as in the phrases, 'making-the-strange-familiar' and 'making-the-familiar-strange'. However, if, following the arguments of Levinas, we accept that strangeness should remain strange, rather than be rendered familiar in the research process, we need to redress our conceptualisation of difference within linguistic ethnography. We propose to approach this discussion through the concept of 'incommensurability'. In doing so we assume no common ground between the researcher and research participant. We see the relationship between researcher and researched as one which is open to the difference each brings. Even where there appear to be similarities between researcher and research participant, for example in terms of language, nationality, race, gender or age, these similarities cannot be assumed as explanatory in understanding the other. That is to say, in developing arguments for human togetherness and common action, the distinctiveness of the individual remains paramount. However, individual distinctiveness does not mean people are unable to develop common action. Biesta (2014: 21) elaborates:

> While Arendt strongly rejects the (communitarian) idea that common action is only possible on the basis of total agreement, total consensus, or total sameness – that would, after all, destroy the very plurality that is the condition for action – she also maintains that common action is not possible on the basis of mere plurality.

Biesta argues for the development of 'a citizenship of strangers' (Biesta, 2012: 684), which seeks political connectivity beyond identity politics. The tension between individuality and plurality is debated here, underpinned by a view of plurality which resists falling into the imposition of sameness.

Typically, the ethnographer approaches research in contexts of 'difference' through concepts such as immersion, a process through which familiarity is said to develop. However, Rapport (2015: 257) asks that researchers reconsider the concept of familiarity, especially that gained through the process of immersion:

> The anthropologist is commonly said to immerse himself or herself in the field setting and there find the research subjects, immersed alike in a culture or an environment or a social structure or a language, in a set of relations or a field of environing forces or a habitus or a discourse or an episteme or a structural class.

Rapport suggests that immersion is a metaphorical construct and contests its appropriateness and accuracy. He suggests that the familiarity which immersion claims to establish brings 'overtones of encompassment and totalism', and further suggests that 'the only thing I know I am immersed in is my experience. I occupy a life-world comprising consciousness and embodiment' (2015: 257). This observation is a challenge to the ethnographer. It refutes the notion of the researcher gaining knowledge through an insider perspective and argues against attempts at capturing cultural or social essences. Rapport's (2010) view is that it is not possible to immerse oneself in another's world because each individual possesses a unique biography. To pretend otherwise is a totalising action. In place of immersion he puts forward the concept of the contact zone, in which individuals, rather than social types, meet. In the contact zone a human being is an 'Anyone' – an individual who moves 'between what is and what might be' (Rapport, 2010: 80). According to Rapport, 'Anyone' experiences multiple and hybrid cultural belongings, and remains open to different belongings, which are observable in contact zones. Relations in Rapport's contact zone evolve through an openness to another's being.

Another concept for handling the tension between strangeness and familiarity in research is empathy. Feminist research orientations have suggested that 'empathy' mediates research processes, making them less 'extractive' and 'objectifying' (Enria, 2016: 320). However, Lather warns against the 'liberal embrace of empathy', which has a tendency to make 'otherness into sameness' (Lather, 2009: 19). Kallio-Tavin (2020) hopes to move the discussion on by distinguishing two distinctive aspects of empathy, 'simulation' and 'projection'. She suggests that while 'simulation' values otherness and strangeness, 'projection' focuses on an egotistical self which claims to understand the other. However, empathy offers little movement forwards for Smith, who suggests that projective empathy runs the risk of 'the self-satisfactions of a beautiful soul' (Smith, 2017: 156–157). In other words, empathy becomes a self-serving attribute which favours ego rather than alterity. As we saw in Essay 6, Brecht (1978) sought to steer theatre audiences away from empathy, and deploys specific techniques of estrangement to guide them towards intellectual critique. For Brecht, the intellectual and the emotional were forces which pulled in opposite directions and constituted the dialectic of the theatre. We have seen that ethnographic drama is equipped to articulate these tensions in the performance of social practice.

Levinas (1998a) argues for the concept of 'proximity' as a means to value difference in research, without relying on predetermined social categories or liberal-minded benevolence. He proposes that we attend to proximity through 'the nudity of face' to conceptualise encounters of difference without essentialising the Other (Levinas, 1998a: 234). Here, the body is at the forefront of action illustrating a disposition and attitude towards encountering the Other. For Levinas, the notion of 'face' proposes that embodied relations have the potential to uproot assumptions based on social types and categories. Face, according to Levinas, is a place for beginnings. It offers openness to difference through a summons to respond to the needs of the Other. To be open to another's face is to adopt a positive disposition towards humanity. It is an obligation which is outside time, and prior to social commitment. It is an 'idealised dyadic structure' (Butler, 2005: 90).

> Over the hands that have touched things, over all things, beginning with the human face and the skin, tenderness spreads. Cognition turns into proximity, into the purely sensible. Matter ... obsesses me with its proximity. (Levinas, 1989: 118–119)

Proximity is not about physical or even social intimacy, but about the suppression of distance in relation to engaging with human difference. For Levinas, 'face' is not to be interpreted through a sociological or linguistic prism. For example, it departs from Goffman's (1955) understanding, which describes face as a social value associated with a role type. It departs too from Brown and Levinson's (1987) account of positive and negative face, which amounts to an in-depth explanation of the maintenance of social order, through politeness theory. Face for Levinas is not conceived as a set of behaviours associated with a social role, or as linguistic performance. Rather, it is a philosophical attempt to conceive of humanness as that which precedes any claim to knowledge, or 'culturo-symbolic construction' (Rapport, 2019: 70). Face is our ability to connect and reconnect, and to see the human potential in each encounter. It is to open up to vulnerability.

In *The Vulnerable Observer: Anthropology That Breaks Your Heart* (1996), Behar argues for emotional involvement in writing about research, arguing that ethnographers should both write about but also read about vulnerability. She asks whether an emotional response lessens or enhances intellectual understandings, before arguing that it brings intellectual rigour to social action. Behar mixes the personal with the professional ethnographic text, in much the same way we do with vignettes throughout these essays. She appeals for the legitimacy with which researchers' autobiographical accounts pay attention to the way the listening subject, namely the researcher, witnesses the other:

the fear of observing too coldly or too distractedly or too raggedly, the rage of cowardice, the insight that is always arriving late, as defiant hindsight, a sense of the utter uselessness of writing anything and yet the burning desire to write something. (Behar, 1996: 11)

Behar champions a genre which embraces the cause of the observer's subjectivity. Acutely aware of the criticisms she is likely to face, she quickly counters these charges, arguing that personal writing is far from simply a decorative flourish, or exposure for its own sake. Her view is that the personal voice, if creatively used, can lead the reader into an 'enormous sea of serious social issues' (1996: 20), and go beyond self-serving, superficial navel-gazing.

Research Vignettes and Field Notes

We will consider two sources of evidence to discuss the themes of strangeness, togetherness and proximity in researcher–researched relations. First, we visit a vignette from Rachel Hu. Rachel and Adrian Blackledge collaborated as researchers throughout the research project. The vignette presented here refers to research in the public library. It describes and reflects on Rachel's relationship with the research participant, Millie. As we saw in Essay 7, during the data collection period the Library of Birmingham was threatened with significant cuts. This created a good deal of uncertainty for staff, whose jobs came under threat. This was the case for Millie. The threatened cuts had an effect on the research team, who had to make contingency plans in case Millie lost her job. These anxieties are all mentioned in Rachel's vignette.

In addition to the vignette we also present several excerpts from Rachel's field notes. Rachel and Adrian wrote over 100,000 words of field notes in the library. Only a tiny fraction of these are presented here. The excerpts have been selected because they bring further detail to some of the tensions Rachel speaks about in her vignette. However, with any selection, there is also curation. In presenting Rachel's voice, and not Millie's, or at least Millie's words only through Rachel's, we are exposed to Rachel's first-hand perspective, but not to Millie's. We have published elsewhere ethnographic accounts of Millie's contributions to the daily life of the library, particularly in relation to her supportive interchanges with staff and visitors (Blackledge *et al.*, 2016; Creese & Blackledge, 2019a, 2019b). Here we focus on the perspective of the researcher, as she reflects on relationships in research.

Rachel Hu, Birmingham

Millie, a customer experience assistant at the city library, is the key participant for this heritage phase. This was sorted by Adrian and Angela with project partner 'Library of Birmingham' (LoB) even before the project officially started. I am quite chuffed at this already-gained access as it means a lot of time and energy has been saved for me, so I don't need to deal with those worrying uncertainties one could come across when looking for a key research participant.

Adrian had previously arranged a meeting with Millie and her manager soon after the project started, so we could build up and reinforce rapport. We had another meeting with them a few days before starting the fieldwork, so they could find out more about the project. Everything went fine, with both Millie and her managers sounding supportive and enthusiastic about the project. However, we were also aware that LoB restructuring was underway due to local council cuts, and anything was subject to last-minute changes, especially library staffing.

The fear that the current LoB restructure could possibly jeopardise our research at LoB haunted us throughout the four months of data collection. But there seemed to be nothing we could do except carry on with our fieldwork as normal. To prepare for the worst scenario, i.e. Millie losing her job before the end of June, Adrian and I did make some contingency plans, but fortunately none of them was needed, as Millie continued working, although she was notified that she must reapply for her own job in early August.

Handling the relationship with Millie wasn't as easy as I thought, especially at the very beginning. The fact that Millie speaks very little Mandarin, and I know even less Cantonese, left us no option but to speak English to each other. Millie is quite outspoken and straightforward, and sometimes she addressed me in front of her colleagues as 'you mainland Chinese', leaving me a bit uneasy, let alone her often-asked, quite stereotyped questions about 'mainland Chinese' darted at me when I least expected, for example when I was happy chatting with the LoB staff at lunch breaks.

I still remember the shock and anger I felt during the lunch break on my first day shadowing her. As if out of nowhere her question suddenly jumped at me while I was happily eating my sandwich: 'have you people stopped killing baby girls since you mainland Chinese prefer boys so much?' I never realised that I am so patriotic towards China. I literally felt like I was being kicked hard in my back tooth. My instinct to speak up for China, like a child defends her mother without a slight hint of hesitation, set me off with quite a serious statement telling her the truth about this topic.

When thinking back on it I realised I might have overreacted a bit at Millie's question, as my words sounded quite defensive, though luckily I felt I managed to hide my anger. I discussed this unpleasant incident with Adrian and Angela, confessing that I shouldn't have taken things personally, especially when there wasn't anything to be personal about. Historical, cultural and economic differences have long existed between China and Hong Kong, and are still there, hence the ideological 'clashes' between Millie and me are nothing new, but normal. On the contrary, these contradictions and clashes could bring out excellent data for our study in terms of superdiversity and heteroglossia.

With the above thoughts stamped on my mind I have been extra cautious talking to Millie since then. Things started to ease bit by bit between us. Gradually Millie has become more relaxed, and likes to chat to me more casually, so I started to enjoy following her around and seeing her fulfil her daily duties.

As time went by, I found we actually shared quite a lot in common, particularly in how to keep our independence in marriage, bring up children, learn new skills and so on. She's quite jokey and chatty, gentle and polite, which makes her pleasant company, hence she's well liked by her colleagues. She seems to have the power to mellow people around her. She's keen to learn new things, and never hesitates to ask questions, although sometimes she can drive me mad by not taking in things, despite repeating them a million times.

I started to see how being non-judgemental and tolerant can work its magic when getting along with a stranger, i.e. Millie in this case, especially when she plays such an important role in this research. I can see her determination, persistence and calm in tackling problems under the 'disguise' of her quite petite figure and gentle manners. This made me want to help her where I could, and we worked on her English during her free time, which Millie was happy about. I could tell Millie gradually opened up to me in the last two months so she was more cooperative than she was at the beginning. Sometimes when listening to Millie talking, I just couldn't help thinking what I could have missed if I hadn't repositioned myself after our first clash. It's not only the precious data which we might not have been able to get but, most importantly, I could have lost this priceless opportunity to adjust myself so I can perform like a professional ethnographer.

Getting along with the LoB staff seemed much easier and enjoyable to me. They were all very relaxed and supportive, friendly and easy to talk to. Meeting them and chatting to them wherever I could provided me with fresh and individual perspectives that I had never come across before. A majority of the LoB staff have been working there for quite a long time and they are experts who know the place and their jobs inside out. They all have deep affection towards the LoB, and you could tell they are emotionally attached to the library. They are a group of friendly professionals who all have high hopes and insightful views for the future development of the library. Meeting up with them and chatting in the staff dining room made me feel they are not librarians anymore. The four months spent with them also changed my impression about the traditional library, and librarians. With the ever-changing technology, and people's needs, maybe it's time for us all to update our views on the role of the library and librarian in our daily life.

Rachel's vignette presents one view of the developing relationship between herself and Millie. She describes a complex and contentious relationship which is unsettled, and unsettling. The relationship worries her deeply. She expresses anxiety about how she should react to Millie. She balances the demands of her professional role and the need to sustain a relationship in the face of personal hurt. In her vignette we are presented with a picture which illustrates more than one way of interpreting the world, as she attempts to resist 'tak[ing] it personally' on the one hand and performing 'like a professional ethnographer' on the other.

Rachel and Millie were unknown to one another when the fieldwork started. We get a sense of Rachel's frustration at her inability to close down the distance between them. Indeed, in Rachel's vignette, Millie appears agentive in maintaining the physical and social distance between them. In linguistic ethnography, 'shadowing' requires that the researcher moves with the research participant through time and space (Dewilde & Creese, 2016). We briefly turn to Rachel's field notes to understand the initial difficulties Rachel faced in shadowing Millie.

Rachel Hu, Birmingham, field notes

Before walking to the counter Millie suddenly stopped and spoke very loudly, as if she was talking to me. I turned back towards her, wanting to ask her what she just said. Seeing that I stopped, she quickly shook one hand behind her back as a secret gesture which could only be seen by me. It's quite a dismissive gesture in Chinese, as it carries the intention of wanting to shut someone up or get rid of someone. I was totally confused by this gesture, as Millie didn't say a word, or look at me. (RH, visit 6)

Gaining Millie's trust is not as easy as I'd expected, and she seems to be suspicious about each move I am making, such as going to lunch with her, or starting audio-recording in her workplace. From her eyes I could read a lot of suspicion, and I could tell she's quite alert and conscious of being shadowed, which is fair enough. (RH, visit 10)

I was hoping this could help with improving our relationship, but she seemed a bit aloof on Wednesday when I came to shadow her, rejecting the opportunity for me to go to lunch with her. (RH, visit 16)

I've managed to persuade Millie to let me shadow her doing the 'boring' Chinese cataloguing for half an hour today. (RH, visit 17)

Rachel put a good deal of effort into shadowing Millie but faced resistance. Millie worked to keep Rachel at a distance physically and socially. She employed several strategies to maintain physical space between them. She avoided eye contact and used a gesture which Rachel interpreted as offensive. Bauman (1993) speaks of 'mismeeting' as a technique to keep strangers at a distance. In mismeeting, no mutual rights or duties are presumed. Mismeeting has a good deal in common with the notion of 'civil inattention' (Goffman, 1971: 331). Civil inattention describes people going about their business while paying only a fleeting glance to others. People can be in one another's presence and aware of one another, without being involved. According to Rachel's account, Millie persistently engaged in 'mismeeting', or 'civil inattention'. In the field note examples we can see how Millie attempted to relegate Rachel to the background, working to keep her out of focus, and outside the staff group. While relegating Rachel to the background did not make her disappear entirely, Millie worked to manage physical space so that Rachel was remote from her bubble of activity. Rachel recorded her thoughts in more detail in her first set of field notes, which record a conversation that took place among a group of Millie's colleagues in the staff room:

> Millie started again prying into the reality of mainland China, if not trying to criticise.
> [Millie] 'What you can see on the telly or newspaper nowadays is that (Chinese) people are happy everywhere, but the corruption, the problems, don't you Chinese want real democracy?'
> She bent her head and wrote down two Chinese characters 'Minzhu / 民主 <democracy>' and asked me to read them out in Mandarin. I repeated the word several times so she could say it as well.
> [Rachel] 'Well I guess in no country in the whole wide world can people say they have real democracy. The gap between the poor and the rich, and the rivalry between social classes, means that there will never be real fairness or equality for everyone in any country. China is no exception, and being a Chinese born there and growing up there I'd like to see things with a more positive and appreciative attitude, especially with the problems any developing country would come across on its way towards becoming a better country. No one can deny its financial development in the past decades, and the efforts the Chinese government is engaging in to build a more legalised society.'
> Millie's strong opinion reminded me of the long-lasting and historical discrimination and rivalry Hong Kong people held against mainland Chinese. I was a bit shocked after I shut my mouth, as I did sound like a spokesman for the Chinese government! Millie's Indian colleague nodded her head, and gave me a sympathetic look, agreeing with me. Millie didn't seem to notice my defence at all, and carried on chatting.
> [Mille] 'A friend of mine lives in Canada, working as an estate agent. She told me almost all her big clients are people from mainland China, who are always after grand property. In most cases they will carry cash, over a million to buy the properties they have chosen. Oh my, they are rich!'
> You can't tell she's jealous or disapproving when she's telling these anecdotes, as if she's seeing it happen with her own eyes.
> [Rachel] 'Anti-corruption is the hottest theme the Chinese government is engaging in now and I bet all the Chinese in or out of China are totally supportive towards the campaign.' I told Millie that almost every day there will be news reporting that another high-ranking official in China is being prosecuted.
> [Tracy, a staff member] 'Corruption can be seen in every country.' Tracy joined in our chat, and took out a big folder full of paperwork. She laid out the folder in front of her and started to read and write in it.
> Millie paused a bit and sighed:
> [Millie] 'All your educated people left China, and how can the rest keep China going?'

I couldn't hold my tongue anymore.

[Rachel] 'Millie, this is not true. Don't forget that China has 13 billion people, and even nowadays it's still a very small fraction of the literate people who choose to study or live overseas.'

I felt I sounded basically very calm and polite, as I knew clearly I am here for the project, and not to debate. (RH field notes, visit 1)

The lunchtime discussion which took place on the first day of fieldwork did not bode well for their future relationship. But it is significant that it took place on the first day. Rachel and Millie are meeting one another as strangers, known to one another only through their professional categories of 'university researcher' and 'customer experience assistant', and through their newly constituted relationship of research participant and linguistic ethnographer. It is immediately apparent that their beliefs are shaped by fundamentally different interpretations of political and social history in relation to China and Hong Kong. Millie and Rachel weave 'historical and socio-public events together with their personal and deeply private side of life' (Bakhtin, 1981: 247), as distant histories and spaces enter their present context. Their narratives show deep emotional attachment to social and historical events. On this first day in the field, dialogue between Rachel and Millie has begun, but the direction of their future relationship is uncertain.

It is immediately evident in the meeting between Millie and Rachel that humans differ significantly, and these differences matter to them. The construction of national identities is at stake here as Millie puts forward a view of China that Rachel cannot accept. This surprises Rachel, producing an unexpected national loyalty. Unquestionably, this is an important theme in both vignette and field note entries. However, just as the voice of 'the patriot' runs strongly through the texts, other voices counter it. Rachel rationalises the ideological 'clashes' she and Millie experience as 'nothing new, but normal'. This explanation allows her to articulate another voice, that of the researcher. Elsewhere in her field notes, Rachel contemplated the need to adjust her approach: 'I will have to adapt my personal feelings and perspectives so it won't affect the research process, especially my relationship with Millie'. The researcher faces a series of dilemmas in building the fledgling relationship with the research participant. Should she be defending her ground and speaking out, or should she keep quiet and protect the research project? These dilemmas cannot be separated from her emotions. Feelings are running high for both researcher and research participant. However, it becomes clear to Rachel that for things to improve, she must move the conversation beyond the social classifications of herself as 'mainland Chinese' and Millie as 'Hong Kong Chinese'.

Levinas warns that symbolic classification entails 'a tyranny of the order of the same' (Levinas, 1969: 300). That is, treating people first and foremost as members of a linguistic, cultural or religious group amounts to denying their unique otherness. Rapport summarises Levinas:

> 'Totality' is the reign of the same, the singular, where everything is a part of a whole or a case under a law – whether religious, economic, or political. Culture is a symbolic totality that negates the infinity of otherness, replacing it with the 'solitude' of sameness – as if all were knowable and categorisable in the same way, in one way. (Rapport, 2019: 72)

Rachel and Millie commenced their relationship as biographical and cultural strangers (Lofland, 1998). In a relationship imposed upon them by the research project, social categories were deployed by them to reproduce their biographical and cultural strangeness to one another. Social categories in play included nationalism and the naming of languages. English, Mandarin and Cantonese were referred to throughout the four-month data collection period by both Rachel and Millie, both keenly aware that each language brought different affordances to them individually, and that proficiency in each language opened up and closed down professional possibilities. This placed further pressure on their relationship, as Rachel's Mandarin/English repertoire was understood to be more prestigious than Millie's Cantonese/English repertoire. Moreover, the distinction between Mandarin and Cantonese reproduced and reinforced their different orientation to Chinese histories. While Rachel and Millie were able to use English to communicate, Rachel appears to view this as a failure, suggesting an inability for them to come together around 'Chineseness'. Moreover, differing perceptions of English created further difficulties, as Millie expressed anxiety about her English proficiency. Her unease is captured in Rachel's following field note entry:

> The counter became quiet and Millie stuck her head in front of my laptop to see what I was writing. After staring for a few seconds she turned and looked at me:
> 'You put down all what I just said? My! My body language, my English and my everything, are you going to note down everything about me?'
> She didn't look impressed so I tried my best to explain why I needed to do so, and convince her that she will have chances to read what I have written about her when we hold the training programme.
> 'My English is different from the others, you know. Why don't you ask the others whose English is much better than mine?'
> Millie did not look convinced.
> 'Their English might be better than yours but they can't speak Cantonese, can they? So we only want you!' I patted Millie's shoulder and we both laughed.
> 'It's my whole profile you want, is it? I will try my best'. Millie seemed relieved and I stopped her by saying,
> 'Be yourself, Millie, that's all we want!' (RH, field notes, visit 3)

Sitting together at one of the library information desks, Millie and Rachel try to get to know one another. From an external perspective there is nothing grand or dramatic happening as they sit together facing the public. Millie glances at Rachel's field notes as she is writing. There is nothing hidden there. The field notes are available to Millie. Rachel does not attempt to conceal them from her. However, they immediately make Millie feel judged. She cannot understand why Rachel is interested in her English and Cantonese, her body language, her 'everything'. Millie appears to feel exposed, in particular around her 'English', which she persistently told Rachel was 'not good'. Millie's anxieties about the potential for the research process to expose her vulnerabilities is captured in the short field note entry. Even though Rachel attempts to reassure her, distrust in the new relationship is taking hold. Commentary on languages serves to reproduce the social distance between them. It is clear that the closeness Rachel hopes to achieve in her relationship with Millie is far from being realised in the first weeks of the research. Neither she nor Millie appeared able to suppress the historical, cultural, linguistic and social categories which divided them in their encounters. It would require different measures to humanise their interactions so that they might encounter one another beyond their roles as researcher and research participant, Hong Kong and mainland Chinese, or Cantonese and Mandarin speaker.

Responsibility to care for the human relationship needed to come from beyond pre-ordained categories. Appiah (2007) argues that when we interact with strangers, we might not share the same beliefs, but we can find points of entry to explore beliefs and values further. Appiah proposes that when a stranger is no longer imaginary, but real and present, ways of communicating open up. Butler (2005) advises us to remember that not all ethical relations are reducible to acts of judgement, and that the very capacity to judge presupposes a prior relation between those who judge and those who are judged. Rachel and Millie would have to first undo their feelings of being judged in order to improve their relations. Moreover, they could not do this in isolation from one another.

While Rachel may feel the responsibility to improve her relationship with Millie, due to the pressures of her ethnographic role, relations could progress only through a mutual willingness to stay within the encounter. Only through gaining the other's perspective could they be exposed to each other as individuals. Only then could they unpick the assumptions made about the other. Through the encounter we are made most susceptible to the vulnerability of others, and to what Levinas refers to as the Other's wounds and outrages. Butler (2005: 136) summarises the impetus towards responsibility even when risks are evident:

> Perhaps most importantly, we must recognise that ethics requires us to risk ourselves precisely at moments of unknowingness, when what forms us diverges from what lies before us, when our willingness to become

undone in relation to others constitutes our chance of becoming human. To be undone by another is a primary necessity, an anguish, to be sure, but also a chance – to be addressed, claimed, bound to what is not me, but also to be moved, to be prompted to act, to address myself elsewhere, and so to vacate the self-sufficient 'I' as a kind of possession. If we speak and try to give an account from this place, we will not be irresponsible, or, if we are, we will surely be forgiven.

In Rachel's account of her relationship with Millie, there is evidence of an attempt to vacate the self-sufficient 'I'. As she says in her vignette, 'As time went by, I found we actually shared quite a lot in common, particularly in how to keep our independence in marriage, bring up children, learn new skills and so on'. Here Rachel provides an account of an improving relationship, based on other social positionings such as motherhood, marriage, family and personal histories. What becomes evident is Rachel's own learning, as she takes responsibility for subduing her own sensitivities in the face of the demands of the other.

Rachel repositions herself in relation to Millie. Over time, the field notes show that while tensions continued to exist, Millie allowed Rachel to close the social and physical distance that existed between them. As Bauman (1993: 157) puts it, 'defence of social space is never foolproof. Boundaries cannot be hermetically sealed'. Rachel and Millie made inroads into the development of their relationship. They started to see one another beyond those initial defining categories of nationhood and languages. As Bakhtin (1963/1984: 59) notes, 'as long as a person is alive he lives by the fact that he is not yet finalised, that he has not yet uttered his ultimate word'. If proximity stands for the unique quality of the ethical situation, and the suppression of distance, the relationship that Millie and Rachel develop shows them both relinquishing control to some degree, in order to become better acquainted. While their voices remain strained, there is a sense of how, against the odds, they begin to develop a bond. The research setting was a space for social interaction and ethical reflection. Reviewing this period, Rachel comments as follows as she engages with an early draft of this essay:

> Indeed, this is how the researcher–researched relationship between me and Millie had developed over those few months while we had to get along with each other almost on the daily basis. Looking back at those days I feel I may have slightly overreacted.
>
> Growing up in two totally different ideologies in Hong Kong and mainland China, which can be contradicting each other, I now feel that Millie was merely sharing her opinions about the topic from what she'd been told and read about, with me being brought up in a totally different political and educational background.
>
> Reflecting on those days with me following Millie around at the library, I now feel that she's really generous to do so, opening up her workplace

and family to me/us with almost no suspicion or hesitation. Always being patient to show me around at different spots of the library, she explained a lot to me about her role and seemed quite happy to have this extra person/me by her side when she's on duty/shift. She welcomed me to her home and cooked a delicious meal for me, telling her life stories and family life. Despite the initial clashes we had at the beginning, we did seem to build a bond between us as time went by.

In this final reflection Rachel considers her own initial projections, and finds that she needs to reconsider the encounter. Walking in Millie's shoes, she develops a new empathy. Contact through field relations enabled the researcher to encounter Millie beyond social categories, and to see her differently.

Summary

This essay has investigated how ethics is located in the co-presence and plurality of others, and depends on contestation for learning. We have seen in Rachel's account that both researcher and research participant struggled to move beyond the political and historical differences which shaped their early interactions. However, we have also seen how these categories did not come to define their relationship. In the relationship between the researcher and the research participant, social interactions are infused with moral dilemmas. Their strangeness to one another was an important site for learning. Their imposed proximity to each other ultimately became an opportunity to look beyond social categories and recognise one another's vulnerabilities. Drawing on presuppositions about the histories and politics of Hong Kong and China served to reinforce stereotypes. But being in constant contact allowed for other kinds of knowledge, and enabled researcher and researched to value one another's difference.

We have suggested that immersion may not be the most productive direction in linguistic ethnography. Instead, both methodologically and theoretically, approaches are required which build a relational ethics which works with the concept of individual uniqueness. However, this also means that through harnessing a plurality of individual debating voices in the public realm, a politics might be developed in a commonality. The relationship between Rachel and Millie is shaped through their interaction with one another. This emerged through their physical coming together, but even more importantly through their capacity to see in one another's face a disposition to build a relationship which incorporated their differences. We saw that the library as a public space holds the potential for engagement with difference and learning, through the possibilities that diversity brings.

Essay 11. Difference

Introduction

Social categories are constructed from ideological fields which gain their significance through the objectifying forces of hegemonic regimes of visibility and audibility (Critchley, 2015). This means that while categories such as gender, race and ethnicity exist as highly relevant concepts, they are nonetheless socially constructed, and subjectively reproduced through objectifying action, rather than 'real' in any concrete sense. The establishment, negotiation and contestation of categories frequently occur through interaction. In order to gain a better understanding of how difference is constructed through mechanisms and strategies of talk, linguistic ethnographers examine how beliefs, commitments and ideologies come into contact, and confront each other through intersecting voices. While linguistic ethnography typically studies difference in relation to the social practices of the researched, this essay looks at difference in relation to the researcher, and considers the construction of social difference within ethnographic teams.

In linguistic ethnography we challenge unfair and unequal social systems by revealing the nuanced way in which social differences are made relevant in human encounters. We do this by resisting a single perspective to explain inequality. Instead, we attempt to reveal multiple and often contradictory perspectives in representing how people act in certain ways, and hold particular sets of values and beliefs. The ethnographic process does not set out to change people but to understand how prior and current social experience shapes the way people construct their worlds. While ethnographers attempt not to sit in judgement on their research participants, they nevertheless bear a responsibility to carry knowledge to wider readerships, and to challenge discriminatory practices and beliefs. As researchers, we do not stand outside the language of representation. Our own experiences bear down heavily on our representations of others. Who we are in this process matters, because ethnographers are never outside the narratives they produce. Geertz (1988: 144) calls this an 'un-get-roundable fact', and suggests that 'all ethnographical descriptions are homemade, [and] are the describer's descriptions, not those of the described'.

Adopting a reflexive approach, linguistic ethnographers interrogate their own frameworks and values. In our linguistic ethnographic research we have consistently adopted reflexive strategies, which we have written about elsewhere (Copland & Creese, 2015, 2016; Creese, 2008, 2010, 2011; Creese *et al.*, 2008, 2009, 2015b; Creese & Blackledge, 2012; Creese *et al.*, 2015a). We view reflexivity not as a self-indulgent, confessional act (Patai, 1994), but as a means of examining what might be overlooked, disregarded or suppressed in the research process. Through revealing our subjectivities, prejudices, cultural affiliations and beliefs, we do not necessarily arrive at more socially just ethnographic accounts (Pillow, 2003), but we attempt to make them more explicit.

The full TLANG research team comprised 33 people, from diverse academic and professional backgrounds. Discourse about difference featured regularly in team discussions and in researchers' written accounts. Researchers within the team regularly mentioned their own histories in relation to nationality, language, culture, race, ethnicity, age, gender and social class. At times, these categories were essential as researchers positioned themselves in team discussions. Another highly salient category, which researchers invoked to draw distinctions within the team, was diversity of disciplinary and professional background. There was a good deal of academic and professional experience within the team, from across the arts and humanities, environmental sciences and social sciences, as well as from the public, charitable, voluntary and business sectors. Interdisciplinarity was a constant feature of the project, but so was *intra*disiciplinarity, especially within the field of applied linguistics, where different academic traditions were represented. In the TLANG project interdisciplinarity and intradisciplinarity were crucial dimensions of response to research questions, emerging data and analysis. The range of perspectives brought by team members made manifest how we ordered knowledge differently. Team meetings were frequently opportunities to displace presuppositions. In this essay we discuss interdisciplinarity within the TLANG research team.

Pragmatism

We turn to philosopher Charles Sanders Peirce (1839–1941) for his theoretical scholarship on pragmatism. Pragmatism is concerned with the practical value of experience. For Peirce, the focus of analysis is not truth, but meaning. The meaning of anything, for Peirce, 'resides in its practical effects – its consequences – and not necessarily the consequences, but our conception of the consequences, because it is that which leads to our actions' (Samuels, 2000: 214). Pragmatism is based on the principle that the expediency and practicality of ideas are key criteria for their merit.

As a logician, Peirce concerned himself with how beliefs are formed in science, arguing that a 'belief' is a habit of mind, 'essentially enduring for some time, and mostly (at least) unconscious; and like other habits, it is (until it meets with some surprise that begins its dissolution) perfectly self-satisfied' (1905/2009: 168). Peirce (1931, 1958) set out to disrupt the seemingly logical order of scientific investigation, which commenced with the scientist positing a 'reasonable' hypothesis, before crowning it with adequate proof. Peirce saw that an individual's intuition could lead too easily to mistaken interpretation of evidence. He warned against a science which failed to seek out its own susceptibility. For Peirce, fallibility should not give cause for despair but, rather, provide an incentive for openness. Peirce viewed 'truth' as a public matter, not as a process of private positive verification (Halton, 2011). Peirce understood that truth is constructed through signification processes. Truth is therefore related to the interpretation of meaning.

Peirce was at pains to point out the communal nature of science, which should draw on wider circles beyond individuals. A person, according to Peirce, 'is not absolutely an individual' (1905/2009: 170) but part of a wider community. Reason comes not from the rationality of isolated individual thoughts, but from the social nature of language, and emerges from the ground up, in the fullness of concrete encounters with the other (Rosenthal, 2003). Peirce saw that every knowledge claim is part of a signification process that is open to further interpretation. He argued that 'all signification, and consequently all inquiry, and its end product, knowledge, are essentially social in character' (Peirce in Bernstein, 2011: 176). R.J. Bernstein explains Peirce's thinking:

> The upshot of his theory of signs is that all signification, which includes all language and thought, is essentially social in nature. This emphasis on the social or communal nature of man reflects Peirce's strong anti-subjectivistic bias. If all reasoning, even when it is internalised in an individual, has an intrinsically social character, and the very life of reasoning is self-criticism, then we see more clearly why constant criticism, conflict with alternative hypotheses and theories, is so vital for achieving warranted beliefs through inquiry. (Bernstein, 2011: 190–191)

For Peirce, a community of inquirers functions to provide a kind of standard and norm for the scientist as they engage in internal dialogue and self-critique. It also requires the individual to background their own instincts and turn to knowledge gained from wider social and physical experience.

Peirce's theory of pragmatism is built around social and communal experience rather than individual intuition. Peirce spoke of three kinds of social experience which inform the construction of knowledge: quality, action and conduct. First, experience can be described in terms of its qualitative immediacy. Peirce characterises this first kind of experience as 'the unanalysed total impression' (in Bernstein, 2011: 178). Examples provided by Peirce include 'the quality of the emotion upon contemplating a fine mathematical demonstration; the quality of feeling of love; or of a prolonged musical note' (in Bernstein, 2011: 179). The second kind of experience Peirce outlines is action. Action is dyadic and involves learning from difference: 'We become aware of our self by becoming aware of the not-self. The idea of other, of not, becomes a very pivot of thought' (in Bernstein, 2011: 180). The third level of experience which Peirce distinguishes from action is conduct. Through rational conduct and intent, a person exerts control over future actions, drawing on a normative body of knowledge. Pragmatism argues that science should not limit itself to opinion but examine its beliefs in order to serve society, and this requires drawing on the availability of sentiments and feelings, contact and otherness, critique and reasoning.

Pragmatism has been described as a method of thinking which links the meaning of a proposition to habits or norms (Bernstein, 2011). Peirce (1905/2009: 170) saw that 'all thought whatsoever is a sign' and that 'the meaning of a proposition is itself a proposition'. Thinking, according to Peirce, is a category of reality which depends on social practice, and takes account of the personal, local and the temperamental. What we find valuable in Peirce's explanation of experience is his willingness to consider 'quality' and the 'emotional' as elements of social practice relevant to scientific endeavour. Emotion is not presented as some kind of pure inner state. Thinking is communal, dialogical and relational. Ideas develop in social and moral space, not in individual minds. All thought is open to connotation, in the same way as spoken discourse. These ideas are particularly interesting in a team approach to ethnography.

Pragmatism warns against atomising, isolating or singling out individual propositions which results in 'meaningless gibberish – one word being defined by other words, and then by still others, without any real conception ever being reached' (Peirce, 1905: 171). Rather, science must begin with the bigger picture and ask what is behind the search for knowledge. Peirce saw that his arguments about science ultimately depended on ethics, which in turn depended on aesthetics (Peirce, in Bernstein, 2011: 191). Behind any experiment lies a goal, end or purpose to be achieved. For Peirce, ethics is the understanding and critique of these ends. Ethics requires a reflection on the human consequences of research outcomes, and calls for critique of the process and transparency of knowledge construction. Peirce argues that aesthetics supersedes ethics because it demands that researchers reveal their reasoning. For Peirce, aesthetics is not about beauty, taste or appreciation, but about critiquing the values, ideals and beliefs the scientist lives by. It is the examination of the standards which the scientist presupposes. Aesthetics asks scientists not only to reveal the ideals behind their beliefs but also to practise those ideals and beliefs. Peirce saw, for example, that to call something 'illogical' was to make a moral judgement. Aesthetics responds to the question of the ultimate justification of science. In connecting aesthetics to science, Peirce blends questions of morality, philosophy and emotion with rationality, logic, reason and judgement.

In any serious inquiry, assumptions are almost inevitably made. Peirce makes an argument for an intersubjective critique of such assumptions. He recognises the dangers of the certitude of the scientist and attempts to 'exercise a control over his control of control' (Bernstein, 2011: 189). Rosenthal (2003: 200) points out that, for Peirce, moral existence emerges from encountering others in social life. Moral action is not determined through abstract philosophical principles; rather, it is built from below, through interaction with others. Indeed, the self in Peircean philosophy cannot survive alone, or find meaning within its own existence. The self is not an independent entity made real through reflection or reason, but instead depends on others for its existence. Science takes place through encountering others.

Within the TLANG research project there were many opportunities for critical reflection. The diversity of the team brought a broad range of experiences to the analysis of developing ideas. We came to depend on one another for contestation, and gained from the varied interpretation of concepts and methodological approaches. In particular, we relied on the disciplinary expertise brought by academic colleagues in business, heritage, sport and law. These areas corresponded to the social domains in which data were collected in the research project, namely shops and markets, libraries and museums, sporting fields and halls, arts centres, and community advice and support services. Academic disciplines can be described as 'thought domains', which are 'quasi-stable, partially integrated, semi-autonomous intellectual conveniences – consisting of problems, theories, and methods of investigation' (Aram, 2004: 380). Aram explains how academic disciplines gain a heightened sense of autonomy, definitiveness and stability through the structuring processes of the university. Supported by institutional and professional practices, 'disciplines tend to reproduce themselves' (Aram, 2004: 381).

Interdisciplinarity

We now turn to three vignettes from researchers in the TLANG project, to examine the concept of 'difference' within a large interdisciplinary team. The vignettes were written by academics who were senior researchers and co-investigators on the TLANG project, providing expertise in the subject areas of law, business, and sport and exercise science. Bharat Malkani was a lecturer at University of Birmingham Law School at the time of the project; Kiran Trehan was Professor of Leadership and Enterprise Development at Birmingham Business School, University of Birmingham; Janice Thompson was Professor of Public Health Nutrition and Exercise at the School of Sport, Exercise and Rehabilitation Sciences, University of Birmingham. Each of these colleagues formed a close collaboration with a different member of the research team, whose expertise lay in sociolinguistics/applied linguistics. Each of the partnered pairs co-led specific disciplinary work in the research project. Reference to these relationships is made in the vignettes. Also referenced is the UK Research Excellence Framework, known as the 'REF', a national quality-assurance exercise designed to determine the appropriate allocation of research funds to universities. The REF has a significant impact on the funding and ranking of UK universities. The vignettes present the perspectives of the three senior researchers.

Bharat Malkani, Law

'Superdiversity' and 'translanguaging' were not words that were part of my lexicon before 2013, so it was with more than just a little trepidation that I joined the Translation and Translanguaging (TLANG) project, headed by the School of Education at the University of Birmingham. My worst fears were confirmed at the first meeting: researchers from disciplines that I didn't even know existed, speaking in terms that were like a foreign language to me (the irony of this, given the research topic, is not lost on me). Three years into the project, though, I find myself confounding my colleagues in the Law School with accounts of multilingualism and applying the knowledge that I've gained to my own research projects.

Much of the project has been a yin/yang experience for me. On the one hand, working in a large, interdisciplinary team with people at various stages of their academic careers has been fascinating and fulfilling: the exposure to different methodologies and ideas has immeasurably benefited me as a researcher, and I have met some wonderful people along the way. On the other hand, I sometimes feel a little bit fraudulent to be named a 'senior' researcher when I'm still learning about some basic ethnographic research methods. Indeed, there are colleagues who are technically junior to me, but much more able than me in this respect. The title 'student researcher' would be more apt.

Another example of how this has been a yin/yang experience lies in the breadth of topics that the team is covering. On the one hand, it has been interesting to learn from the teams working in sports and business, which are subjects that I would never otherwise encounter in my working life. I've enjoyed attending events like the launch of the project, and the first 'networking assembly', where I've heard thought-provoking talks on subjects that fall outside my field of research. But on the other hand, in the ruthless world of the Research Excellence Framework (REF), I sometimes feel that I'm losing valuable time that should be spent on my own research outputs. This creates a startling paradox for an academic. I know that I'll benefit in the long term from full engagement with my colleagues on the team, even when we're discussing subjects that I'm not involved in, but I'm also aware that if I don't produce my REF outputs, there is no hope of career progression.

In addition to the substantive knowledge that I've gained by working on this project, I've also picked up editorial experience, and I'm in the process of organising workshops and networking assemblies for the law stage of the project. Cajoling authors into submitting their drafts on time, and reading and rereading their submissions has made me much more aware of the other side of the table when it comes to publishing. For all those editors who have published my work in the past: I'm sorry for missing deadlines and not following author guidelines stringently! At the time of writing this, the organisation of the workshops is in its nascent stage, as we're just lining up dates and venues, but I'm both nervous and excited about the forthcoming events. But not as nervous and excited as I am about receiving the data from the law sites. Having played a small role in helping team members identify appropriate sites, it will be interesting to see what the research brings. Confidentiality issues, not unexpectedly, put a spanner in the works when trying to locate research sites, and I found the discussions of what constitutes 'legal advice' or 'legal information' to be eye-opening. We had to stay away from 'legal advice' centres because of the confidentiality issues, and so some time was spent thinking about other legal settings. In the Law School, academics have particular definitions of these sorts of things, so it was interesting to hear what non-lawyers understood by 'legal advice', as compared to 'legal information'. I'm confident that the sites should generate interesting insights into superdiversity and the law, and I'm looking forward to the next stage of the research.

Observing the principal investigator (Angela Creese) keeping the team together, and the project running, has given me ample ideas for how to run a big project, should I ever do so in the future. I've never envied her task: ensuring that everybody is doing their job on time, organising events and meetings, following up with people who need following up (I'm guilty as charged on this count). However, I have envied the fact that Angela has been able to pull together a project that clearly interests her greatly, and it has inspired me to coordinate a large research project on issues that I want to devote my time and energy to. Look out funders and colleagues – I'll soon be coaxing you into parting with your money and time.

Kiran Trehan, Business

One of my key images of contributing to TLANG is the role and impact of emotions in interdisciplinary research. The form of this vignette is presented as a short narrative. I hope it illustrates that interdisciplinary research is not simply about subject areas and scholars from different disciplines coming together to explore, share and collaborate. Rather, it involves emotional labour, and must be critical by design, integrated and embedded within the wider context.

In at the deep end. I lie in bed, it's 6:30 a.m. Far too early to be getting up on a cold morning. It's not quite Winter yet, but there's still a chill in the air. I spy out of the window a dreary day. I haven't slept well, but there it is, the familiar feeling in the pit of my stomach. I'm excited and anxious about my first project meeting – how did I get involved in this project, what do I know about language, linguistics and translanguaging? Clearly, I am more than out of my depth, and the initial excitement turns to fear. I remind myself why I said 'yes' to being a senior researcher on the project. I wanted to learn and be part of an interdisciplinary team, and at the time was thrilled to be asked to be part of what looks like an exciting opportunity.

I arrive at the meeting. On the surface everything looks great and exciting – how often do you get such an eclectic group of academics in the same room to work together? There is an edge of anxiety that I can feel and sense in the room. I'm intrigued and curious about what's going on, but now is not the time to raise it, so I stay focused on the task. We each take our seat and play a part. Yet there is no script. It is interesting to observe the roles we take on … some do the meeting and greeting – checking everybody in – making them feel like old friends that have come round for coffee, introducing the newcomers so that they feel part of the group. There's a good buzz in the room. The meeting goes extremely well. The group is vocal and the contributions are impressive. There is an interesting tension behind the friendly and relaxed façade presented by some members, and the warm challenges by other colleagues, as we explore the opportunities and complexities of the work streams. It feels genuine, authentic and hugely exciting. I leave in awe of the tasks ahead and seduced by the opportunity to work in a different context, with people who have been talking a different language which somehow I am beginning to unravel.

Business, language and TLANG – match made in heaven? [8 months into the project]. As I walked back to my office with a serious stomp in my step, my obvious frustration must have shown. My colleague asks if I am okay. 'You look a bit distracted!' I shut the door of my office and flop down in my chair. How much longer can I keep banging my head against the wall? We have the workshop to plan and deliver and the case study to write. There is so much rich material. The hours and toil the team have put in, and I just want to make sure we do justice to it all.

Because of no fault of my own, another meeting missed, another deadline passes, another phone call that didn't take place. I feel like I am still on the starting blocks. Should I speak to Angela? That's the last thing I want to do. I pride myself in being a good team player, so I need to work harder in trying to engage with my partner on the project. He is central to writing the case study so that it reflects our shared, interdisciplinary interests in business and linguistics. And so that it meets the project's outputs. I feel unsettled again. In truth, I am questioning the dynamics, power relations and my own self-doubts. I have to work harder and not get seduced by the intellectual discussions that I love having with my TLANG partner. As great as the ideological discussions are, we still have to deliver a case study report.

To dance or not to dance? – A critical question [end of the project]. This brief reflection has attempted to offer a glimpse into the life of a researcher working in an interdisciplinary team. What it does not do is tell the whole story. Interdisciplinary research is not without its risks. Those big moments of self-doubt, frustrations and anguish run alongside moments of laughter, hope, excitement and imagination. The words from a song called 'I hope you dance' capture the essence of my lived experience on the TLANG project:

> *I hope you never lose your sense of wonder*
> *When one door closes, I hope one more opens*
> *I hope you never fear the mountains in the distance*
> *Never settle for the path of least resistance*
> *When you come close to selling out reconsider*
> *And when you get the chance to sit out or dance*
> *I hope you dance*

Working on the TLANG project has been one of the moments in my academic career which I will treasure, for which I will forever be grateful, because I have experienced and learnt that a genuine commitment to interdisciplinarity requires criticality, an openness to risk, the ability to speak about the unspoken and to question the systems, structures and institutions in which research is crafted, maintained and disrupted.

Janice L. Thompson, Sport

I came to the TLANG project as an outsider. I am not a linguist, and until joining the group I knew nothing about translanguaging – I wasn't even familiar with the term! I knew absolutely no one on the team and had just arrived at the University of Birmingham. I was invited to be a part of the original grant application to the AHRC as a senior researcher to represent the area of 'sport'. Even this invitation was somewhat unexpected and anxiety-provoking, as my academic background is in exercise physiology and nutrition, and not sport *per se*. My research involves developing and implementing healthy eating and physical activity interventions to reduce obesity and type 2 diabetes in diverse communities. As such, I have extensive expertise in working with superdiverse communities and in trying to get people to be more active. Although I participated in competitive sports when I was younger, am currently an avid sports fan, and am physically active for my own personal health and enjoyment, I wasn't sure I could deliver what might be expected of me. But as I'm a risk-taker and love taking on new challenges, I figured I'd give it a go!

I have spent a number of years working in interdisciplinary teams, and from both a professional and personal view feel this is the most effective and rewarding approach to conducting research. So, I have not experienced any challenges in being a part of an interdisciplinary team. What has been somewhat new to me is feeling as if I have no shared contexts or professional experiences in common with other research team members. I'm accustomed to being a 'minority' with regards to my gender, ethnicity and culture in various professional and personal settings. But within the TLANG team, I believe I'm the only member of the team who comes from an exercise/physical activity disciplinary background, and I get the impression that I am one of the few who has spent most of my life competing in team and individual sports. However, I have not conducted a proper survey of the sporting history of all team members, and so I cannot confirm whether my assumption is supported by actual data. The teams I typically work with in my own research are quite disciplinarily diverse, but most if not all members will have shared experiences with, and views about, the main outcomes of interest, which are typically health- and behaviour-related. So my biggest challenges have been around learning a new professional 'language', and integrating into a new research 'culture' – specifically the language spoken by linguists and other social scientists working in the area of translanguaging. And what I've found so surprising is the limited knowledge some of the team members have about various sports, and their lack of personal experiences around the predominance of physical and non-verbal communication when engaging in sport.

These challenges have been both frustrating and incredibly rewarding. My frustration stems from wanting to fully understand what is going on in the research, and to contribute in a meaningful way despite knowing nothing about linguistics and translanguaging. Initially I found this very difficult to do because I didn't understand much of what was being discussed in meetings, assemblies and other exchanges. However, the fact that the team has been incredibly welcoming, respectful of my expertise and patient when dealing with my constant bombardment of questions has made this experience incredibly rewarding. And they have also been engaged listeners, fully taking on board my suggestions for how data interpretation could be impacted by sport-specific cultural norms and complex real-time interactions that are impossible to capture with existing data-collection methods. Being a member of the TLANG team has given me the opportunity to learn about areas of research and communication that I didn't know existed, and has opened my mind to how I might approach my own research differently. And one of the things I value most about the TLANG team, which is not present in many interdisciplinary teams, is the mutual respect and deep level of trust that the team members have in each other. Differing views and interpretations are not only accepted but are encouraged, and no one feels they are superior to any member of the team, no matter what their role and 'position' might be. Despite my lack of confidence at the beginning as to whether I could contribute to the various aspects of the project in a meaningful way, the team members have never doubted me, and I now feel like I am a viable and valuable member of this unique and ground-breaking team and project. I look forward to learning even more about academic disciplines and research methods that are new to me, and to use the TLANG experience to enhance my approaches to my own research area.

Despite the difference in style, there is a good deal of overlap in the three researchers' accounts of working in an interdisciplinary research team. Common themes are reflections on the experience of working in interdisciplinary teams; the social and changing nature of scientific concepts; and the team as a community. We take each of these in turn.

Experience

Peirce reminds us that science is a social and communal activity based on experience with others. The three researchers speak of their professional experience on the TLANG project in a number of ways, which, following Peirce, can be described in terms of quality, action and conduct. Kiran Trehan highlights the emotional experience of joining a research project outside her core disciplinary interests, and argues that these emotions are part of the labour which contributes to the research. Her account brings, in Peircean terms, a 'qualitative immediacy' to her experience of joining the team, and provides a 'total impression' of taking part in team meetings. For example, she senses an 'edge of anxiety' in the first team meeting. Bharat Malkani speaks of a yin/yang experience of the project overall, and the need to face up to his 'worst fears' as he joins a team of linguists. Janice Thompson speaks of 'anxiety-provoking' moments, but also the buzz of 'new challenges'. Beyond the emotional experience which contributes to TLANG's scientific endeavours is the experience of working with others. Peirce describes this kind of experience as learning from difference. Kiran speaks about how exposure to difference, and the disruption of certainty, leads to creativity and risk-taking. However, she also describes how becoming aware of 'the other' is not straightforwardly simple. She describes the experience of collaborating with another team member, which is at least temporarily characterised by frustration. The third kind of social experience which contributes to science according to Peirce is 'conduct'. Here Peirce is concerned with how a body of knowledge influences thinking. Normativity and social pressure to conform are evident in the research vignettes. For example, Bharat describes the gain of working outside his discipline, in relation to his own learning. He speaks of enjoyment and of provocation. But he also points to 'ruthless' demands which reinforce disciplinary boundaries and determine 'career progression.' Such demands cause him to question the investment of time he makes in taking part in the interdisciplinary research project.

Social nature of concepts

The most obvious way in which the three researchers are confounded by working in a large interdisciplinary team is through responding to the language of the research project. A lack of familiarity with core concepts causes the researchers 'trepidation' and unease. Bharat, Kiran and Janice describe learning what amounts to a new language as they engage with new concepts. This experience proves difficult, but is also rewarding. Bharat describes the way new ideas go on to become pivotal in his thinking about his 'home' discipline of law. Janice describes learning a 'new professional "language"'. However, she is already more comfortable with some concepts (e.g. 'superdiversity') than others (e.g. 'translanguaging'). Bharat gives an account of how concepts very familiar to him such as 'legal advice' or 'legal information' take on different meanings in the hands of non-specialists in law. He found this to be 'eye-opening' because, 'in the Law School, academics have particular definitions of these sorts of things', which are interpreted differently by non-lawyers. Janice also points to the 'unexpected' nature of disciplinary definitions. While the TLANG team refer to her expertise generically in relation to sport and exercise, she carefully defines her specialism in relation to exercise physiology and nutrition. She also points to her surprise at what appears to be the research team's lack of experience of participating in and watching sport. However, she reminds herself that this is an observation which may be based on presupposition and needs further exploration. In fact, many TLANG team members had played or still took part in competitive team and individual sports, and were avid sports fans, but their positionality as ethnographers who deny ready-made expertise, and typically establish a weak ontology towards knowing (Kelz, 2016), gave Janice a very different impression. In their efforts to gain the perspective of the participants in the sports phase of the project, where they observed, and in some instances participated in, volleyball, football, karate, capoeira and basketball, the TLANG ethnographers backgrounded their experience and knowledge until later, in the interpretive and writing processes.

It is this kind of interdisciplinary discussion and analytical process which Peirce puts at the heart of his philosophy of pragmatism. Evident in the researchers' accounts are reflexive critique and self-doubt. Kiran asks, 'what do I know about language, linguistics and translanguaging?', while Bharat speaks of feeling 'fraudulent' as a senior researcher who is 'still learning about some basic ethnographic research methods'. Janice similarly describes herself in terms of not being a linguist, but also in relation to her newness to the team and the university. She describes how interdisciplinary work 'has opened my mind to how I might want to approach my own research differently'. Peirce welcomes such fallibility, and sees that openness produces better science. Indeed, such questioning aids the robustness of the science being undertaken. Certainly, the disciplinary orientations that Bharat, Kiran and Janice brought extended the learning of the whole team.

Research teams as communities

Peirce believed that every knowledge claim is a process of interpretation. He saw that a community of inquiry could serve as a way to increase knowledge and understanding through engaging individual researchers in self-critique, and examination of norms. Peircean pragmatism highlights the affordances of interdisciplinary approaches to the construction of knowledge. Bharat, Kiran and Janice speak of the challenges of taking part in research outside of their disciplinary homes and the risk of exposure this brings. But there are other gains to be had from the interdisciplinary research community. Bharat speaks of developing new editorial and leadership skills, developing his capacity and confidence to propose and lead large research projects in the future. Kiran reflects on overcoming a temptation to dwell only on ideas and theory, however seductive these might be. She acknowledges other pressing agendas, such as practicality, deadlines and meeting project outcomes. In her short account of the difficulties of collaborative working she reminds herself of the bigger picture, and reflects on the consequences of taking one path and not another. As she reveals her reasoning, we get a sense of the aesthetics shaping her values, ideals and beliefs. In their vignettes Bharat, Kiran and Janice reflect on the human consequences of their engagement in the project, and on the need for ethical critique and transparency.

Ethical Responsibility

We return to the philosophical thoughts of Levinas, and specifically his conceptualisation of alterity, or the Other. As a Jewish intellectual living during the period of the Third Reich, Levinas's philosophy must be interpreted within the frame of war, but posited as a search for peace (Critchley, 2015). Levinas argued against philosophical directions which account for humanity's existence in terms of sameness. In effect, he challenged the imposition of social categories as the basis on which to speak about people. Observing first-hand what 'degenerate forms of the ideal' (Bernstein, 1994: 36) produced politically, Levinas opposed the totalising bio-political distinctions of categories put in place by Nazism, which 'denied Jews any right to choose their identity … reducing all Jews to a single, undifferentiated category with one common destiny' (Bernstein, 1994: 36). Instead, Levinas developed a 'humanism of the other', predicated on relationships between individuals, and on their differences. As conceived by Levinas, differences between people are resources which free the individual from self-interested entrapment, egotism and narcissism. As we saw in Essay 9, Levinas's philosophy proposes an ethical responsibility to care for the human relationship, even in the face of hostility. Welten (2020: 357) describes Levinas's philosophy as a response to the ultimate violence of the Holocaust, 'a violence that is not committed against individuals only, but against the dignity of humanity as such'. Butler explains (2005: 90):

> We might say, 'even the Other who brutalises me has a face', and that would capture the difficulty of remaining ethically responsive to those who do injury to us. For Levinas, however, the demand is even greater: 'precisely the Other who persecutes me has a face'. Moreover, the face is turned toward me, individuating me through its address.… Thus responsibility merges not with the 'I' but with the accusative 'me'. Who finally takes on the suffering of others, if not the being who says, 'Me [*Moi*]'?

In other words, responsibility for the Other cannot be passed on, traded off or taken over. It is 'my' responsibility alone. And this quality of being responsible for the Other is what makes 'me' ethical. As Bauman puts it (1993: 77), 'It is through stretching myself towards the Other that I have become the unique, the only, the irreplaceable self that I am'. For Levinas, subjectivity shifts so that self comes into being not through his or her own agency and consciousness, but through responsibility alone. Responsibility has a particular kind of meaning for Levinas. As Butler summarises (2005: 91), 'responsibility is not a matter of cultivating a will, but of making use of an unwilled susceptibility as a resource for becoming responsive to the Other'. Levinas provides more detail:

> To be human means to live as if one were not a being among beings.... It is I who support the Other and am responsible for him.... My responsibility is untransferable, no one could replace me.... Responsibility is what is incumbent on me exclusively, and what, humanly, I cannot refuse. This charge is a supreme dignity of the unique. I am I in the sole measure that I am responsible, and non-interchangeable. (Levinas, 1985: 100)

Levinas is radical because he upends the way we conceive of ethical relations. He starts with the accusative case 'me' in the encounter, rather than the nominative 'I', suggesting, 'Everything is from the start in the accusative ... I am "in myself" through the others. The awakening is not in the "I am I", but in the "I am for"' (Levinas, 1998a: 103). This means that at the most primary level 'we are acted upon by others in ways over which we have no say. It is this passivity, and impingement which inaugurates us into who we are' (Butler, 2005: 90). This willingness to be commanded, this unfreedom, this 'trauma' is what makes humans ethical. It is to be for the other, without the assurance that she will be for me. Welten (2020) argues that, for Levinas, ethics is an ethics of vulnerability. It is to have a care for the human relationship which remains open to the cry of the other. Butler (2005: 97) shows that:

> Levinas' 'me' emerges not through seduction but through accusation and persecution, and although a possibility for murderous aggression is constituted in response to this scenario, it is twinned with an ethical responsiveness that seems to be there from the start, a constitutive feature of a primary human susceptibility to the Other.

What Levinas does is to recast the Other as the crucial character in the process through which the moral self comes into its own:

> A formation in passivity, then, constitutes the prehistory of the subject, instating an ego as object, acted on by others, prior to any possibility of its own acting. This scene is persecutory because it is unwilled and unchosen. It is a way of being acted on prior to the possibility of acting oneself or in one's own name. (Butler, 2005: 87)

Welten argues that Levinas counters classical Western conceptualisations of subjectivity. Rather than the primacy of self's construction of the

Other, it is the Other who constructs it/me. In other words, the subject should be understood in terms of its original medieval meaning, as 'subjectum, subjected to the other' (Welten, 2020: 361). With this reversal, the subject is no longer in control of representation. The subject loses the power to categorise or essentialise through symbols of language which inevitably diminish the Other's uniqueness. The Other is to remain unique and non-categorisable in Levinas's humanism of the Other. The alterity of the Other should not be eroded through the essentialising power of language. For Levinas, the ethical demand emerges not through language but through the proximity of the human face, which he views as the ultimate signification process, more central than language.

From Levinas's perspective, morality cannot be discursively established, let alone proved. His humanism is 'pre-ontological', that is, without cause or principle (Butler, 2005). For Levinas, the human relationship has no particular history or setting. The moral force emerges prior to any possibility of social action or individual choice. It 'is the first reality of the self, a starting point rather than a product of society' (Bauman, 1993: 13). Signification happens primarily through sensory proximity of the human face, and through its potential to remain open to others. Levinas speaks to the possibility of the ethical connection, almost in spite of social context. His is an assertion of shared humanity which is outside the interactional moment, but nevertheless conceived in earthly human relations. Levinas's utopia, for that is what it is, is grounded in the encounters people have. It describes the disposition to be open to difference.

So how is the philosophy of Levinas relevant to linguistic ethnography and to investigation of the situated interaction in social space? Our response lies in the invitation to address more overtly the ethical in our research, and to consider agency in relation to listening to the other. For example, where interaction is difficult, where no common ground can be assumed, we ask, might there be something beyond the social which can explain the moral desire to continue the dialogue, despite the vulnerability it exposes? Similarly, when we are at the limits of our knowledge and experience in encounters with others, what prompts us to build trust in the face of hostility and difficulty (Butler, 2005)?

We now turn to considering Levinas's work in relation to another vignette from the TLANG project. London-based researcher Daria Jankowicz-Pytel describes the research she undertook in a London community centre. The centre provides advice and information to people originally from Eastern Europe. The organisation advocates for people who need help with navigating British institutional and administrative systems.

Daria Jankowicz-Pytel, London

The last phase of the project involved collaboration between two key research participants, Michalina and Barbara, in an advice centre in

London. Both Michalina and Barbara were trained advisors, offering guidance to people on a range of issues, including benefits, immigration and welfare rights.

The research partnership started joyfully, but soon revealed complex positionings. I began to wonder how far Michalina's participation in the project was her own decision, and how far it was imposed on her. At first, pushing myself into this relationship seemed uncomfortable and intimidating – I felt I was an outsider and an intruder. Later, I realised it was a great position for an observer, offering a wide-angled perspective. I understood that these tensions were not personal. Rather, they were unremarkable, and a natural and necessary mechanism of the organisation. In other words, the institution was run by strong, professional women protecting their vulnerable clients. Indeed, the two women's roles in the organisation's structure were clearly defined: Michalina worked on relations with clients, and Barbara on relations with stakeholders and funders. Any initial tensions I experienced were put aside. I saw that the two women built their relationship around trust, loyalty and the responsibility they felt to protect and support vulnerable clients.

Trust was an important and changing factor. Initially, the lack of trust was an issue for us all. I found myself relying on the 'shields' provided by the university, which made data collection more 'legitimate', 'meaningful' and, by implication, 'harmless'. I also sensed that the concerns of Barbara and Michalina about the research were diminished by the authority of university governance, and its responsibility for any potential mess. However, our relationships developed beyond this. Once the trust-building process started between me, Michalina and Barbara, the interactions became informal. When I got access to their kettle, and to silly jokes shared across the team, I noticed we were all more comfortable! However, the arrival of two other TLANG co-investigators, neither of them Polish speakers, both university professors, again changed the atmosphere. Things became more uncomfortable. I saw that although interactions continued in Polish, their language towards me became much more formal. In the presence of others from the research team, Michalina maintained social distance, which vanished again when I returned to observing her alone. I could see she preferred to be observed by me only, and I suspect the argument about limited room space was sometimes just an excuse to keep the other co-investigators away.

I often felt I could identify with Michalina in some ways. There was this sense of shared knowledge about the reality of the 'old Poland' (1980s–1990s). For example, the context for sarcastic jokes about pointless queues – shelves in shops during Communism were empty, so a queue meant something was offered for sale – whatever it was, it was a good idea to queue – for tea, for soap, for washing machines – grotesque, tacky glass-holders identical in each and every Polish household; or spitting with tobacco when smoking cigarettes without a filter. Our shared knowledge was also a context for bitter memories, as I could see sad similarities between Michalina's and my mother's life stories, which were reminders that I am happy to be right here and now. On the other hand, little tangible things like the old-fashioned crystal fruit bowl (exactly like the one my beloved Gran used to have in her kitchen), the habit of drinking tea 'the Polish way' with sugar and lemon, or the music of Michał Lorenc played next door to Michalina's office. All these brought back the past Poland into present-day London, and made me realise I miss people and places, which are only memories. It also made me understand I am part of something that doesn't exist anymore, and if this is my 'Polishness', it exists neither here nor in Poland. Yet, I don't feel 'British' either. Polish language seemed to link all these dispersed worlds into one meaningful world to me, the one in which I live. I could tell Michalina's feelings were similar.

Michalina had the skill to find things from people just by falling silent, including from me. Sometimes I wondered who interviewed whom. Michalina kept her private life securely away from the project, therefore I focused on her work routine. I felt inexperienced in dealing with other people's tragedies, and I struggled to manage my emotions during observations of the advice meetings. Limited space in the advice room, direct eye contact with clients, and uncomfortable silences during interactions between counsellor and client seemed to shape emotions in the room. I only realised my own emotional reactions through retrospective writing. In this process I understand I learn by doing but only if I notice; self-reflection appeared to be the tool which helped me controlling and redefining my role as a researcher.

Michalina and I developed a friendly relationship in the project. However, this varied, appearing to weaken and strengthen at times throughout the project. I was puzzled. It was reinforced after the EU referendum, when moods shifted. Barbara and Michalina rolled up their sleeves to work with the media and fight against skewed images of 'bloody-foreigners' which negatively portrayed Polish migrants in the UK.

In her vignette Daria finds a solidarity and connection with Michalina. Despite the ups and downs of their relationship in terms of trust, we gain a sense of sincerity and integrity. This is in keeping with the ethos established in the advice centre overall. They shared values of respect across the different relationships in play, including between colleagues, researcher and researched, and between advisor and client. The vulnerability of people who need assistance because of poverty, disadvantage, exclusion or exploitation is met with sympathy. Michalina is addressed by the clients, and is responsible for dealing with the issues they raise. In Levinas's terms, we might say that Michalina backgrounds herself in relation to visiting clients. Her obligation and responsibility for others are foregrounded. Although the stories of the clients are not narrated directly in the vignette, we arrive at a sense of individual tragedies through Daria's emotional reaction. Through these narratives Daria reflects on her own learning. Proximity, literal in this case, opens up a set of new relations and deep connection despite the fact that advisor, researcher and client are strangers to one another. The complexities of the migrant's journey and the emotions they create in Daria are further revealed and understood through her follow-up actions of writing and thinking about their experience.

While these emotions appear somewhat traumatic, there are also light-hearted experiences. Daria builds on her shared background with Michalina in relation to symbols of Polishness, including objects, music, traditions, people and practices. However, we also see Daria's unwillingness to be located in any one national category. She resists the simple category of nationality to describe her own and Michalina's identity positionings, speaking of 'dispersed worlds'. Daria also reports on the imposition of other identities. While Michalina remains open to the vulnerabilities of her clients, ready to approach them openly and non-judgementally, she is not able to overcome the categorisation which she imposes on the other two co-investigators who also visit the site. The two non-Polish-speaking senior academics from the university are never able to shrug off the hierarchical categorisation of 'professor'. They are unable to escape the metanarrative of formality, expertise and social distance that such a category attracts socially. This has an impact on what is possible in the field site, and their presence is necessarily reduced.

Summary

Both Peirce and Levinas were concerned with the tyranny of an individualism which highlighted self, ego, sovereignty and autonomy. Both set out to dislodge the subject from its principal position. Both developed an approach to meaning that was relational, interactive and intersubjective. Levinas, like Peirce, believed that ethics begins with encountering alterity in human dialogue. However, they also differ substantially. Unlike Peirce, who emphasised shared norms and communities of inquirers, Levinas stressed relations between unique human beings. While Peirce foregrounds the social dimension of shared understandings, Levinas describes what happens when we are at the limits of interpreting difference. Indeed, Levinas is concerned with the harm that social and normative interpretations can deliver when taken to extremes. Nevertheless, both Peirce and Levinas anchor their philosophy in mundane and everyday encounters between people, and adopt an anti-subjectivist stance towards the individual. We have combined the two philosophical directions in this essay because both scholars provide theoretical insights into the way difference is conceptualised. While social, normative and communal aspects of understanding put forward by Peirce are central to interpretive processes for documenting patterns of language use in social context, equally important is the conceptualisation of people in the research process as unique individuals whose identities exist beyond categorisation.

Essay 12. Movement and Affect

Introduction

As we saw in Essay 6, one of the phases of the TLANG research project asked questions about communication in sport in contexts of superdiversity. Several members of the research team joined in with the sporting activity they were observing. This was the case for Zhu Hua, who participated weekly in a beginner's karate class in London, and Jolana Hanusova, who joined a capoeira class in Leeds. As we turn to their field notes and vignettes, we consider how Zhu Hua and Jolana emphasised the intensity of learning new sports. We will see their narratives shift between observations of cultural life and a focus on 'sensing' their own and others' bodies. Their participation in the community venues modified the nature of data collection. They discarded their pen and paper, their iPad and computer, and followed the instructor's movements and directions. The result was that their field notes recorded affect and manner as much as propositional content and meaning. As their bodies were put under pressure, the two researchers focused on embodied sensations and emotional feelings – aching muscles, sore joints, sound, musicality, rhythm, the stretch of fabric, joy, exhaustion, frustration, anxiety and pleasure. Their observations moved away from rationality and towards the senses.

Theatre of Affect: Interdisciplinary Connection in Sport and Art

In the perceptible realms of the arts such as poetry, prose fiction and theatre, we see a keen interest in what the senses bring to meaning and interpretation. Throughout these essays we have stressed an approach to signification which highlights the body. We turn to a particular strand of theatre studies here for further clarification. Einarsson (2017: 101) explains how the playwright and novelist Samuel Beckett shifts signification from 'meaning-oriented' to 'presence-oriented' art, as the audience is transported 'away from the disembodied, propositional sphere of knowledge and rational thinking, into the firmly embodied realm of experience'. Beckett turns to the body not in order to communicate less but because we 'know more than we can possibly capture in words' (Einarsson, 2017: 20). Beckett reconfigures the possibilities of signification to foreground sense, including the sensing body, over and above the linguistic referent. For Beckett, the choreographed body is not for reflection but for attention, demanding spectators' corporeal involvement. It is a realigning of the body in relation to the mind (Einarsson, 2017).

In Beckett's dramas the poetic forms of the body are artistic objects which reveal human relations. The body is said to function in the same way as prosody in language – able to highlight intensities during physical interaction, allowing interlocutors to sense meaning beyond words. In his plays Beckett questions the nature and status of language, preferring instead to emphasise the quality, manner and pace of movement. He achieves this through the use of mis-movements, 'to disrupt, irritate, and jolt spectator-perception, specifically with the intention of undermining semantic content, and keeping the audience in a state of suspension as to the meaning of it all' (Einarsson, 2017: 16). Language is of course crucial to Beckett, but it is often to the organisation of rhythm that he turns. Beckett draws vitality 'not from the poetic forms of metaphor, but from the music hall and circus, and from action and gesture, to create their own kind of intricate balletic choreography' (Einarsson, 2017: 102).

Beckett sought to destabilise, confound and subvert linguistic expression, by shaping an idea 'over and against its potential meanings' (2017: 83). Einarsson describes it like this:

> Notably, Beckett's well-known resistance towards interpretation seems analogous to this description of affect as preverbal sensation, which 'fills the being before the mind can think'. The theatre of affect seems founded on the recognition that we perceive and make sense of much more in the theatrical presentation than our minds (or language) enable us to access, and so we can never arrive to fully understand it. (2017: 125)

Einarsson suggests that at a certain point, the 'dramatic ammunition' (2017: 109) of Beckett's plays becomes less a struggle with words and more a concern with the rhythmic structures of visual and auditory elements in performance. Affect, then, is linguistically tangible through its manner, prosody and quality. In Beckett's world, linguistic and semiotic approaches are critiqued for disregarding the extent to which perception itself can be experienced as meaningful. The implications of Beckett's paradigmatic shift from the propositional to the non-propositional are therefore more far-reaching than a backgrounding of words. Beckett's theatre of affect asks us to give up intellectual distance in favour of sharing in the communal experience of life, in much the same way that Levinas does in his philosophy of relational ethics, and Peirce does in his version of pragmatism. Writing ethnography through drama, poetry and narrative provides us with a similar direction.

Seeking Indeterminacy in Ethnographic Writing

The portrayal of the human experience in all its complexity demands an interpretive openness. Such openness may be pursued through the creative arts. Great novels develop our ethical and moral sense by engaging with the details of people's lives, capturing their ordinary truths and tiny alterations (Bernstein, 1994). Morson (2013) points out that in distinguished works of literature, ethics are not mechanical, abstract or systematic, but intricate, shifting and contextual. In the novel we are attuned to the authenticity of values and decisions alien to our own. We read about particular cases, and bring our interpretive acumen to the ethical conditions under which the characters operate. Here we revisit the arguments for polyphony which we proposed in Essay 3. We suggested that in the polyphonic novel, the narrator gives up the right to the final, authoritative word and gives equal importance to the voices of characters. As we have seen in Essay 9, Morson (2013) cites the Russian realist novels of Tolstoy and Dostoevsky as examples in which characters are immersed in a polyphony of conflicting, contingent voices.

Unlike sociological case studies, novels consider the 'irreducible importance of particulars', the 'rich sense of the psychological and social milieu of living people' and the prosaic value of 'irrelevancies' (Morson, 2013: 28). According to Morson, the ethical engagement required of reading about different lives in all their complexity is very different from the 'phony neutrality' with which social scientists present others encountered in distant times and places (Morson, 2013: 1). Bernstein argues that the most appropriate way to retain complexity is through the polyphony of voice:

> Fiction is precisely what can reject fixity, and it offers the most unqualified enactment of our longing for fluid possibilities and limitless sideshadows. The desire to be free, at least in one's imagination, from the tyranny of one's own deepest convictions, and the moral obligations they impose, is part of the pleasure of novels that pluralise the confines of a strictly linear biographical narrative. (Bernstein, 1994: 112)

Both Bernstein and Morson are particularly wary of linguistics because of its propensity to isolate the linguistic sign to explain signification. Linguistics stands accused of omitting the wider ethical and moral topographies which shape people's lives. Unsurprisingly, these scholars suggest that we suspend the energy devoted to sociological case studies and linguistic analyses, and find other ways of writing social life. They suggest forms of literary writing which retain the density and mystery of social life, and resist determinism and presupposition. They propose that the social sciences need new ways of writing, which deal with difference non-judgementally, and capture the ever-changing nature of truth, so that we widen our experience as well as our sympathetic repertoire. As Morson puts it:

When one reads a novel, one identifies with characters. In so doing, one experiences from within what it is like to be a member of the opposite sex, belong to another social class, work in an unfamiliar profession, live in a different society, or take other assumptions and values for granted. One experiences feelings and perspectives that one either knew about only by hearsay, or never even suspected. (Morson, 2013: 208)

In his 1994 book *Foregone Conclusions: Against Apocalyptic History*, Bernstein refers to literature which takes the Holocaust as its subject matter. He argues against literary accounts of history which are 'predestined', insisting that writers should not use hindsight to judge decisions made by those whose future was still to be known. He critiques two related writing techniques for their stance toward time in relation to the Holocaust. In the first, which he terms 'foreshadowing', the narrator speaks about the present not for itself, but as 'the harbinger of an already determined future' (Bernstein, 1994: 2). This technique allows the writer to handle characters and events not in terms of the lived moment but through the lens of an already determined future. The second, which he names 'backshadowing', is a variant of foreshadowing, in which inherited values and shared knowledge are used to judge participants in historical events, as though they had access to the same knowledge as the writer in the present. More recently, the historical novelist Hilary Mantel (*The Guardian*, 2020) made a similar point in relation to her protagonist Thomas Cromwell (chief minister to Henry VIII from 1532 to 1540), arguing that historical figures must be viewed as products of their own time and not retailored to fit ours. Writing specifically about the Holocaust, Bernstein warns against judging the history of pre-Shoah European Jewry through the lens of backshadowing, 'as though they too should have known what was to come' (1994: 16). Instead, Bernstein argues for a writing style in which events are presented not as predestined in the light of the Holocaust, but described without the 'acquired certainty' of that future knowledge (Bernstein, 1994: 23). To achieve this, he advances the concept of 'sideshadowing'. Sideshadowing is a writing technique which recreates contingency, and resists categorisation:

sideshadowing champions the incommensurability of the concrete moment and refuses the tyranny of all synthetic master-schemes: it rejects the conviction that a particular code, law or pattern exists, waiting to be uncovered beneath the heterogeneity of human existence. Instead of the global regularities that so many intellectual and spiritual movements claim to reveal, sideshadowing stresses the significance of random, haphazard, and unassimilable contingencies, and instead of the power of a system to uncover an otherwise unfathomable truth, it expresses the ever-changing nature of that truth, and the absence of any predictive certainties in human affairs. (Bernstein, 1994: 4)

As 'a gesturing to the side', sideshadowing attempts to hold onto a present 'dense with multiple, and mutually exclusive, possibilities for what is to come' (1994: 1). It values the present for what it is. In making his argument, Bernstein argues for the multiplicity of narrative voice. He critiques the absolute authority of first-person Holocaust testimony, suggesting that individual accounts are too often held to represent an undifferentiated Jewish people, and can be read in moralising, homogenising and generalising ways. Bernstein finds an alternative in narrative fiction, which he believes, at its best, can provide an ethical basis for responding flexibly and undogmatically to the plurality of social life. He calls this approach a prosaics of the quotidian, which:

> requires a willingness to remain receptive to the voices from the shadows, in order to safeguard itself from becoming either a new kind of reductionism, or a blind affirmation of whatever has triumphed sufficiently to flourish in the glare of actuality. (Bernstein, 1994: 7)

The concept of the prosaic is also developed by Morson, who similarly argues that the value of the novel is in its presentation of 'irrelevancies', or 'what Bakhtin called "the surplus of humanness", which cannot be transformed into norms' (Morson, 2013: 29). For Morson,

> the most important events in life are not the grand, dramatic, and striking ones. They are, instead, the prosaic, undramatic, and ordinary ones we often do not so much as notice. (Morson, 2013: 3)

What does this have to do with writing linguistic ethnography? Ethnography is not fiction. It is not a novel, or a drama or a poem unless it is actively translated as such by ethnographic researchers or people working in the creative arts. And, as we have suggested elsewhere in this book, we believe the creative arts, and ethnographic drama in particular, offer a promising direction for reporting, representing and interpreting ethnographic research findings. There is a need to 'crack the armature' of established ways of writing and 'break free from the expectations scripted by previous successes' (Bernstein, 1994: 112). In what follows, we return to, and consider the potential of, the ethnographic field note and the research vignette to represent the plurality and unfinishedness of social life.

In these essays we distinguish between field notes and vignettes as modes of representation. As we have seen, in the TLANG research project vignettes were meta-summaries which documented researchers' reflections on their relations in the field. Vignettes were therefore resting points, in which researchers were encouraged to review ground covered. Field notes, on the other hand, were written on a regular and ongoing basis, usually synchronic with observation, or written soon after leaving the research site. They were records of researchers' engagement in the heat of the moment, rather than noticings recollected in tranquillity. Both field notes and vignettes were sources of evidence, each rendered as data through interpretive analysis by the research team.

Editors and publishers of academic journals typically require that interpretive research is written in a particular genre. In ethnographic accounts, the voices of research participants are normally edited and curated by the author, and presented as evidence to support specific arguments and conclusions. The academic genre rarely welcomes ambiguity and contradiction. Morson (2013) and Bernstein (1994) propose that great literature avoids over-determination through strategies such as sideshadowing, which cast historical events as unfinished and open to interpretation. We approach a discussion of field notes and vignettes with the tensions identified by Bernstein and Morson very much in mind. That is, we explore how field notes and vignettes might be read as instances of sideshadowing, refusing to be reduced to a single argument or empirical certainty. We suggest that field notes are able to represent the plurality of multiple perspectives and voices. We approach the analysis of field notes and vignettes through ethnographically informed discourse analysis. In doing so, we retain polyphony and multiplicity, contingency and ambiguity. We do not seek to 'tidy up' the messy verbiage of everyday encounters, but to represent them as they are. Ethnographic accounts of social life often produce an in-progress aesthetic. We are drawn to the possibilities of telling the stories of those with whom we collaborate in ways beyond the tried and tested research article. As we have demonstrated in the essays in this collection, we are rethinking the genres available for reporting linguistic ethnographic research. As Bernstein puts it:

> The urge to find a new way to tell our stories is not due to any faddish longing after novelty, or to a careless dismissal of the masterpieces of the past, but rather to an urgent need to find a narrative strategy that adequately expresses the full range of intellectual premises of our own epoch as persuasively as earlier stories corresponded to, or self-consciously challenged the basic convictions and assumptions of their times. The task for us as both story-dwellers and storytellers, that is as individuals who learn to understand ourselves and our world through the stories we tell and are told, is how to construct the meanings we require in our personal and collective narrative without hypostatising those narratives as absolute and inevitable. (Bernstein, 1994: 124)

Writing Sport

In this section we consider field notes and vignettes from two members of the research team, Zhu Hua and Jolana Hanusova. Zhu Hua was co-investigator for the London team, along with Li Wei, and worked alongside researchers Daria Jankowicz-Pytel and Agnieszka Lyons. Jolana Hanusova was a researcher on the Leeds team, along with co-investigators Mike Baynham and James Simpson. Other members of the Leeds team were Jess Bradley, John Callaghan and Emilee Moore. The London team

198   Part 3. Relations in Linguistic Ethnography

observed a karate coach, Stefan. Stefan was born into a Polish Roma family. He started learning karate in his teens in Poland and had become a Sixth Dan (rank) and Karate Sensei (teacher), instructing in karate clubs in London. He spoke Polish, Polish Romani and English, and was highly proficient in specialised Japanese karate terms. The Leeds team observed a capoeira group. They worked closely with one of the instructors, Tiago. Born in Maputo, Mozambique, Tiago had lived in Leeds for several years at the time of data collection. Tiago was a speaker of multiple languages, including Ronga and Changana (local languages in and around Maputo), Portuguese (the language of education in Mozambique) and English, which he started learning as an adult. At the age of 14, he discovered capoeira, a sport that combines dance, acrobatics and music.

London-based researchers Zhu Hua and Daria Jankowicz-Pytel both took part as beginners in Stefan's weekly karate classes. The sessions were held in an East London community hall, where children aged 4–15 gathered to learn and train. Zhu Hua and Daria stood out as the oldest members of the class. In Leeds, Jolana joined a small group of adults meeting in a local community setting for weekly capoeira sessions.

The participation of researchers in karate and capoeira brought another dimension to data collection and analysis. The physicality, movement and proximity of the researchers to other participants created a new dynamic. Researchers were immersed in the demands of the sport, resulting in their having less time to make notes. In the case of capoeira, music and rhythm also featured prominently in the sessions. Another point of interest noted by researchers in this phase was the multilingual nature of the sports classes, with researchers often surprised by the repertoire of languages and other semiotic resources in play for teaching and learning karate and capoeira.

Zhu Hua, London, field notes

Today's observation will test the true meaning of participatory observation. Daria and I have been talking about taking part in karate sessions, and today is the day. We managed to get to the place in plenty of time, arriving almost at the same time as Stefan (key research participant and teacher) and Don (teacher assistant). Stefan disappeared to change his clothes and Don went to get mats out of the small storage room. The room is clearly marked as space for karate stuff. When the double doors are closed, you cannot tell that the storage room is for karate, but once the doors are open, one door became a notice board with a poster of the master, leaflets with names of karate moves, and the Dojo code.

There are two cupboards inside the storage room. There is lots of stuff packed in the cupboards (not in any particular order or structure, in fact, and if I'm honest, things seem to be randomly piled on top of each other) and Stefan spent a long time getting something out and putting it in his carrier bag. I could not see what he was trying to get out. He was wearing a white T-shirt with the karate association logo on the back. I have brought a white top and some trousers which could 'pass' as karate *gi* (karate outfit). I showed Stefan my *faux* karate *gi* and he approved it. He pointed at the trousers and explained to me that the legs need to be wide. Knowing that as participant observer I do not need to take notes as I used to, and am consequently free of my notebook and pen, I feel quite liberated and have more 'mental' space to look around and get involved. I was secretly hoping that my memory would help me with my field notes later on.

Daria and I went on to help Don to turn the mats into a carpet. Stefan was the chief designer. He divided the room into a main stage and a side stage. For the main stage, he put a red square mat in the centre, some blue mats around the red one and then some red mats at the outside. The side stage is blue mats only. Colours are used to mark boundaries of the stages. The trick is to connect the edges of the mats. While Don, Daria and I were working on the side stage, Stefan came over and watched us. He said 'No' when we were trying to press down some mats, presumably in the wrong way. For a moment, I felt quite inadequate: things which look simple are not simple.

Once the mats were done, the children began to arrive. I went to change clothes. The room was surprisingly warm, given that it was a cold day. On my way back from the toilet facilities, I noticed a poster on the notice board which features one of the Karate Kid movies. What a coincidence. When the TLANG team presented the research design in Senate House, at the beginning of the project, I used a picture of the Karate Kid to talk about what we were planning to cover. The present time was connected with the past time. The poster is an advert for Stefan and his coaching without mentioning his name. It talks about 'instructor with a 6th Dan' and over 35 years of experience. The word 'free' repeats twice. On the left side is a list of USP (unique selling points) of karate: self-defence, discipline, confidence, fun and exercise, which seems to be a different list from the 'Dojo code' on the door of the storage room.

When I came back, Daria was talking to a little boy, Simon, and his grandma. I could not help joining in. He looked about four years old and must have been the youngest student. His grandma was explaining to me that they speak Russian. Simon had had a long day at school. They did swimming. He has brothers and they play-fight all the time. Simon was not interested in joining in our conversation, and he seemed a little absent-minded, occasionally yawning. Stefan shouted 'line up' and grandma said 'help' to us. I know that she was asking us to help her grandson if needed.

We all lined up. Daria and I stood in the back row, separate from the line of children. Stefan started sorting out the children according to the colours of their belts. He walked to the children who stood in the wrong place, put his hand on their shoulder or back, and gently dragged/walked them over to the place where they should be. White, red and orange. Stefan then addressed the whole group in Polish, with Don as the translator. He talked about the grading exam, and told the children that it was not an option: you either do it or do not take the lessons at all. He then showed the children how to kneel down (i.e. left leg first, then right leg) and how to get up (right leg then left leg – I hope my memory is correct). Once the children seemed to have it right, he got the whole group in a kneeling position, and Don started giving instructions (I think in Japanese): bow to the master (they moved their kneeling positions slightly to face the picture of the master). At this point I began to understand why they have a picture on the door.

After this, Stefan got up and asked the group to spread out into a big circle. A little girl went up to Stefan and whispered into his ear. Stefan seemed to understand and asked her to stay in a different place. The warm-up started. Stefan positioned himself on the red square mat in the middle (this is why he wanted one square mat in the middle – it is the centre of the main stage and reserved for the master). The beginning of the warm-up was quite nice and slow: toes, legs, neck, etc. But then the tough ones came: push-up 10 times, and then jumping up, and then another several rounds of push-ups and jumping up, with each round getting faster. The children were following his instructions, although I could see several cheeky ones were cheating when Stefan was not looking at them. There was no way Daria and I could follow this part. I cannot even do one single push-up, let alone 10 in a row. Just when I thought that this was a bit awkward, Stefan came over and said something in Polish to Daria, who told me that Stefan said we do not have to do it, since it would give us sore muscles the next day. In the middle of the warm-up, a girl arrived late. She bowed and sat down on her knees, and patiently waited for Stefan to let her join in.

After the warm-up, Stefan organised 'monkey crawl', which involved running on legs and hands. Children were divided into three groups: two groups facing each other at either side of the main stage, and the third group with smaller children just on their own. When the first group of children began to crawl at a good speed, Stefan shouted Don's name, and pointed at the heater. Don moved quickly and sat on the heater, so that children would not knock their heads. Very health-and-safety-minded. I could tell that the children loved the monkey crawl. They were giggling and competing with each other, trying to get to the other side first. Simon, the youngest, did perfect monkey crawl, although I could tell that in order to be the first one to come back to the same place, he turned round only two-thirds of the way. How competitive he was. Stefan was watching and doing the pep talk. A girl's belt became loose. Stefan took it and turned it into a whip. He was pretending to smack the children with the belt if they were slow. A lively activity.

After that, Stefan led a *Kata* [a detailed pattern of movement] together with the whole group. I copied Stefan very carefully. After two rounds, Stefan began to divide the whole group into two. So the first round was in fact a test of ability. He lined up four children in each row. He would go to a student and say 'you' and, sometimes with a push, point to another place. The children would move to where Stefan pointed. The only people left were two boys, Daria and me. Presumably, we were the ones who needed special help. Stefan handed us over to Don, a 15-year-old, who would be our instructor for the next few minutes. We moved to the side stage. It all seemed well planned.

Needless to say, the special group varied in ages and heights. It included Simon, and another small boy, who must be 5 or 6 years old, and Daria and me, who were surely the oldest. Don, a young coach, tackled this diverse group with confidence. He is only 15 years old, but seems to be very experienced in coaching. He would demonstrate, and then ask us to copy. His instructions were mostly in English-only, with occasional Japanese terms for the moves. The challenging bit (to me, anyway) was when he asked group members to do the moves one by one. There was no hiding place. The first couple of moves were easier. But then it got complicated. Realising that we might not be used to copying things through mirror images, Don asked Daria and me to stand in the same direction as him. It helped a bit. He also spent a bit of time explaining what blocking moves are for.

It began to make sense to me. After several moves, Don began the task of getting the group to remember the names of moves in Japanese. He would say: can you do the move of xxxx (the move in Japanese)? The one who got it right would get one point. This turned into a Japanese lesson. To be honest, when I was learning the moves, I did not pay any attention to their names. In any case, Stefan's instructions on the main stage were very loud, and I could not hear Don's instructions clearly. Simon, the other boy, and especially Daria were very good in recalling the terms. The final activity was more of a fitness challenge. Don asked us to do one move and then follow it up with five push-ups or sit-ups. It was tough, but the boys took to the task seriously. In the middle of it, Stefan shouted stop, and did a gesture of stop as well. We then all lined up, and that was the end of the lesson. A good sleep for the night, and sore legs next day for sure.

What is immediately striking in Zhu Hua's field notes is her range of interest. There is a sense of urgency at getting it all down, a desire to capture the energy and liveliness of the class, a sense of many different directions to follow. She is 'liberated' and 'free' from the technology of pen and paper, and able to find 'more "mental" space to look around and get involved'. This means to participate through movement. Much of the field note entry records the body – moving, bowing, warming up, touching, pushing, crawling, jumping, walking, dragging, kneeling. Mention is also made of pace – speeding up, slowing down, repeating, copying and demonstrating. A range of emotions are recorded – joy at 'mak[ing] sense' of the exercise routines, but also inadequacy, as the exercises became 'tough' and muscles became 'sore'. Ultimately, 'there was no hiding place' for the researcher as novice karate student. The reader of these field notes is invited to experience the intensities and sensations that emerge through the emphasis on the body. The karate was done in the community hall, and Zhu Hua's notes do not dwell on the cultural production of karate but, rather, on the manner of exercise. In other words, her attention here shifts to affect, as she describes her own and others' movements and mismovements (Einarsson, 2017).

While bodies take centre stage, other narratives bubble along in the sideshadows. Simon, the youngest karate player, and his grandmother, keep their distance from centre stage where Stefan stands in the red square instructing the whole class. Simon – a young, 'tired', 'yawning', Russian-speaking child whose grandmother views him as potentially vulnerable in a large class of older children, and who recruits the help of two researchers to keep an eye out for him – features as an auxiliary character throughout the field notes. While Simon is never centre stage, Zhu Hua returns to him several times in her field note entry, for example recording his skill at monkey crawl. Another prominent storyline is of inanimate objects, including the storage room, cupboards, doors, poster-boards, posters, lists and mats. This list of objects features strongly in developing several themes. First, the objects contribute to an account of status and rules for displaying respect. For example, the display of the Dojo code and a picture of the Sensei (teacher) reinforce ranks of knowledge and authority. Second, the objects connect different scales of time and space, from the London community hall to the global community of karate. The poster also serves as a reminder that the community hall is not simply a place to learn, but a research site, as Zhu Hua recalls its appearance in an earlier TLANG research presentation. Third, the mats transform the space from a community hall to a karate venue as they are placed in particular colour order. From the shadows these objects are given prominence by Zhu Hua, without providing an explanation. The objects bring colour, texture and materiality to the story. A final storyline which develops throughout the vignette refers to Don, who is allocated the role of the researchers' teacher by Stefan. Don becomes the tutor for Zhu Hua and Daria, and for the two youngest children in the class. His multilingualism in Polish, English and Japanese, his skill and patience in working with the group, and his importance to Stefan as an assistant, all attract commentary.

We might view each mini-narrative as an example of sideshadowing. The researcher is happy to capture the contingencies and ambiguities of the moment, without the urge to determine any particular line of argument. Nevertheless, the account lingers on moral and ethical issues. In story 1 there is engagement and kindness between strangers, as adults discuss the care of a young child. Storyline 2 shows a concern with order, and the structuring of space and time, as the researcher takes a position in relation to an apparent absence of organisational skills:

> There are two cupboards inside the storage room. There is lots of stuff packed in the cupboards (not in any particular order or structure, in fact, and if I'm honest, things seem to be randomly piled on top of each other) and Stefan spent a long time getting something out and putting it in his carrier bag.

Storyline 3, with its dimension of age, opens up another space for concern with values and beliefs. When Don, a 15-year-old instructor and 'young coach', becomes the teacher, he tackles 'this diverse group with confidence'. While he is only 15 years old, he is nevertheless 'very experienced in coaching'. Here, Zhu Hua writes in a manner which explores her values and allows the reader to consider theirs at the same time. In her field notes she extends her sympathy to Don, who has been put in charge of a challenging group: 'Simon, and another small boy, who must be 5 or 6 years old, Daria and me, who were surely the oldest'. The field notes do not explicitly develop an analysis of age and competence, but this topic is clearly implicit. While all three storylines are infused with moral values, they do not seek to take the moral high ground. Data are in-progress and unfinished, conclusions not settled.

We now turn to Zhu Hua's vignette, written at the end of data collection in the sport phase of the research project. She picks up and develops some of the themes in the field notes.

Zhu Hua, London
The highlights of this round are definitely the participant observations. Daria and I joined the karate lessons in the last week of November. We stood alongside 4- and 5-year-olds, and were taught by a 15-year-old coach who did not hesitate to make it clear, very politely, that our moves were not right. Despite his age, he was very good at teaching a diverse group of various abilities and experience. Participating as a student gave me a new perspective on what is going on in the lesson. It legitimatised my place of observation, from having been in a corner of the room, to now be right under the key participant's nose. I could see better what was going on, and where the instructor was directing his attention. It also helped me to share the experience of the students, and to find out what it was like to learn the basic moves, which were in fact not that simple, to memorise the names of the moves aurally, and to experience what it was like to discipline yourself when you are exhausted by endless rounds of push-ups, jump-ups and sit-ups.

This round of data collection requires not just Polish and English, but also Japanese and Romani, in which none of us in the team have expertise. I learned Japanese a long time ago, and was okay to pick up some basic words, but I was not so good with some of the technical terms and the alphabetical writing of Japanese. Daria, on the other hand, seems to make the best use of her shared Polish with the key participant. She was able to text Stefan and find out the meaning of the Japanese words through Polish, and then translate it into English in her field notes. I also found myself relying more on common sense to work out what was going on when Polish was spoken in class. Daria is very good at technology. She is adept at using her iPad to take pictures and to video, and the quality of the pictures and videos is excellent. Thank goodness for that! Being able to capture multimodal data is very important to this phase of the research, as the key research participant quite often uses non-verbal means to communicate, and it is difficult to describe movements in words.

It was difficult to build rapport with the key research participant, and to have a real sense of getting to know him, since our interactions were mediated or translated, and lacked spontaneity. But despite this, I began to see his warm-heartedness and determination through the way he interacts with his students (he is very observant and notices everything that is going on in the room); the way he cares about his students (he walked over at the end of class to check the student who did not feel well during the session, and he soothed a child who was crying because he thought he was hurt); and the way he teases his students (he sometimes laughs at his own pretended strictness in class).

The vignette is less tentative than the field notes. It offers a summary of the themes in the field notes, including participant observation, age, teacher competence, multilingualism and learning by doing. It also takes a more authoritative tone, and begins to build arguments related to translanguaging, multimodality and the importance of technical knowledge for recording data. It ends by describing the kindness and care the key research participant shows his students.

In the next example we visit a capoeira class in Leeds through the field notes and vignette of Jolana Hanusova.

Jolana Hanusova, Leeds, field notes

I arrived at the centre around 19:50. Silvio (the *mestre* – master) is already there with two other men. Silvio starts talking about the old songs. 'There are a lot of different songs, but people don't pay attention to them. It is the language of the people from the dark side of society. There are songs about a guy called Pedro Mineiro, lots of songs about him. The language is full of dialects, words with different meanings. If people don't study the meaning of the songs, they won't understand the old masters.'

Silvio started playing a song. I had never heard it before – but then, I know just a very few, whereas Silvio must know dozens and dozens of them. Before the song, he swapped my *pandeiro* (tambourine) for his drum, and showed me how to play it – two taps on the edge, one strike with the open hand in the middle, one tap at the edge. I got it, but then did not know how to fit into the rhythm with the tune – the Tanzanian guy helped me.

I forgot to note when Tiago (key participant) arrives. I think it's around this time. I stand up and go to him with the recording equipment, then he joins us. Silvio asks what the word 'besouro' (beetle) means. It's a bug. According to the myth, a *mestre* named Besouro had mystic powers, and people believed he could disappear from the police, as there was always a bug flying around when he did. The myth grew. He was then killed in Maracangalha.

Silvio explained that capoeira has nothing to do with martial arts. The Tanzanian guy says that calling it a 'martial art' makes it easier to explain. 'Maybe', says Silvio, 'but for me, martial arts is karate and kung fu. I have debated a lot about it with the other *mestres*.'

The Tanzanian guy asks, 'so how would you describe capoeira?' Silvio says 'it's Brazilian culture. We fight too. We pretend a fight into a dance. But I wouldn't go as far as martial art. Street fight, maybe.' The Tanzanian guy says, 'but the base of capoeira should be the same, everybody should agree on it, no?'

Silvio explains, 'When you go to history, each group has its own history. Mine was formed in 1995. Each group only teaches the history of their group – of what was before, during slavery. Besouro was not a thief, he worked, but he liked to fight.' Silvio points to at the drum. 'This is actually a *conga*, not an *atabaque*. Conga was used by the Africans in Cuba. *Caxixi* (small percussion instrument) is used with the *berimbau* (the main instrument in capoeira), and *agogô* (cowbells) come from candomblé. Candomblé, capoeira, and samba are one.'

Natalia walks in the room around this time. Silvio is continuing, 'in the *quilombos* (settlements formed by runaway slaves), there were white people living there as well. People think that the *quilombos* were isolated, but Zumbi (one of the leaders) had gunpowder. How could he have got the gunpowder? Only through trading with the whites.'

Somebody asks, so what's *pisada de Lampião*? I know that in this context, *pisada* means a kick. I know it because I remember Silvio telling us last time. This is like revision – it's like at school. Silvio says, 'Okay, everybody take a chair!' Silvio sprawls on his chair: 'now imagine you are soaking in the sun ... in Copacabana ... or Ipanema. Drinking beer. But in Brazil, everything can become a weapon. Even a beer bottle, when you break it. In the São Paulo state, people fight a lot with machetes. Isn't that so?' (turning to Natalia, who is from Campinas). Natalia agrees with him.

'So, you are sitting in the chair, and someone comes with a machete. What do you do?' He raises his right hand, gets down from the chair to the left, stays near the floor, and kicks back with the left from the low position. We watch him; he gets back to the chair and breaks the movement into parts, with us following him. Then to the other side. He repeats the movement a few times, then leaves his chair and leaves us to practise it. He comes to each of us, pretending a machete attack with his hand (slowly), to add context to the exercise and give us motivation to get down from the chair.

The next exercise is without a chair. It is a sequence of movements, avoiding a kick, getting out of the way, and a counterattack. It is quite complicated. I am trying to follow the Tanzanian guy practising on my right. He spots me watching him and breaks down his movements to make it easier for me to follow him.

Silvio then pairs us up – I'm with Natalia – and Silvio shows us the attacker's perspective as well. He leaves us to practise. Natalia and I are doing our best; we are clearly not at this level, as one of the moves is standing on one's hands, with the other person attacking the exposed abdomen with their head. By this time we are all sweating.

Silvio gathers us at the side of the room, indicates for me to come to him, stretches out his arms, and gestures for me to do the same. We take each other's hands, fingers intertwined, above our heads. Then Silvio starts to roll his body so that he is standing with his back to me, bending backwards. This motion forces me to do the same. We walk down to the end of the room in this way. This exercise is meant to stretch the back, but I feel rather like it's meant to break the back. It is making me dizzy like I haven't been for a long time. But it's good fun. I do the same exercise with Tiago – it's easier, he is tall, so I don't need to bend that much.

Then Silvio starts a fight with Tiago (not in a *roda*, or circle, as there are not enough people). They fight in a relaxed way. I ask the Tanzanian guy to practise with me, and he agrees. There are very few things I can do, but I really enjoy it still. It's all about getting away from his kicks. He corrects my circular kick, telling me to 'aim forward, rather than upward, otherwise you're not really a danger to the other person'. I escape in a non-capoeira way, just simply getting away. I ask, 'can I do that?' The Tanzanian guy says 'you can do anything, really. But don't forget that you would normally be playing in a *roda*, so there wouldn't be that much space'.

The receptionist comes in to remind us that we then need to leave as quickly as possible. We take our things and make our way out. Everyone is too tired for a drink.

In these field notes Jolana, like Zhu Hua, describes the body at length. Body parts, including hands, abdomens, heads, fingers, backs become pivotal points of interest. Bodies are directed backward, forward, upwards, left, right, and low to the ground. Bodies roll, bend, stretch and circle. They sweat and are made dizzy. Teaching happens through sequencing, motioning, repeating and practising. Researchers and researched operate outside their comfort zones. Also similar to Zhu Hua is the way the researcher forgets herself in the activity of exercise. While Jolana does not describe freedom from her notepad in the way Zhu Hua does, her comment, 'I forgot to note when Tiago … arrives. I think it's around this time. I stand up and go to him with the recording equipment', points to her absolute concentration, even in the moment of learning to play the instrument and joining a new rhythm. Jolana is immersed in the 'embodied realm of experience', which 'fills the being before the mind can think' (Einarsson, 2017: 125). The arrival of Tiago wrenches Jolana away from her learning, as she focuses on her role as a researcher and sets him up with a digital voice recorder and microphone.

In addition to movement, Jolana highlights sound, image, objects and people. Attention is given to music, lyrics, instruments, the telling of stories about capoeira traditions, mythical figures, dialects, the heat of the sun, and to slavery, defence, segregation and life on the street. In another set of field notes, Jolana asks, 'Is capoeira a kind of theatre/performance in sport?' In Jolana's narrative, the reader is exposed to capoeira's theatre. In much the same way as Beckett's theatre of affect dwells on movement and mis-movement to shift the balance from propositional meaning to physical presence, Jolana's field notes describe affect, experience and sensation:

- fingers intertwined, above our heads
- like it's meant to break the back

- making me dizzy
- like I haven't been for a long time.

Jolana's field notes produce a visual and poetic effect which foregrounds the fluidity of performance in the sporting activity. We now turn to Jolana's vignette, in which she gives an account of how the research team came to select Tiago as a key participant, and what happened after the data collection stopped.

Jolana Hanusova, Leeds

I have a passion for Brazilian culture, especially when it comes to music and literature. Capoeira is something I have long been curious about, as references to it can be found in both books and songs. Capoeira is usually described as a Brazilian martial art, but it also combines elements of dance, and it is accompanied by songs sung to the distinctive sound of the *berimbau* – a bow-shaped instrument with a single metal string. The songs are in Portuguese, and they often speak about the hardships of the African slaves during the colonial period of Brazil, which is when the roots of capoeira date back to.

Capoeira was one of the first things that came into my mind when we were thinking of ideas for the sports phase of the project, in which we wanted to explore the use of the Portuguese language in the sports context. I could also think of a potential key participant – a friend of mine with a similar obsession with Brazilian culture had introduced me some time ago to Tiago, a capoeirista from Mozambique, and a native speaker of Portuguese.

After initial conversations, we knew Tiago would make a great key participant, as he took an immediate interest in the project, and he was very open in sharing with us his views. He loved to speak about capoeira and what it means to him. During one of our chats he told me: 'Capoeira is more than a sport, it is a whole way of living. It teaches you lots of life skills. When I come across a difficult situation now, I stop and look at it from different angles before acting. And that I've learned from capoeira.'

However, if I ever thought of capoeira as a dance or a philosophy, this changed when I first practised it, despite my initial expectation that I would just be observing our key participant and taking notes, as I did in the previous phases of the project. One of my first observations was to take place at a capoeira workshop in York, organised by the Leeds capoeira school, outside their regular classes. I had agreed with Mike (TLANG co-investigator and team member Mike Baynham) that he would do the job of taking notes and I would take part in the workshop. I enjoyed it greatly, and despite not being able to follow many of the exercises, it revealed to me what doing capoeira feels like physically, and that things that look easy might not be easy to do at all. I could also experience the whole dynamics of the workshop and the interaction between the participants. The *mestre* would always be addressed formally, with great respect. Among the other participants, there was an atmosphere of

> mutual support, especially from the more experienced capoeiristas like Tiago towards the beginners.
>
> After this experience it did not make any sense to be sitting in a corner taking notes during the regular classes. But I would still grab my notebook whenever I could to make a quick note to help me to remember a particular phrase, or the order of the songs. But I've also had to learn to memorise what was happening in the class, so that I can describe it in my field notes the day after.
>
> Through participating in the classes, I became more of a member of the group, rather than a researcher or an observer, and became perceived as such by others – despite my occasional taking notes and assisting Tiago to attach the voice recorder before the beginning of the class. And very soon I started feeling a part of the group myself, as I was getting to know the people better not only during the class, but also from our chats afterwards when we would often head to the social club for a pint, before going home for a well-deserved shower. And before the four-month period of observation was over, I had decided to become a member of the group, and carry on with capoeira in the future.

Jolana speaks of her journey towards membership of the capoeira group. The vignette deals with the dynamic of strangeness and proximity. Her impulse to become involved, to get close, opens up new understandings. Revelations extend beyond propositional context, to sensuous experiences of bodies engaging with one another. Expression and affect are conditioned by proximity as much as through words.

Summary

In this essay, we have explored ways of writing ethnography. We argue that vignettes reveal complexity, moral ambiguity, contradiction and contingency. They allow us to keep the familiar strange, without falling into the trap of making the strange familiar. Vignettes widen examples of signification, allowing us to retain the sensing present, disrupting the apparent logic of unifying academic storylines. Indeed, vignettes retain polyphony. They produce texts which emphasise the manner, affect, movement, values and beliefs of researchers and research participants, in voices rich with prosody and unfinished meaning.

We agree with Morson and Bernstein when they argue that sociological case studies and linguistic analyses might benefit from less deterministic forms of writing. Field notes and vignettes are equipped to capture contradictions, flaws and moral dilemmas. The focus in field notes on the incidental reduces the tendency to look too soon for cause and effect. Field notes seek to look and see, and resist the urge to decide on hierarchies of relevance. They retain instances of moral positioning which add depth to researchers' accounts. They live in the moment as the researcher brings context to life, helping to resist presupposition and dogma. This is particularly salient when the researcher participates in physical activity, attempting to convey meaning, including perceptions gained from sensing bodies in movement and proximity to others.

Field notes and vignettes are crucial in the preparation and writing of full-length ethnographies. And yet they are sometimes viewed as less scientifically stringent than linguistic transcripts and interviews, falling below the evidentiary standards required of social scientific accounts (Rampton *et al.*, 2004). We argue the contrary. Field notes and vignettes reveal complexity, moral ambiguity, contradiction and contingency. They widen examples of signification, allowing us to retain the present in linguistic ethnographic accounts, and disrupting the apparent logic of unifying storylines. Field notes and vignettes bring an in-progress aesthetic to accounts of social life. We return to Jolana Hanusova for a final example from her field notes:

> Silvio took out two razors and put them down on the floor in the middle of the circle. The razors were old-fashioned steel razors which folded like a knife. Silvio told us that razors were used in capoeira in the '30s and '40s, when capoeira was still illegal. You can't talk about capoeira without talking about these. It was very common that people would carry razors. That's why, unlike in jiu-jitsu and other sports which usually end up with people wrestling on the floor, this wouldn't happen in capoeira – because people would have taken out the razors by then. They would carry them in their shoes, for example.
>
> I asked whether people used to fight with razors attached to their feet. Silvio took one of the razors and held it between his toes.
>
> 'That's just for show really, because it can slip out easily, and you could cut yourself. And the wounds from the razor heal from the outside towards the inside, so extremely badly, and you would end up with a scar. I know because I've got a few.'
>
> Around this point I realised that the theoretical part of capoeira was going to be quite substantial, so I sneaked out to get my notebook and started taking brief notes. I must have looked like a nerd.

Field notes and vignettes bring a presence to research which allow the reader to experience the manner, affect, movement, values and beliefs of researchers and research participants, in voices rich with prosody and unfinished meaning. They are a primary means of recording and interpreting observations in linguistic ethnography.

References

Aabø, S. and Audunson, R. (2012) Use of library space and the library as place. *Library and Information Science Research* 34, 138–149.

Alexievich, S. (2005) *Voices from Chernobyl: The Oral History of a Nuclear Disaster*, trans. K. Gessen. New York: Picador.

Alexievich, S. (2015) On the battle lost. https://www.nobelprize.org/nobel_prizes/literature/laureates/2015/alexievich-lecture_en.html.

Alexievich, S. (2016) *Secondhand Time: The Last of the Soviets*, trans. B. Shayevich. New York: Random House.

Alford, C.F. (2004) Levinas and political theory. *Political Theory* 32 (2), 146–171.

Appiah, K.A. (2007) *Cosmopolitanism: Ethics in a World of Strangers*. London: Penguin.

Aram, J.D. (2004) Concepts of interdisciplinarity: Configurations of knowledge and action. *Human Relations* 57 (4), 379–412.

Arendt, H. (1977) What is freedom? In H. Arendt, *Between Past and Future: Eight Exercises in Political Thought* (pp. 143–172). Harmondsworth: Penguin.

Arendt, H. (1998) *The Human Condition*. Chicago, IL: University of Chicago Press.

Audunson, R. (2005) The public library as a meeting-place in a multicultural and digital context – The necessity of low-intensive meeting-places. *Journal of Documentation* 61 (3), 429–441.

Audunson, R., Essmat, S. and Aabø, S. (2011) Public libraries: A meeting place for immigrant women? *Library and Information Science Research* 33. https://doi.org/10.1016/j.lisr.2011.01.003.

Bailey, B. (2012) Heteroglossia. In M. Martin-Jones, A. Blackledge and A. Creese (eds) *The Routledge Handbook of Multilingualism* (pp. 499–507). London: Routledge.

Bakhtin, M.M. (1963/1984) *Problems of Dostoevsky's Poetics*, ed. C. Emerson. Manchester: Manchester University Press.

Bakhtin, M.M. (1981) *The Dialogic Imagination: Four Essays*, ed. M. Holquist. Austin, TX: University of Texas Press.

Bakhtin, M.M. (1986) *Speech Genres and Other Late Essays*, ed. M. Holquist and C. Emerson. Austin, TX: University of Texas Press.

Bartlett, T. (2012) *The Concepts of Voice, Heteroglossia and Polyphony in Literature, Sociology and Linguistics: An SFL Perspective*. Cardiff: University of Cardiff.

Bauman, Z. (1993) *Postmodern Ethics*. Blackwell: Oxford.

Bauman, Z. (2007) The liquid modern adventures of the 'sovereign expression of life'. In S. Andersen and K. van Kooten Niekerk (eds) *Concern for the Other: Perspectives on the Ethics of K.E. Løgstrup* (pp. 113–138). University of Notre Dame Press.

Becker, A.L. (1995) *Beyond Translation: Essays Toward a Modern Philology*. Ann Arbor, MI: University of Michigan Press.

Behar, R. (1996) *The Vulnerable Observer: Anthropology That Breaks Your Heart*. Boston, MA: Beacon Press.

Bernstein, M.A. (1994) *Foregone Conclusions: Against Apocalyptic History*. Berkeley, CA: University of California Press.

Bernstein, R.J. (2011) *Praxis and Action: Contemporary Philosophies of Human Activity*. Philadelphia, PA: University of Pennsylvania Press.

Biesta, G. (2012) Becoming public: Public pedagogy, citizenship and the public sphere. *Social and Cultural Geography* 13 (7), 683–697.
Biesta, G. (2014) Making pedagogy public: For the public, of the public, or in the interest of publicness? In J. Burdick, J.A. Sandlin and M.P. O'Malley (eds) *Problematizing Public Pedagogy* (pp. 15–25). New York: Routledge.
Biesta, G.J. (2016) *The Beautiful Risk of Education*. London: Routledge.
Blackledge, A. and Creese, A. (2019) *Voices of a City Market: An Ethnography*. Bristol: Multilingual Matters.
Blackledge, A. and Creese, A. (2021a) *Interpretations – An Ethnographic Drama*. Bristol: Multilingual Matters.
Blackledge, A. and Creese, A. (2021b) *Volleyball – An Ethnographic Drama*. Bristol: Multilingual Matters.
Blackledge, A. and Creese, A. (2022) *Ode to the City – An Ethnographic Drama*. Bristol: Multilingual Matters.
Blackledge, A., Creese, A. and Hu, R. (2015) *Voice and Social Relations in a City Market*. TLANG Working Paper 2. https://tlang.org.uk.
Blackledge, A., Creese, A. and Hu, R. (2016) *Protean Heritage, Everyday Superdiversity*. TLANG Working Paper 13. https://tlang.org.uk.
Blackledge, A., Creese, A. and Hu, R. (2017) *Translanguaging, Volleyball, and Social Life* (WP 19). https://tlang754703143.files.wordpress.com/2018/08/translanguaging-volleyball-and-social-life.pdf.
Blackledge, A., Creese, A. and Hu, R. (2018) *Translating the City*. TLANG Working Paper 34. https://tlang.org.uk.
Block, D. (2017) Political economy in applied linguistics research. *Language Teaching* 50 (1), 32–64.
Blommaert, J. (2010) *The Sociolinguistics of Globalisation*. Cambridge: Cambridge University Press.
Brecht, B. (1978) *Brecht on Theatre*. London: Bloomsbury Academic.
Brintlinger, A. (2017) Mothers, father(s), daughter: Svetlana Aleksievich and the Unwomanly Face of War. *Canadian Slovak Papers* 59 (3–4), 196–213.
Brown, P. and Levinson, S. (1987) *Politeness: Some Universals in Language Usage: 4* (Studies in Interactional Sociolinguistics, Series Number 4). Cambridge: Cambridge University Press.
Burnside, J. (2019) *The Music of Time: Poetry in the Twentieth Century*. London: Profile Books.
Busch, B. (2022) A few remarks on working with auto-socio-bio-ethnography. In J. Purkarthofer and M-C. Flubacher (eds) *Speaking Subjects in Multilingualism Research: Biographical and Speaker-centred Approaches* (pp. 290–303). Bristol: Multilingual Matters.
Bush, D. (2017) 'No other proof': Svetlana Aleksievich in the tradition of Soviet war writing. *Canadian Slavonic Papers* 59 (3–4), 214–233.
Butler, J. (2005) *Giving an Account of Oneself*. New York: Fordham University Press.
Butler-Kisber, L. and Stewart, M. (2009) The use of poetry clusters in poetic inquiry. In M. Prendergast (ed.) *Poetic Inquiry: Vibrant Voices in the Social Sciences* (pp. 1–12). Rotterdam: Sense.
Cahnmann, M. (2003) The craft, practice, and possibility of poetry in educational research. *Educational Researcher* 32 (3). https://doi.org/10.3102/0013189X032003029.
Clifford, J. (1986) Introduction: Partial truths. In J. Clifford and G. Marcus (eds) *Writing Culture: The Poetics and Politics of Ethnography* (pp. 1–19). Oakland, CA: University of California Press.
Copland, F. and Creese, A., with Rock, F. and Shaw, S. (2015) *Linguistic Ethnography: Collecting, Analysing and Presenting Data*. London: Sage.
Copland, F. and Creese, A. (2016) Ethical issues in linguistic ethnography: Balancing the

micro and the macro. In P. De Costa (ed.) *Ethics in Applied Linguistics Research: Language Researcher Narratives* (pp. 161–178). London: Routledge.

Creese, A. (2008) Linguistic ethnography. In K.A. King and N.H. Hornberger (eds) *Encyclopedia of Language and Education* (2nd edn) (vol. 10, pp. 229–242). New York: Springer Science and Business Media.

Creese, A. (2010) Linguistic ethnography. In E. Litosseliti (ed.) *Research Methods in Linguistics* (pp. 138–154). London: Continuum.

Creese, A. (2011) Making local practices globally relevant in researching multilingual education. In F.M. Hult and K.A. King (eds) *Educational Linguistics in Practice: Applying the Local Globally and the Global Locally* (pp. 41–55). Bristol: Multilingual Matters.

Creese A. and Blackledge, A. (2012) Voice and meaning-making in team ethnography. *Anthropology and Education Quarterly* 43 (3), 306–324.

Creese, A. and Blackledge, A. (2019a) Stereotypes and chronotopes: The peasant and the cosmopolitan in narratives about migration. *Journal of Sociolinguistics*. https://doi.org/10.1111/josl.12376.

Creese, A. and Blackledge, A. (2019b) Translanguaging and public service encounters: Language learning in the library. *Modern Language Journal* 103 (4), 800–814. https://doi.org/10.1111/modl.12601.

Creese, A., Bhatt, A., Bhojani, N. and Martin, P. (2008) Fieldnotes in team ethnography: Researching complementary schools. *Qualitative Research* 8 (2), 223–242.

Creese, A., Bhatt, A. and Martin, P. (2009) Multilingual researcher identities: Interpreting linguistically and culturally diverse classrooms. In J. Miller, A. Kostogriz and M. Gearon (eds) *Culturally and Linguistically Diverse Classrooms: New Dilemmas for Teachers* (pp. 215–233). Bristol: Multilingual Matters.

Creese, A. and Blackledge, A., with Bhatt, A., Jonsson, C., Juffermans, K., Li, J., Martin, P. Muhonen, A. and Takhi, J.K. (2015a) Researching bilingual and multilingual education multilingually: A linguistic ethnography. In W.E. Wright, S. Boun and O. García (eds) *Handbook of Bilingual and Multilingual Education* (pp. 127–144). Malden, MA: Wiley/Blackwell.

Creese, A., Takhi, J. and Blackledge, A. (2015b) Reflexivity in linguistic ethnography. In J. Snell, S. Shaw and F. Copland (eds) *Linguistic Ethnography: Interdisciplinary Explorations* (pp. 266–285). London: Palgrave Macmillan.

Critchley, S. (2013) *Infinitely Demanding: Ethics of Commitment, Politics of Resistance.* London: Verso.

Critchley, S. (2015) *The Problem with Levinas.* Oxford: Oxford University Press.

Critchley, S. (2020) *Tragedy, the Greeks, and Us.* London: Profile Books.

Dentith, S. (1995) *Bakhtinian Thought: An Introductory Reader.* London: Routledge.

Denzin, N.K. (1997) *Interpretive Ethnography: Ethnographic Practices for the 21st Century* Thousand Oaks, CA: Sage.

Denzin, N.K. (2003) *Performing Ethnography: The Politics of Culture.* London: Sage.

Denzin, N.K. and Lincoln, Y. (2005) The discipline and practice of qualitative research. In N.K. Denzin and Y. Lincoln (eds) *The Sage Handbook of Qualitative Research* (pp. 1–32). Thousand Oaks, CA: Sage.

Deumert, A. (2018) The multivocality of heritage – moments, encounters and mobilities. In A. Creese and A. Blackledge (eds) *The Routledge Handbook of Language and Superdiversity* (pp. 149–164). London: Routledge.

Deumert, A. (2022) The sound of absent-presence: Towards formulating a sociolinguistics of the spectre. *Australian Review of Applied Linguistics* 45 (2), 135–153. https://doi.org/10.1075/aral.21039.deu.

Dewilde, J. and Creese, A. (2016) Discursive shadowing in linguistic ethnography. Situated practices and circulating discourses in multilingual schools. *Anthropology and Education Quarterly* 47, 329–339.

Einarsson, C.P. (2017) *A Theatre of Affect: The Corporeal Turn in Samuel Beckett's Drama*. Stuttgart: Ibidem-Verlag.
Emerson, R., Fretz, R. and Shaw, L. (2011) *Writing Ethnographic Fieldnotes* (2nd edn). Chicago, IL: University of Chicago Press.
Enria, L. (2016) Co-producing knowledge through participatory theatre: Reflections on ethnography, empathy and power. *Qualitative Research* 16 (3), 319–329.
Erickson, F. (2018) Ethnography. In B. Frey (ed.) *The Sage Encyclopedia of Educational Research, Measurement, and Evaluation* (pp. 601–620). Thousand Oaks, CA: Sage.
Fairclough, N. (1995) *Critical Discourse Analysis: The Critical Study of Language*. London: Longman.
Faulkner, S. (2009) *Poetry as Method: Reporting Research Through Verse – Developing Qualitative Inquiry*. London: Routledge.
García, O. (2009) *Bilingual Education in the 21st Century: A Global Perspective*. London: Wiley/Blackwell.
Geertz, C. (1973) *The Interpretation of Cultures*. New York: Basic Books.
Geertz, C. (1988) *Works and Lives: The Anthropologist as Author*. Stanford, CA: Stanford University Press.
Glissant, E. (1997) *Poetics of Relation*. Ann Arbor, MI: University of Michigan Press.
Goffman, E. (1955) On face-work. *Psychiatry* 18 (3), 213–231.
Goffman, E. (1971) *Relations in Public*. Harmondsworth: Penguin.
The Guardian (2020) Hilary Mantel: 'Being a novelist is no fun. But fun isn't high on my list'. https://www.theguardian.com/books/2020/oct/04/hilary-mantel-wolf-hall-mantel-pieces.
The Guardian (2022) David Hare: 'There is an awful lot of pious theatre at the moment'. Interview with Matthew Reisz, 6 August. https://www.theguardian.com/books/2022/aug/06/david-hare-there-is-an-awful-lot-of-pious-theatre-at-the-moment.
Hall, S. (2007) Living with difference. *Soundings* (37), 148.
Halton, E. (2011) Pragmatic e-pistols. *European Journal of Pragmatism and American Philosophy* 3 (2), 41–63.
Hamilton, M.L., Smith, L. and Worthington, K. (2008) Fitting the methodology with the research: An exploration of narrative, self-study and auto-ethnography. *Studying Teacher Education* 4 (1), 17–28.
Heaney, S. (1989) *The Government of the Tongue*. London: Faber & Faber.
Heaney, S. (2003) *Finders Keepers*. London: Faber & Faber.
Herzog, A. (2020) *Levinas' Politics: Justice, Mercy, Universality*. Philadelphia, PA: University of Pennsylvania Press.
Hobson, R.F. (1985) *Forms of Feeling: The Heart of Psychotherapy*. London: Routledge.
Hymes, D.H. (1972) On communicative competence. In J.B. Pride and J. Holmes (eds) *Sociolinguistics* (pp. 269–293). London: Penguin.
Hymes, D.H. (1980) *Language in Education: Ethnolinguistic Essays* (Language and Ethnography Series). Washington, DC: Center for Applied Linguistics.
Inoue, M. (2003) The listening subject of Japanese modernity and his auditory double: Citing, sighting, and siting the modern Japanese woman. *Cultural Anthropology* 18 (2), 156–193.
Ishiguro, K. (2017) *My Twentieth Century Evening and Other Small Breakthroughs. The Nobel Lecture, Delivered in Stockholm 7th December*. London: Faber & Faber.
Jaspers, J. (2018) The transformative limits of translanguaging. *Language and Communication* 58, 1–10.
Jaworski, A. and Coupland, N. (1999) Introduction. In A. Jaworski and N. Coupland (eds) *The Discourse Reader* (pp. 1–38). London: Routledge.
Johnson, C.A. (2012) How do public libraries create social capital? An analysis of interaction between library staff and patrons. *Library and Information Science Research* 34, 52–62.

Kallio-Tavin, M. (2020) Art education beyond anthropocentricism: The question of nonhuman animals in contemporary art and its education. *Studies in Art Education* 61 (4), 298–311. https://doi.org/10.1080/00393541.2020.1820832.

Karpusheva, A. (2017) Svetlana Aleksievich's 'Voices from Chernobyl': Between an oral history and a death lament. *Canadian Slavonic Papers* 59 (3–4), 259–280.

Kelz, R. (2016) *The Non-sovereign Self, Responsibility, and Otherness: Hannah Arendt, Judith Butler, and Stanley Cavell on Moral Philosophy and Political Agency*. New York: Palgrave Macmillan.

Kelz, R., Knappe, H. and Neupert-Doppler, A. (2022) Temporality and democratic sustainability. In P. Nanz, H. Knappe and B. Bornemann (eds) *Handbook of Democracy and Sustainability* (pp. 107–112). London: Routledge.

Krasnov, V. (1980) *Solzhenitsyn and Dostoevsky: A Study in the Polyphonic Novel*. Athens, GA: University of Georgia Press.

Kubota, R. (2016) The multi/plural turn, postcolonial theory, and neoliberal multiculturalism: Complicities and implications for applied linguistics. *Applied Linguistics* 37 (4), 474–494.

Kubota, R. and Miller, E.R. (2017) Re-examining and re-envisioning criticality in language studies: Theories and praxis. *Critical Inquiry in Language Studies* 14 (2–3), 129–157.

Kulick, D. (2005) The importance of what gets left out. *Discourse Studies* 7 (4–5), 615–624.

Lather, P. (2009) Against empathy, voice and authenticity. In A.Y. Jackson and L.A. Mazzei (eds) *Voice in Qualitative Inquiry: Challenging Conventional, Interpretive, and Critical Conceptions in Qualitative Research* (pp. 29–38). New York: Routledge.

Levinas, E. (1969) *Totality and Infinity: An Essay on Exteriority*, trans. A. Lingis. Pittsburgh, PA: Duquesne University Press.

Levinas, E. (1985) *Ethics and Infinity: Conversations with Philippe Nemo*, trans R.A. Cohen. Pittsburgh, PA: Duquesne University Press.

Levinas, E. (1989) Ethics as first philosophy. In S. Hand (ed.) *The Levinas Reader* (pp. 75–87). Oxford: Blackwell.

Levinas, E. (1996) *Emmanuel Levinas: Basic Philosophical Writings*. Bloomington, IN: Indiana University Press.

Levinas, E. (1998a) *Otherwise Than Being, Or, Beyond Essence*, trans. A. Lingis. Pittsburgh, PA: Duquesne University Press.

Levinas, E. (1998b) Dialogue on thinking-of-the-other. In *Entre Nous*, trans. M.B. Smith and B. Harshav (pp. 201–217). New York: Columbia University Press.

Levinas, E., Wright, T., Hughes, P. and Ainley, A. (1988) The paradox of morality: An interview with Emmanuel Levinas. In R. Bernasconi and D. Wood (eds) (2002) *The Provocation of Levinas: Rethinking the Other* (pp. 168–181). London: Routledge.

Lindbladh, J. (2017) The polyphonic performance of testimony in Svetlana Aleksievich's *Voices from Utopia*. *Canadian Slavonic Papers* 59 (3–4), 281–312.

Lofland, L.H. (1998) *The Public Realm: Exploring the City's Quintessential Social Territory*. Hawthorne, NY: Aldine de Gruyter.

Løgstrup, K.E. (1956/1997) *Beyond the Ethical Demand*. Notre Dame, IN: University of Notre Dame Press.

Long, N. (2015) For a verbatim ethnography. In A. Flynn and J. Tinius (eds) *Anthropology, Theatre, and Development. The Transformative Potential of Performance* (pp. 305–333). Basingstoke: Palgrave.

Malpas, J. (2017) In the vicinity of the human. *International Journal of Philosophical Studies* 25 (3), 423–436.

Maréchal, G. and Linstead, S. (2010) Metropoems: Poetic method and ethnographic experience. *Qualitative Inquiry* 16 (1), 66–77.

Maynard, K. (2009) Rhyme and reasons: The epistemology of ethnographic poetry. *Etnofoor* 21 (2), 115–129.

Maynard, K. and Cahnmann-Taylor, M. (2010) Anthropology at the edge of words: Where poetry and ethnography meet. *Anthropology and Humanism* 35 (1), 2–19.

Morson, G.S. (2013) *Prosaics and Other Provocations: Empathy, Open Time, and the Novel*. Brighton, MA: Academic Studies Press.

Muldoon, P. (2006) *Horse Latitudes*. London: Faber.

Myers, H. (2017) Svetlana Aleksievich's changing narrative of the Soviet–Afghan war in Zinky Boys. *Canadian Slavonic Papers* 59 (3–4), 330–354.

Myers, H. (2018) Telling and retelling a war story: Svetlana Alexievich and Alexander Prokhanov on the Soviet-Afghan War. Unpublished dissertation, Columbia University.

Nancy, J.L. (2007) *Listening*. New York: Fordham University Press.

Ochs, E. and Capps, L. (2001) *Living Narrative: Creating Lives in Everyday Storytelling*. Cambridge, MA: Harvard University Press.

Office for National Statistics (2011) *2011 Census for England and Wales*. London: UK Data Service.

O'Reilly, S. (2020) *Linton Kwesi Johnson Awarded PEN Pinter Prize 2020*. London: British Library.

Patai, D. (1994) When method becomes power (response). In A.D. Gitlin (ed.) *Power and Method: Political Activism and Educational Research* (pp. 61–73). London: Routledge.

Paterson, D. (2018) *The Poem: Lyric, Sign, Metre*. London: Faber.

Pavlenko, A. (2019) Superdiversity and why it isn't: Reflections on terminological innovation and academic branding. In B. Schmenk, S. Breidbach and L. Küster (eds) *Sloganizations in Language Education Discourse: Conceptual Thinking in the Age of Academic Marketization* (pp. 142–168). Bristol: Multilingual Matters.

Peirce, C.S. (1905/2009) What pragmatism is. In *The Logic of Interdisciplinarity: 'The Monist'-Series* (pp. 230–244). Berlin: Akademie Verlag.

Peirce, C.S. (1931) *Collected Papers of Charles Sanders Peirce, Vols I–VI*, ed. C. Hartshorne and P. Weiss. Cambridge, MA: Harvard University Press.

Peirce, C.S. (1935) *The Collected Papers of Charles S. Peirce, Vol. 2*. Cambridge, MA: Harvard University Press.

Peirce, C.S. (1958) *Collected Papers of Charles Sanders Peirce, Vols VII–VIII*, ed. A.W. Burks. Cambridge, MA: Harvard University Press.

Phipps, A. and Saunders, L. (2009) The sound of violets: The ethnographic potency of poetry? *Ethnography and Education* 4 (3), 357–387.

Pillow, W. (2003) Confession, catharsis or cure? Rethinking the uses of reflexivity as methodological power in qualitative research. *Qualitative Studies in Education* 16 (2), 175–196.

Prendergast, M. (2009) 'Poem is What?' Poetic inquiry in qualitative social science research. *International Review of Qualitative Research* 1 (4), 541–568.

Prendergast, M., Leggo, C. and Sameshima, P. (eds) (2009) Poetic inquiry: Special issue. *Educational Insights*, 13 (3).

Purkarthofer, J. and Flubacher, M-C. (eds) (2022) *Speaking Subjects in Multilingualism Research: Biographical and Speaker-centred Approaches*. Bristol: Multilingual Matters.

Rampton, B., Tusting, K., Maybin, J., Barwell, R., Creese, A. and Lytra, V. (2004) *UK Linguistic Ethnography: A Discussion Paper*. https://www.lancaster.ac.uk/fss/organisations/lingethn/documents/discussion_paper_jan_05.pdf

Rapport, F. and Hartill, G. (2012) Crossing disciplines with ethnographic poetic representation. *Creative Approaches to Research* 5 (2), 11–25.

Rapport, N. (2010) Apprehending anyone: The non-indexical, post-cultural, and cosmopolitan human actor. *Journal of the Royal Anthropological Institute* 16, 84–101.

Rapport, N. (2015) Anthropology through Levinas: Knowing the uniqueness of ego and the mystery of otherness. *Current Anthropology* 56 (2), 256–264.

Rapport, N. (2019) Anthropology through Levinas (further reflections) on humanity, being, culture, violation, sociality, and morality. *Current Anthropology* 60 (1), 70–79.

Reyes, A. (2014) Linguistic anthropology in 2013: Super-new-big. *American Anthropologist* 116 (2), 366–378.

Richardson, L. (1997) *Fields of Play: Constructing an Academic Life.* New Brunswick, NJ: Rutgers University Press.

Richardson, L. and St Pierre, E. (2005) Writing: A method of inquiry. In N.K. Denzin and Y.S. Lincoln (eds) *The Sage Handbook of Qualitative Research* (pp. 959–978). Thousand Oaks, CA: Sage.

Riley, D. (2000) *The Words of Selves: Identification, Solidarity, Irony.* Stanford, CA: Stanford University Press.

Rosa, J. (2019) *Looking Like a Language, Sounding Like a Race: Raciolinguistic Ideologies and the Learning of Latinidad.* New York: Oxford University Press.

Rosenthal, S.B. (2003) A time for being ethical: Levinas and pragmatism. *Journal of Speculative Philosophy* 17 (3) (Essays from the Meeting of the Society for the Advancement of American Philosophy), 192–203.

Saito, Y. (2015) Aesthetics of the everyday. In E.N. Zalta (ed.) *The Stanford Encyclopedia of Philosophy.* http://plato.stanford.edu/archives/win2015/entries/aesthetics-of-everyday.

Saldaña, J. (2005) *Ethnodrama: An Anthology of Reality Theatre.* Walnut Creek, CA: AltaMira Press.

Saldaña, J. (2011) *Fundamentals of Qualitative Research.* Oxford: Oxford University Press.

Samuels, W.J. (2000) Signs, pragmatism, and abduction: The tragedy, irony, and promise of Charles Sanders Peirce. *Journal of Economic Issues* 34 (1), 207–217.

Silverstein, M. (1992) The indeterminacy of 'contextualization': When is enough enough? In P. Auer and A. Di Luzio (eds) *The Contextualization of Language* (pp. 55–75). Amsterdam: John Benjamins.

Simon, S. (2012) *Cities in Translation: Intersections of Language and Memory.* Abingdon: Routledge.

Smith, D. (2017) 'After you, sir!': Substitution in Kant and Levinas. *Journal of the British Society for Phenomenology* 48 (2), 149–161. https://doi.org/10.1080/00071773.2016.1256602.

Solzhenitsyn, A. (1963) *One Day in the Life of Ivan Denisovich*, trans. M. Hayward and R. Hingley. New York: Praeger.

Solzhenitsyn, A. (1968a) *The First Circle*, trans. T.P. Whitney. London: Collins Harvill.

Solzhenitsyn, A. (1968b) *The Cancer Ward*, trans. R. Frank. New York: Praeger.

Solzhenitsyn, A. (1972) *August 1914*, trans. M. Glenny. London: Bodley Head.

Svenska Akademien (2015) Press release. The Nobel Prize in Literature 2015. https://www.nobelprize.org/prizes/lists/all-nobel-prizes-in-literature.

Tahmasebi-Birgani, V. (2014) *Emmanuel Levinas and the Politics of Non-Violence.* Toronto: University of Toronto Press.

Voloshinov, V.N. (1973) *Marxism and the Philosophy of Language.* Ann Arbor, MI: Seminar Press.

Welten, R. (2020) In the beginning was violence: Emmanuel Levinas on religion and violence. *Continental Philosophy Review* 53, 355–370. https://doi.org/10.1007/s11007-020-09491-z.

Williams, Q. (2021) They bodied that different English in difference. https://youtu.be/w3SXTXeGNFY. Presentation at Ethics and Aesthetics of Encountering the Other: New Frameworks for Engaging with Difference (AH/T005637/1). https://ether.leeds.ac.uk/ether-resource-library/519-2.

Wortham, S. (2001) Language ideology and educational research. *Linguistics and Education* 12 (3), 253–259. https://doi.org/10.1016/S0898-5898(01)00055-9.

Index

Aabø, S. 107
Advice centre 74–75, 77, 86, 89, 108, 136, 149, 180, 188, 190
Advocacy 8, 74–75, 77, 86, 89
Aesthetics 60, 130, 177, 186
Affect 139, 192–193, 201, 206, 208, 209
Agency 20–22, 26, 130–131, 136, 153, 158, 160, 187
Ainley, A. 214
Alexievich, S. 19, 34, 37–38, 41, 51
Alford, C.F. 129, 134, 140
Alienation 92, 99
Alterity 22, 26, 132, 134, 137, 162, 186, 188, 191
Ambiguity 3, 4, 13, 16, 132, 135, 147, 153, 159, 197, 208
Ambivalence 3, 35, 136, 140, 159
Anthropology 132, 163
Appiah, K.A. 127, 171
Arabic 7, 8, 50, 155
Aram, J.D. 178
Arendt, H. 159, 160, 161
Arts 4, 9, 10–11, 12, 62, 192, 194
Audio-recording 24, 33, 42, 45, 48, 53, 82, 91, 109, 110, 114
Audunson, R. 107, 108
Austerity 5, 15

Backshadowing 195
Bailey, B. 36
Bakhtin, M.M. 34–37, 42, 51, 52, 169, 172
Bartlett, T. 34
Barwell, R. 215

Bauman, Z. 3, 147, 148, 153, 158, 159, 167, 172, 186, 188
Becker, A.L. 138
Beckett, S. 19, 192–193, 206
Behar, R. 17, 127, 142, 163, 164
Bernstein, M.A. 186, 194–197
Bernstein, R.J. 176
Bhatt, A. 212
Bhojani, N. 212
Biesta, G. 24, 25, 26, 129, 138, 160, 161
Birmingham 5, 7, 8, 12, 13, 107, 128, 160, 178
Blackledge, A. 4, 34, 46, 49, 51, 61, 74, 75, 92, 109, 110, 114, 142, 164, 175
Block, D. 131
Blommaert, J. 6, 7
Blythe, A. 82
Body 11, 90, 94, 96, 137, 138, 163, 171, 192, 193, 201, 206
Brecht, B. 19, 92, 93, 94, 98, 100, 103, 106, 122, 123, 162
Brintlinger, A. 37
Brown, P. 163
Burnside, J. 14, 19, 28, 71, 73
Busch, B. 142
Bush, D. 38
Business 7, 15, 149, 150, 154, 178, 180, 181
Butchers 8, 14, 33, 40, 51, 53, 54, 55, 71, 72
Butler, J. 24, 25, 131, 133, 134, 141, 163, 171, 186, 187, 188
Butler-Kisber, L. 59

Cahnmann, M. 25, 60
Cameron, D. 113
Cantonese 7, 8, 53, 75, 165, 170, 171
Capoeira 185, 192, 198, 204–209
Capps, L. 4, 129
Cardiff 7, 8, 12, 149, 150, 154
Categorisation 5, 133, 191, 195
Census 7
China 8, 33, 56, 159, 165, 168, 169, 172
Chinese 8, 43, 48, 51, 56, 57, 65, 74, 75, 87, 89, 165, 167, 168, 170, 171
Choreography 100, 193
Civil inattention 167
Clifford, J. 38, 39
Collaboration 9, 10, 12, 18, 144, 178, 188
Communicative repertoires 7, 90
Community centre 5, 7, 8, 74, 75, 83, 86, 87, 89, 188
Complexity 13, 18, 21, 22, 23, 38, 55, 59, 119, 134, 136, 142, 143, 153, 157, 194, 208, 209
Connectivity 136, 161
Consciousness 37, 38, 40, 53, 130, 136, 162, 187
Conservative Party 112, 113, 119, 123
Contact zone 162
Conviviality 11, 47
Cooper, Y. 112, 113, 119
Copland, F. 175
Co-presence 173
Coupland, N. 19
Creative Arts Labs 9, 10
Creative practice 10, 13, 18, 22
Creativity 18, 21, 24, 25, 27, 39, 82, 83, 107, 152, 184
Creese, A. 4, 12, 74, 75, 91, 93, 109, 110, 114, 142, 164, 167, 175, 180
Critchley, S. 129, 135, 174, 186

Cultural heritage 7, 15, 149, 150
Culture 13, 23, 38, 39, 87, 88, 107, 131, 139, 150, 153, 162, 170, 175, 182, 183, 204
Czech 7

Dance 10, 14, 18, 100, 181, 207
Defamiliarisation 23
Dentith, S. 35
Denzin, N.K. 76, 92
Deumert, A. 18, 19, 21, 23, 25, 142
Dewilde, J. 167
Dialogism 39, 52, 53
Difference 3, 5, 8, 9, 15, 24, 60, 88, 129, 132–133, 147, 151, 159–161, 173, 174, 177, 184, 186, 191
Digital communication 8, 33, 40, 56, 57, 149
Discourse 19, 21, 23, 26, 36, 52, 53, 54, 55, 69, 83, 109, 112, 118, 119, 123, 128, 129, 132, 137, 139, 175, 197
Disposition 3, 15, 127, 129, 144, 163, 173, 188
Diversity 4, 5, 6, 37, 38, 49, 53, 55, 57, 107, 140, 173, 175, 178
Documentary prose 19, 33, 34, 37, 38
Dostoevsky, F. 34, 35, 37, 38, 145, 194
Drama 4, 12, 14, 15, 18, 20, 49, 74–79, 83, 86, 88, 92–93, 106, 114–115, 135–136, 193, 196

Ego 22, 25, 26, 29, 134, 141, 142, 143, 162, 187, 191
Einarsson, C. P. 192, 193, 201, 206
Emerson, R. 42
Emotions 12, 16, 92, 95, 144, 153, 163, 176, 177, 190, 191
Empathy 23, 95, 98, 99, 100, 103, 144, 147, 162, 173

Empiricism 18, 19, 25, 142
Encounters 3, 4, 15, 21, 41, 127, 129, 130, 142, 147, 148, 149, 154, 159, 163, 171, 174, 188
English 8, 53, 75, 78, 152, 165, 170, 171, 198, 202, 203
Enlightenment 107, 158
Enria, L. 162
Entertainment 47, 92, 122
Epic theatre 92
Erickson, F. 39
Essmat, S. 107
Estrangement 92, 95, 96, 97, 99, 100, 102, 103, 162
ETHER 130
Ethical-aesthetic perspective 13, 17–22, 26, 27, 130
Ethics: ethical subject; ethical behaviour; relational ethics
Ethnographic drama 20, 74–76, 81, 82, 92, 93, 98, 114, 115
Ethnographic writing 3, 13, 38, 39, 60, 142, 194
Ethnography 142, 144, 145, 146, 148, 149, 161, 174, 189
Ethnotheatre 92
Exegesis 87, 88

Face 26, 137, 139, 142, 163, 186
Fairclough, N. 54
Familiarity 161, 162
Faulkner, S. 60
Fiction 17, 34, 35, 38, 60, 68, 83, 114, 142, 194
Field notes 65, 67, 69, 75, 76, 90, 91, 99, 109, 114, 164, 167, 168, 170, 171, 196, 197, 198, 203, 204, 207, 208, 209
Field relations 15, 127, 146, 152, 159, 173
Flubacher, M. C. 142
Foreshadowing 195
Football 7, 8, 185
Fretz, R. 42
Fujianese 7

García, O. 138
Geertz, C. 39, 174
General election 110, 112, 118, 119
Gestus 93, 94, 100, 101
Glissant, E. 21, 88
Goffman, E. 163, 167
Goodness 129

Hakka 7
Hall, S. 133
Halton, E. 176
Hamilton, M. L. 127, 142
Hare, D. 82, 114
Heaney, S. 28, 65, 67, 68, 72
Herzog, A. 139, 140, 141
Heterogeneity 195
Heteroglossia 14, 36, 37, 39, 49, 51, 53, 55, 165
Hierarchy 35, 50
Hobson, R. F. 148
Hokkien 7
Holocaust 186, 195, 196
Hong Kong 8, 90, 108, 160, 165, 169, 171, 172
Hu, R. 6, 44, 46, 51, 61, 65, 74, 75, 77, 109, 110, 160, 164, 167, 168–173
Human subject 19, 23, 128, 130, 133, 147
Humanism 26, 129, 136, 186, 188
Humanity 15, 26, 28, 129, 133, 134, 135, 138, 146, 163, 186, 188
Hymes, D.H. 6, 139

Icon 20, 22
Identity 20, 25, 107, 134, 141, 161, 186, 191
Ideologies 5, 19, 36, 51, 52, 89, 132, 149, 172, 174
Imagination 11, 12, 18, 24, 25, 39, 63, 68, 83, 107, 142, 181 194
Incommensurability 161, 195
Indeterminacy 4, 22, 129, 138, 194
Indexicality 4, 19–22, 36, 130, 132, 133, 139

Individual 3, 4, 15, 23, 26, 41, 55, 108, 123, 128, 130–131, 134, 136, 141, 144, 161, 162, 170, 173, 176, 182, 190, 191
Inoue, M. 20, 132
Interdisciplinarity 16, 175, 178, 182
Interpretant 22
Interpretation 22, 39, 76, 82, 83, 89, 133, 138, 146, 153, 176, 183, 185
Interpreters 8
Intersubjectivity 4
Interviews 24, 33, 40, 51, 53, 86, 110, 115, 209
Intradisiciplinarity 175
Inversion 26, 132
Involvement 95, 130, 139, 163, 193
Iraq 8, 150
Ishiguro K. 23, 27

Japan 132, 201, 203
Jaspers, J. 131
Jaworski, A. 19
Johnson, B. 112, 113
Johnson, C.A. 107, 108

Kallio-Tavin, M. 162
Karate 7, 8, 185, 192, 198–199, 201, 202
Karpusheva, A. 37
Kelz, R. 130, 136, 137, 141, 146, 160, 185
Knappe, H. 27
Knowing 16, 19, 21, 25, 137, 139, 171, 185
Krasnov, V. 35, 36, 37
Kubota, R. 130, 131
Kulick, D. 136

Labour Party 111, 112, 113
Lange, D. 19, 40, 41
Languaging 138
Lather, P. 162
Latinidad 132
Latinx 20, 132

Law 136, 178, 179, 180, 185
Leeds 192, 197, 198, 204, 207
Levinas, E. 15, 25, 26, 29, 129, 130, 134, 136, 137–140, 142, 146, 163, 169, 186–188
Levinson, S. 163
Liberalism 25, 26, 130, 134, 141
Library of Birmingham 107–110, 114, 115, 117, 119, 160, 164, 166, 173
Libraries 106, 107
Lincoln, Y. 76
Lindbladh, J. 35
Linguistic diversity 6, 8, 140
Linstead, S. 25, 60
Listening subject 128, 130, 132, 163
Lofland, L.H. 170
Løgstrup, K.E. 24, 147, 158
London 7, 12, 149, 150, 188, 197, 198
Long, N. 76

Making strange 23, 102
Malaysia 8, 33, 90
Malpas, J. 149
Mandarin 7, 8, 43, 46, 48, 75, 77, 78, 80, 83, 86, 160, 168, 170
Mantel, H. 195
Manyness 18
Maréchal, G. 25, 60
Maynard, K. 25, 60, 72
Meaning 33, 34, 36, 65, 67, 75, 88, 129, 138, 148, 175, 176, 177, 178, 192, 193
Metacultural 20
Metaphor 16, 60, 66, 90, 134, 162, 193
Metapragmatic 20
Methodology 5
Metonym 60, 66
Migration 8, 50, 51, 52, 74, 87, 140, 189
Miliband, E. 111–112, 118, 119
Miller, E. R. 131

Mismeeting 167
Morality 3, 4, 136, 149, 158, 159, 177, 188
Moral spacing 15, 148, 159
Morson, G. S. 144, 145, 194, 195, 196, 197, 208
Movement 14, 16, 91, 94, 100, 102, 104, 192, 193, 198, 201, 205, 206
Mozambique 8, 198, 207
Muldoon, P. 62
Multilingualism 8, 179, 202, 204
Multimodality 204
Multiplicity 3, 143, 196, 197
Museums 9, 178
Music 14, 18, 25, 28, 33, 71, 72, 73, 138, 176, 190, 192, 198
Myers, H. 34, 37

Nancy, J.L. 28, 129, 138
Narrative 142, 143, 169, 174, 194, 196, 197
Nationalism 170
Neoliberalism 130, 141
Netherlands 8
Nexus of discourses 123
Nobel Prize in Literature 34, 36

Ochs, E. 4, 129
Office for National Statistics 7
Ontology 23, 142, 146, 159, 185
Opacity 21, 23, 88,
Openness 138, 142, 145. 146, 162, 163, 176, 185, 194
Opera 9, 11
O'Reilly, S. 72
Othering 5, 9, 127, 128, 132, 133

Patai, D. 175
Participant observation 203, 204
Paterson, D. 19, 28, 63, 66, 67, 69, 70, 71
Pavlenko, A. 131
Peirce, C.S. 20, 22, 175–178, 183, 184, 185, 191

Performance 11, 14, 18, 22, 47, 48, 74, 76, 82, 90, 92, 98, 100, 119, 123, 193, 206, 207
Philosophy 3, 133. 134, 135, 138, 143, 177, 186, 188
Phipps, A. 59
Photographs 8, 24, 33, 40, 91, 109, 142
Pillow, W. 175
Playwright 25, 27, 77, 82, 83, 92, 114, 192
Plurality 16, 35, 36, 57, 160–161, 173, 196
Poetry 14, 17, 25, 28, 59–61, 65, 67, 69, 71, 72
Poland 8, 143, 150, 189, 190, 198
Polish 8, 150, 151, 189, 190, 191, 198, 199, 200, 203
Politics 27, 107, 111, 113, 140, 141, 157, 161
Polyphony 16, 18, 34, 35, 36, 37, 38, 39, 41, 42, 51, 53, 194, 197
Polyvocality 39
Portuguese 7, 8, 198, 207
Pragmatism 175, 176, 177, 185, 193
Prendergast M. 59, 60
Proust, M. 27
Proximity 96, 137, 138, 160, 163, 164, 172, 173
Public engagement 10
Purkarthofer, J. 142

Race 132, 161, 174, 175
Racial capitalism 20
Raciolinguistics 19
Radical empiricism 25
Rapport, N. 67, 136, 139, 161, 162, 163, 170
Recontextualisation 79, 82, 90
Referential 18, 139, 142
Reflexivity 23, 131, 175
Relational Ethics 5, 28, 127, 128, 130, 133, 134, 140, 173, 193

Representation 3, 9, 11, 12, 14, 15, 18, 24, 27, 33, 35, 38, 55, 59, 60, 67, 74, 75, 82, 83, 92, 93, 100, 119, 128, 139, 174
Responsibility 5, 21, 23, 26, 131, 134, 137, 140, 144, 145–146, 155, 171, 186–187, 190
Reyes, A. 131
Rhyme 59, 60, 62, 63, 72, 98
Rhythm 40, 59, 67
Richardson L. 130, 142
Ricoeur, P. 140
Romani 7, 8, 198, 203
Rosa, J. 19. 20, 132
Rosenthal, S. B. 148, 176, 178

Saito, Y. 23
Saldaña, J. 83, 88, 92
Samuels, W.J. 175
Saunders, L. 59
Semiotic landscape 40, 55, 56
Semiotic repertoires 8
Shadowing 104, 109, 110, 167
Sideshadowing 195, 197, 202
Silverstein, M. 20, 21, 22
Simon, S. 89
Slovak 7, 8
Slovakia 8
Smith, A.D. 92
Smith, D. 146, 162
Social media 7, 11, 33, 56, 82, 109, 149, 157
Solzhenitsyn, A. 36
Sovereignty 25, 130, 136, 191
Spanglish 132
Spatiality 13
Speaking subject 39, 132
Spectre 19, 24
Sport 90, 95, 149, 178, 182, 185, 192, 197, 198, 207
Stereotypes 132, 172
St Pierre, E. 142
Strangeness 160, 161, 162, 164, 170, 173

Strangers 8, 128, 129, 161, 167, 169, 170, 171, 190, 202
Stewart, M. 59
Subjectivity 4, 13, 19, 20, 21, 23, 25, 26, 127, 128, 129, 132, 138, 140, 164, 187
Sudan 8
Superdiversity 70, 110, 179, 184, 192
Symbol 22, 39
Syria 144, 157, 158

Tahmasebi-Birgani, V. 26, 29, 137, 138, 140, 141
Temporality 13, 26, 27, 28
Theatre 9, 76, 82, 83, 88, 92, 93, 95, 98, 105, 114, 122, 192, 193, 206
Thought domains 178
TLANG 5, 6–9, 12, 13, 33, 74, 107, 129, 130, 135, 136, 140, 144, 160, 175, 178, 183, 185, 192
Tolstoy, L. 145
Tragedy 135
Translanguaging 5, 8, 92, 138, 179, 180, 182, 184
Translation 18, 24, 44, 82, 133
Transparency 21, 88, 177, 186
Trope 39, 66, 161
Trust 24, 25, 83, 107, 130, 144, 147–148, 158, 159, 188, 189
Truth 4, 21, 24, 35, 37, 39, 67, 82, 83, 114, 175, 176, 194, 195

Uncertainty 135, 149, 158
Unfinishedness 13, 196

Ventriloquation 82
Verfremdungseffekt 98, 102
Video-recording 15, 24, 33, 76, 82, 91, 92, 109, 114, 149
Vignettes 128, 142, 149, 153, 159, 164, 178, 179, 186, 192, 196, 197, 208

Volleyball 5, 90–93, 98, 100, 102
Voloshinov, V.N. 54, 55
Vulnerability 16, 24, 26, 163, 171, 187, 188, 190

Welten, R. 141, 142, 186, 187, 188
White European 21
Williams, Q. 24, 129
Wortham, S. 131

50% OFF!

To order the companion volumes at 50% discount just use the code BLCR50 on our website www.multilingual-matters.com.

Just use the code BLCR50 on our website www.multilingual-matters.com

For Product Safety Concerns and Information please contact our EU Authorised Representative:

Easy Access System Europe

Mustamäe tee 50

10621 Tallinn

Estonia

gpsr.requests@easproject.com